An Introduction to the Anthropology of Melanesia

Culture and Tradition

Melanesia is a fascinating culture area, and has always been a popular fieldwork site for the anthropologists, including W. H. R. Rivers, Bronislaw Malinowski, Margaret Mead, and Gregory Bateson. A surprising number of the most important theoretical contributions to the subject were also first formulated with reference to Melanesian studies, and undergraduate students today still learn much of their basic anthropology from Melanesian examples. Paul Sillitoe's *Introduction to the Anthropology of Melanesia* of which this is the first volume, is intended for students and general readers with some grounding in the issues and ideas that inform the discipline. Each chapter focuses on a topic common to many cultures in the region, such as the role of so-called big men, ancestor cults, male initiation, and exchange, and these ideas are fleshed out with apt ethnographic examples. The range of materials handled is quite exemplary, and each case is provided in sufficient depth to make good sense of it for readers not already familiar with the region. This book will be useful as an introductory or intermediate level for undergraduate courses in general anthropology, and Pacific cultures.

PAUL SILLITOE is Professor of Anthropology at the University of Durham. He has conducted extensive anthropological field research in the Southern Highlands of Papua New Guinea. His books include *Give and Take* (1979), *Roots of the Earth* (1983), *Made in Niugini* (1988), and *A Place Against Time* (1996).

An Introduction to the Anthropology of Melanesia

Culture and Tradition

Paul Sillitoe

Department of Anthropology, University of Durham

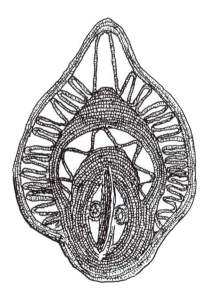

CAMBRIDGE
UNIVERSITY PRESS

PUBLISHED BY THE PRESS SYNDICATE OF THE UNIVERSITY OF CAMBRIDGE
The Pitt Building, Trumpington Street, Cambridge CB2 1RP, United Kingdom

CAMBRIDGE UNIVERSITY PRESS
The Edinburgh Building, Cambridge, CB2 2RU, United Kingdom
http://www.cup.cam.ac.uk
40 West 20th Street, New York, NY 10011–4211, USA   http://www.cup.org
10 Stamford Road, Oakleigh, Melbourne 3166, Australia

First published 1998

Printed in the United Kingdom at the University Press, Cambridge

Typeset in Plantin 10/12pt [CE]

A catalogue record for this book is available from the British Library

Library of Congress Cataloging-in-Publication Data

Sillitoe, Paul.
An introduction to the anthropology of Melanesia / Paul Sillitoe.
    p. cm.
ISBN 0 521 58186 9 (hbk.) – ISBN 0 521 58836 7 (pbk).
1. Melanesians – Social life and customs. 2. Ethnology – Melanesia.
GN668.S55   1998
306′.0995 – dc21   97-35251 CIP

ISBN 0 521 58186 9 hardback
ISBN 0 521 58836 7 paperback

For friends in Melanesia,
heirs to *ol pasin bilong tumbuna*

Contents

Maps

Figures

Tables

Plates

The logo featuring in this book is based on a yam mask from the Maprik
region of Papua New Guinea.

Thereafter he mooned about the Java Sea in some trading schooners, and then vanished, on board an Arab ship, in the direction of New Guinea ... He remained so long in that outlying part of his enchanted circle that he was nearly forgotten before he swam into view again in a native proa a portfolio of sketches under his arm. He showed these willingly, but was very reserved as to anything else. He had had an 'amusing time', he said. A man who will go to New Guinea for fun – well!

Joseph Conrad, Victory: An Island Tale

Preface

Melanesia is a region in the south-west Pacific Ocean, occupying about the same area of the globe as Europe. Another name for the region, which dates from the early days of Western exploration, is the Black Islands. It reflects the region's place in the European imagination, from its discovery up to the present day. Among the impressions that inform its reputation are images of wild people, savage and primitive, who revel in black customs, and the legends emphasising dark customs live on. Even as the twentieth century comes to a close the region continues to exercise this fascination. Reports of undiscovered primitive people still appear in the Western press: 'A nomadic Stone Age tribe believed to be untouched by civilisation has been discovered by a government patrol in wild mountainous jungle of Papua New Guinea ... Naked, except for a few strips of bark and leaves, the Liawep people ... [were] found last month living in bush huts under a large human-faced rock which they worshipped as a god' (*Independent* 26 June 1993). This book aims to help replace these imaginative excesses with an understanding of this region's intriguing cultures built up by anthropologists working there over the past century. An anthropological **introduction** to the indigenous peoples and cultures of Melanesia, it is intended for both those who have some background in anthropology and those with none.

Readers with some grounding in the issues and ideas that inform the discipline may have heard something about the engrossing ethnography of Melanesia and wish to learn something more about it. The region has played a prominent role in the history and intellectual development of the subject from its inception. It was one of the first places where extended fieldwork, now acknowledged as the hallmark of anthropology, was practised, by the Russian Miklucho Maclay on the coast near present-day Madang in 1871 (not, as many students of anthropology are erroneously taught, by the well-known Pole Bronislaw Malinowski, who worked in the Massim nearly fifty years later). The varied ethnographic reports produced since then, being informed by their authors' backgrounds, the ideas prevalent when they wrote, and so on, constitute not a consistent record but a patchwork body of knowledge which presents an overview text like this one, with some interesting challenges. Those with no previous knowledge of anthropology may also wish to learn something about Melanesia, and to this end the book includes brief introductory comments on anthropological topics such as the study of stateless polities, non-centralised dispute resolution, swidden agriculture, rites of passage, and so on, to set the ethnography in a broader disciplinary context.

The book will contain little new for those familiar with the region. The exception is the proposal that we drop the term 'ceremonial exchange' and stop talking about 'gift economies' because these are inappropriate to the practices to which they refer and cloud important issues. They are confusing not only to an introduction to the region but also in intellectual debates about it. Instead it is suggested that we refer to sociopolitical exchange (or sociopolitical modes of exchange, complimenting the well-known domestic mode of production). It focuses on traditional or premodern aspects of Melanesian society, reflecting in considerable part the region's ethnographic record, in which accounts of these institutions feature prominently. Several anthropologists have been privileged to observe some Melanesian societies before they started to change enormously following extensive contact with the outside world and have written accounts of largely 'traditional' cultural orders. They represent the classic ethnography that has contributed to Melanesia's anthropological celebrity and engaged the imagination of the general reader.

The intention is **not** to suggest that Melanesian societies were ever static. Although many anthropologists have written in a one-time frame, few if any of them thought that the societies they studied had no history and were not experiencing change. The rate of change in premodern contexts would have been slow on the whole, certainly as viewed from the brief time spans of most anthropological fieldwork. Furthermore, the full force of the change consequent upon the intrusion of the Western world may not have been felt for some years after initial contact, and it is in this interval that anthropologists have observed and reported on relatively traditional societies. Many of these cultures have subsequently changed considerably as a consequence of what anthropology contemporarily calls globalisation; modern communications are allowing the world's cultures to influence one another as never before.

Recent interest in globalisation has focused on the recontextualisation of aspects of Western life and the associated technology as people struggle to incorporate them into their own cultural traditions. The other side, commonly heard in the South-West Pacific, is people's lament for the loss of their cultural identity in the face of this global onslaught. This book chimes in with this lament. Throughout Pidgin-speaking Melanesia, people commonly refer to their culture as *pasin bilong tumbuna* (literally fashion belong ancestors or our ancestors' customs) and talk about the need to maintain *kastom*. They perceive that they are losing their cultural identity. The documentation of traditional aspects of their cultures is not, from this perspective, any romantic essentialism harking back to some 'primitive' past but a record that will feature crucially in their search for their cultural identity in a rapidly changing world. We can sense something of the same concern and confusion over these trends worldwide in the apparent strengthening of the resolve to protect ethnic and national identities. This preoccupation with safeguarding distinct cultural characters while simultaneously embracing worldwide shifts of perspective and influence reflects something of the intriguing human urge to reconcile opposites: becoming the same yet remaining different.

A wrestling with opposites characterises a considerable part of Melanesian social life. It gives rise to some intriguing paradoxes which contribute to its ethnographic fascination. There are the region's fluid categories, which not only challenge our conception of classification but even call into question attempts to define it geographically or characterise sociocultural groups within it. There is the tension evident in stateless political contexts between individuals' desire to press their own advantage at the possible expense of others and their concern with maintaining amicable social relations with them. There is the resolution in sociopolitical exchange of the potential conflict between competition and sociability. There is the existence of inequalities within fiercely egalitarian social environments. There is the paradoxical behaviour of people in disputes, vigorously siding with their relatives while simultaneously pressuring them to reach agreeable settlements. The emphasis on socially integrative reciprocal relations has a disruptive aspect too, expressed in the revenge ethic, and the violent lives of some relate to initiation ceremonies in which kinsmen, with parental connivance, terrorise and abuse young relatives towards whom they normally act protectively.

Some scholars have argued that many anthropologists have largely overlooked history, but few if any have ever denied that the history of the region must be significant in understanding it. It is just that reliable historical documentation has been sparse in many regions until relatively recently. There is little evidence of the changes that had occurred before Europeans arrived, except for that to be gleaned from oral histories, which are shallow and frequently feature mythical elements that are difficult to assess, and archaeological finds, which are currently sparse and difficult to interpret. When the full force of outside contact is felt, the pace of change increases dramatically and that change, unlike precontact history, is documented with the start in a Western sense of a historical record.

In relation to historical contexts and time frames, it is pertinent to note that the ethnographic accounts in this book are presented in what anthropologists call the **ethnographic present tense**. This is a convention in anthropology that has been criticised, but the criticism appears to be founded on a misunderstanding. The ethnographic present is **not** intended to suggest any timeless premodernity; it represents the time around which the anthropologist conducted the fieldwork and produced the ethnography in question. Few anthropologists neglect to document the changes that have occurred since European contact (for example, the use of steel tools and other manufactured goods) and may rely on people's memories for information on practices recently ended (for example, on stone axe technology, head-hunting rituals, and so on), and they customarily report this information in the ethnographic present, as relating to what they, or the people with whom they live, have witnessed.

The anthropological convention of the ethnographic present obviates the need for constant and confusing changes of tense in writing and justifications for the use of one tense and not another. On some occasions what anthropologists study becomes history before they even commit it to print; this is particularly the case where tribal societies change rapidly in the modern world. The ethnographic record in their notebooks becomes a pastiche of what was observed and has passed into desuetude, what continues, and what has been modified, and it is difficult to know how to handle information on a society of which some aspects have changed while others continue. In the Massim region, for example, people continue to participate in an anthropologically renowned exchange institution called the *kula* but in contexts radically different from the one first reported; whereas people once travelled in outrigger canoes and communicated with conch shells, today they use outboard launches and telephones. What is past and what is present?

The change that occurs over time, particularly following the outside world's intrusion, further promotes sociocultural variety. No society is unchanging, and documenting the variation that occurs over time inevitably presents problems; this is the essence of history as a discipline. These problems are compounded throughout the South-West Pacific by the startling diversity of cultures found here. This variety contributes to its fascination for anthropologists, but it presents further difficulties for an introductory text like this one. The problem is how best to acquaint the reader with this ethnographic variety. This book addresses this conundrum as an ethnographically founded introduction to the region, not a comparative sociology, reflecting the author's experiences as a fieldworking anthropologist.

Each chapter discusses a topic common to many societies throughout the region using ethnographic data on one society as an illustration. The ethnographic example serves to draw out issues relating to the topic that are common across Melanesia, while playing down any local idiosyncrasies. This approach mirrors the state of our ethnographic knowledge of the region which is patchy, and is preferable, I think, to one that attempts a broad comparative overview that might give the false impression of comprehensive ethnographic coverage. It would also result in a burdensome catalogue of available ethnographic evidence which, rather than furthering understanding of Melanesian society, would hinder it with a flood of miscellaneous ethnographic illustration.

This approach limits this introduction to a relatively small range of ethnography in its exploration of regionally relevant themes. The implication is not that it includes in the author's judgement the best and omits the rest. Many excellent anthropological studies have been undertaken in Melanesia, but an introduction like this must restrict its coverage. Two concerns guided the selection. One was to achieve a good spread geographically and culturally across the region, and the other was to select studies that dealt in sufficient detail with the topics to be addressed to draw out themes central to the region. Some very difficult choices had to be made in the light of these considerations. Readers of this book who are stimulated to read further will find a wealth of ethnographic writing on Melanesia awaiting them.

It is probable that some readers, in addition to taking exception to the selection of ethnographic material, will also disagree with the selection of topics. Again, although limitations of space have resulted in the omission of some topics from this introduction, it nonetheless covers those that I think are central to achieving a balanced introductory understanding of the Black Islands and their people. Despite Melanesia's cultural variety, there are constant underlying themes detectable across it. A prominent one, for instance, is the centrality of the exchange of things in social life. Certain classes of objects are very important to Melanesians. They vary greatly from one place to another, ranging from strings of button-sized sea-shell discs arranged in tyre-like coils to ochred crescents cut from pearl-shell valves and from elaborate ornaments of dogs' teeth to enormous decorated yam tubers, but the contexts in which people transact them and the principles underlying their exchange are similar everywhere. Other themes covered range from gather-hunting to swidden agriculture and from beliefs in ancestor spirits and fear of endemic sorcery to acephalous politics and informal dispute-settlement procedures.

A *caveat* may be in order here. Each chapter is not a potted ethnography on the society featured. No attempt is made to cover everything from kinship to religious beliefs, economic organisation to political order, and so on. The ethnography selected is used only to explore the theme of the chapter, and to elicit points of general relevance to the Melanesian region. This approach again reflects the nature of the region's ethnographic record, which contains considerable information on some issues in some cultures and little to nothing about others.

Every effort is made to remain faithful to the ethnographic facts as recorded in the literature, but the ethnographer's interpretation of these facts is not always presented without criticism or revision. Some might argue that it is too optimistic to imagine that one could remain true even to the ethnographic facts, because what constitutes them is not necessarily clear. All ethnographic accounts inevitably include an element of subjectivity. Anthropologists' observations are partial, and they always interpret them to some extent. Therefore their upbringing, gender and so on, as well as the intellectual preoccupations current in the age in which they write, condition the ethnographic record. Contemporary post-modern criticism questions the status of the descriptions and explanations of outside observers of what they think they see and hear in other societies, arguing that there is an involuntary subjective element and unavoidable ethnocentric judgement in any selection of ethnographic 'facts' and their interpretation according to the intellectual canons of an alien culture. The rapid turnover of theories in the social sciences, each informing interpretations differently and focusing attention on varying ethnographic issues, exacerbates this inconsistency. There is no escaping this criticism. It relates to the critique of Orientalism and the metropole's definition of the Other. This introduction compounds it with its arbitrary selection of ethnography depending on the availability of ethnographic research judged relevant to points I consider important for understanding something about the anthropology of Melanesia. Perhaps the justification for this presentation and interpretation of a selection of ethnography from Melanesia is that one Westerner's illusions are as valid as another's, and furthermore, that the encounters of several other anthropologists who have worked in the region conform closely to my own experience.

Whatever the philosophical status of anthropological knowledge, this introduction puts a particular spin on the ethnographic facts. The objective is to develop a coherent perspective of Melanesian society. Although this interpretation tries not to privilege any time, theory, or perspective but to cover both dated issues such as culture and personality and topical ones such as gender and inequality, it attempts to set these within the context of some relevant current post-modern theoretical preoccupations. It would be inappropriate, in a text like this, to engage in the 'deconstruction' of works to reveal how the personal backgrounds and current intellectual interests of ethnographers inform their interpretations of other cultures, effectively substituting one illusion for another. Nonetheless, it is important for the reader to be aware of these contentious interpretive issues. To this end, the following accounts include apposite comments on the ethnographers and their times to contextualise the record. Another device adopted is to remind readers, at appropriate junctures, of the tendency to draw conclusions on the basis of one's own experiences by drawing parallels between the Melanesian institutions discussed and episodes in readers' own lives.

It is my hope that this book will not only be interesting and informative but also may stimulate further reading on this fascinating and relatively little-known part of the world. Each chapter concludes with some references for further reading on the ethnography and topics discussed. The book comes from a range of university lecture courses with a Pacific content that I have given over several years, notably a first-year course entitled 'Anthropology and Ethnography', and a second-year one entitled 'Regional Studies: Oceania'. I thank the students who attended these series of lectures for asking questions and making comments that helped, sometimes inadvertently, to clear up issues and clarify my presentation. I also thank my wife, Jackie, for reading through the manuscript, commenting on its suitability as an introduction and improving on the text where necessary to make it clearer. Assistance from Durham University Publications Board with meeting the costs of the plates is gratefully acknowledged.

1   Introduction to Melanesia

Melanesia is a region in the South-West Pacific made up of a number of islands varying in size from the world's second-largest island, New Guinea, to small coral islets like the Solomon's Reef Islands (Map 1.1). Different writers put the region's boundary in different places; it is not easy to define precisely, on geographical, cultural, biological, or any other grounds, where Melanesia ends and the neighbouring regions (of Indonesia, Micronesia, Polynesia and Australia) begin. The 'Black Islands' stretch from the western tip of New Guinea (and in some senses include a few of the Indonesian islands here) to Fiji in the east and from the Torres Straits in the south to Mussau Island in the north, but there are a few small islands in the east, among them Tikopia and Ontong Java, which are customarily assigned to Polynesia on cultural grounds. The problem we have in defining Melanesia's place on the globe relates to a dilemma that recurs time and again in studying the region; drawing a boundary demands arbitrary decisions because any one part of the area fades into another without any abrupt linguistic, cultural, or other changes.

Given this albeit imprecise idea of what constitutes Melanesia, on what general grounds do we define it? It is, to start with, a historical category which evolved in the nineteenth century from the discoveries made in the Pacific and has been legitimated by use and further research in the region. It covers populations that have a certain linguistic, biological and cultural affinity – a certain ill-defined sameness, which shades off at its margins into difference. This sameness is, however, by no means cultural uniformity; Melanesia is one of the most varied regions, in almost every sense, on earth. 'It is literally impossible to make more than a handful of generalizations that will apply to even the majority of the societies' (Chowning 1977: 2).

The natural environment

The natural environment of Melanesia repeats the theme of variation, displaying a striking diversity over short distances. A useful initial

Map 1.1   Melanesia: geographical location. (After Brookfield and Hart 1971.)

distinction to make is between small and large islands. Some of the small islands are coral atolls, others volcanic peaks. They usually have a limited range of ecological habitats – some have the palm-fringed lagoons and beaches of popular imagination, others dense rain-forest cover, or, where populated, regrowth and grassland. The large islands, in contrast, are characterised by high, rugged interior mountain chains, far and away the largest and most spectacular of which is the central cordillera running spine like though New Guinea. Three gross regions are identifiable on these larger islands:
(1) the coast (or, rarely, the lowlands);
(2) the lowland plains of the great rivers; and

Plate 1.1 The coast: the beach at Kaibola on the Trobriand Islands, with a man leaning against a canoe used in overseas *kula* exchange journeys.

(3) the highlands (particularly in New Guinea) or the interior mountains.

The **coast** varies from inviting beaches to impenetrable mangrove, from steep cliffs where mountains plunge into the sea to raised coral reefs and from equally inaccessible swamps to grasslands and bushy regrowth (Plate 1.1). The great **river plains** are less varied, characterised by large, meandering rivers, sometimes with islands of floating vegetation, enormous areas of swampland with isolated backwaters, and some savanna, grassland and forest (the river systems on the south coast of New Guinea flow through one of the world's most extensive swamps). The **highlands** are stupendous, with ranges of precipitous mountains

Plate 1.2   The highlands: a vine suspension bridge stretching across the
fast-flowing Was River in the montane forest near Pinjip in the Southern
Highlands of Papua New Guinea.

clothed in majestic rainforest, the highest topped with alpine grassland
and sometimes snow; the broad valleys running between them often
contain wild rivers (Plate 1.2). The mountainsides support extensive
areas of human-made grassland and secondary regrowth. One can do no
better to evoke the nature of this country than to quote two of the New
Guinea highland's first explorers: 'Take Switzerland drop it down into
the southern ocean near the equator, overspread its peaks and gorges
with a rank growth of tropical vegetation, put in a wide barrier of
malarial swamps to guard its borders, pollute it with tropical diseases,
add a malignant assortment of poisonous snakes and insects for variety'
(Leahy and Crain 1937: 49).

Whereas the region's vegetation is like that of the tropics of South-East Asia, the wildlife is part of the unique Australian faunae complex. The animals evolved in isolation because of the deep seas separating the western tip of New Guinea from the Indonesian islands, divided by the so-called Wallace line (named for the naturalist Alfred Wallace). The sea never dried up here during the Pleistocene; Australasia was never connected to South-East Asia by a land bridge that animals could cross. The furry creatures of Melanesia are largely marsupials, animals that rear their young in pouches, such as tree kangaroos, wallabies, and possums, together with rats, dogs, and pigs introduced by humans. Pigs feature prominently in the lives of most Melanesians. The bird life, in contrast to the mammalian, is among the most colourful and varied in the world. The best-known are probably the majestic birds of paradise, while others include megapodes, brilliantly plumed parrots, hornbills and, largest of all, the flightless cassowary. In the seas there are many tropical fish, an important food source for coastal people including: tuna, barramundi, flying fish, various shellfish, sharks, turtles, dugongs and, in estuaries, enormous crocodiles.

Being almost on the equator makes Melanesia a hot place and one subject to monsoons, that is, characterised by two seasons depending on wind direction, one considerably wetter than the other. However this description applies only to a few places, with October to March being the wet season. Elsewhere the mountains break up the air masses, giving rise to less predictable local weather patterns. On the coast and at lower altitudes it is hot (mean maximum around 30 °C) and humid, and there are frequent and sometimes heavy falls of rain the year round. In the highlands and at higher altitudes it is warm (mean maximum around 25 °C), commonly sunny in the mornings, with cloud build-up and rainstorms in the afternoons and occasional frost.

The people

The inhabitants of Melanesia display considerable physical variation, making characterisation of their biological make-up difficult except in the broadest terms. They are short people, the average height for males being about 1.65 m and females about 1.6 m, although to call them pygmies (as some writers have some populations) is confusing and inaccurate. They are stocky and well-built, especially in the highlands. As the Greek-derived name 'Melanesia' for the region intimates, they are dark-skinned, ranging from almost coal-black to caramel-brown. Finally, the frequently heard name 'Papua' reminds us that they are frizzy-haired (Malay *papuwah*). Their features have been characterised

Plate 1.3   A Non-Austronesian or Papuan woman: a Bogaia mother from
the Strickland Gorge region carrying a screaming child on her shoulders.

as rugged – the nose generally broad across the tip, the lips prominent, the eyes dark brown. Men frequently have luxuriant beards. With regard to serological and other single-gene-marker evidence, there is little to tell because of the small amount of research undertaken in Melanesia. As one authority has dryly observed, 'For distributions, and the precise description of populations and subspecies, certain species of Melanesian birds are far better known than Melanesian man' (Howells 1973:161).

According to our current knowledge, it seems, for one thing, that significant numbers of Melanesians exhibit blood-group B. On the basis of this and other biological evidence, we can be sure that there is no direct connection between the so-called Oceanic Negroids of Melanesia and the people of Africa, whom they resemble physically in some regards. For distant relatives we must look to the small Negrito populations of South-East Asia and to the Australian Aborigines. It appears, on current evidence, that they evolved the characteristics they share with Africans (dark skins, tight curly hair, and so on) independently of them, perhaps as selective responses to similar tropical environments.

Some writers with an interest in the prehistoric peopling of Melanesia have tried to divide the population into racial types, corresponding to different waves of prehistoric migration into the region. These racial classifications usually propose three broad groups. The **Negritos**, remnants of the first arrivals, purportedly occur in isolated highland pockets and are short, muscular, heavy-featured and dark brown. The **Papuans**, descended from the next large prehistoric wave of immigrants, are slightly taller, a more coppery-brown, heavy-boned and reported sometimes to have hooked noses (Plate 1.4). The **Melanesians**, descendants of the last people to arrive, are supposedly the tallest and lightest-skinned of all Melanesia's inhabitants, of gracile build and less woolly-haired than others. We need not bother ourselves over much with these distinctions, for whatever the differences among the various racial stocks involved in the peopling of Melanesia by immigrants from South-East Asia they have interbred extensively and blended with one another over thousands of years. As a result, examples of all three physical types can be found in the same community and – worse still for racial classifications – diagnostic features of all three types in the appearance of individuals! Different physical and genetic types flow imperceptibly one into another, and small local populations display a staggering internal variety in biological character and appearance which resists tidy-minded regional classifications.

Plate 1.4 An Austronesian or Melanesian man: a Trobriand Islander
renowned for his knowledge of garden magic, stacking up yam tubers for a
harvest exchange.

Languages

Linguists study peoples' languages with a view to establishing and
corroborating relationships and tracing origins. Here again we have
problems regarding definitions. Linguists distinguish two major language groupings in Melanesia which they usually call **Austronesian**
(sometimes called Malayo–Polynesian or Melanesian) and **Non-
Austronesian** (or Papuan).

It is not known with any certainty where these two major groupings
came from nor when they first appeared in Melanesia, but linguists
agree that the Non-Austronesian was the first to arrive. The languages
so classified today descend from those of the early immigrants from
South-East Asia, but sufficient development has occurred locally over
the thousands of years that they have been spoken in Melanesia to
produce today's staggering range of languages, many of them unrelated
linguistically to any common protolanguage speculated to have existed

Table 1.1. *Non-Austronesian and Austronesian languages compared.*

	Austronesian (AN)	Non-Austronesian (NAN)
Phonetics	simple	varied
Vocabulary	certain common words shared (e.g., *tama* 'father', *ika* 'fish')	varies greatly between languages
Word order	subject – verb – object	subject – object – verb
Verbs	simple structure	complicated with range of aspects, moods and tenses
Gender	not differentiated	nouns may mark elaborately
Pronouns	share common basic forms	no shared forms
Possession	expressed by 'of' (e.g., 'axe of man') or possessive pronoun (e.g., 'man his axe')	expressed by ''s' equivalent (e.g., man's axe)
Article	present	rare
Counting	based on 5	bases vary: 2, 4, 8, or parts of body

long ago. The situation with the Austronesian grouping is less confusing because all of its languages belong to the same family. Nonetheless, where and when Austronesian originated is in dispute; suggestions include western Melanesia, where we find the greatest diversity in these languages (taken by some linguists as indicating the place of origin), but the more common view, which accords with the available archaeological and physical anthropological evidence, is that the prototype Austronesian language originated somewhere in South-East Asia and reached Melanesia with later immigrants. In any case, where we find Austronesian languages today they invariably show marked traces of Non-Austronesian influence. All of today's Melanesian languages are, to some extent and in significant regards, 'home-grown'.

The Non-Austronesian languages are found over a considerably larger area than the Austronesian ones. We find Austronesian speakers on many of the smaller islands, but they do not penetrate far into the interior of the region's largest island, New Guinea (which many take as clear evidence that they arrived later). The implication is not, however, that Austronesian languages have a limited global distribution: they are found in Indonesia, Polynesia, Micronesia, the Philippines, Malaysia and even Vietnam and Taiwan. Secondly, there are the considerable structural differences between the languages in each grouping (Table 1.1): briefly, Austronesian languages have simple structures, whereas Non-Austronesian ones have complex ones (such that, for instance, in some languages an elaborately conjugated and conditioned verb can comprise a whole sentence).

When we refer to these two major linguistic groups we are talking on a high level of abstraction. The actual languages comprising them and spoken today in Melanesia vary greatly. Indeed, the large number of different languages spoken across the region (some writers calculate that nearly half the world's languages occur here) has led some to call it the modern Babel. There are at least several hundred languages, and some authorities think there may be more than a thousand. It is difficult to know for certain, not only because many of the languages have yet to be described, but also because of the problems we have in deciding when one language ends and a new one begins – that is, distinguishing between dialect and language. We face similar difficulties regarding cultural traits, deciding where one culture or society ends and another starts. These problems illustrate again the difficulties we encounter when we try to classify; instead of becoming clearer things can become murkier.

The people themselves often make no attempt to make these distinctions among themselves, often having no names for what we perceive as different linguistic or cultural groups. The names given to these entities and now prominent in the anthropological literature are often contrived and sometimes comical in their derivation. Those who have christened these linguistic and cultural groups have often seized upon some frequently heard but unintelligible word to label them. The patrol that discovered the Wola called them the Wen, having heard them say '*wen, wen*' (soon, soon) as they walked along, trying to tell the strangers that they would soon reach the next place on the path. The Gnau of the Torricelli Mountains were named for their word *gnau* ('no'), presumably they were expressing negative feelings about the newcomers. The nearby Arapesh were more welcoming, perhaps; their word *arapesh* means 'friends'. So too, apparently, were the Siane of the Eastern Highlands, their word *siane* being a greeting – although it also means 'there are buttocks', suggesting a possible insult to the outsiders. And among the Orokaiva the word *orokaiva* means 'peace', suggesting that they feared attack.

A hypothetical cultural and linguistic model illustrates the problems that attend the drawing of boundaries around these groups (Figure 1.1). We can imagine a series of sociocultural and/or speech communities (A to J), the differences between which relate to geographical distance between them. The people in group D can understand and relate readily to those in C and E, for although they speak different dialects and have somewhat different customs the differences between them are not large (similarly, G can easily comprehend F and H); D can understand and relate to B, and with some effort, F, too, for there are several differences

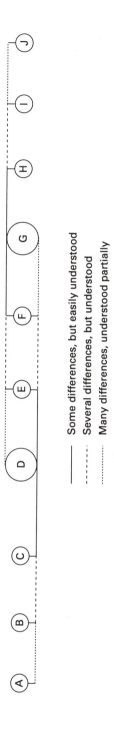

A B C D E F G H I J

—— Some differences, but easily understood

------ Several differences, but understood

·········· Many differences, understood partially

◯ Speech communities/cultures

Figure 1.1   A model of linguistic and cultural boundaries.

between them (similarly, G can E and I); and D can only partially understand and comprehend the practices of A and G, for there are many differences between them (similarly, G can D and J). D cannot understand or participate in the culture of H, I, or J (similarly G from A, B, or C); they are foreigners. It is difficult to draw boundaries and talk of different languages and cultures when one dialect and cultural tradition flows into another (and our chain could extend perhaps to Z or wherever some physical barrier prevents regular neighbourly interaction). It is inappropriate to think in firm categorical terms, although we habitually do so. We can expect some problems when we try to conceive of some aspects of Melanesian life and culture, for in some senses we have to cultivate different conceptions – think more flexibly with fluid categories.

Origins

The problems that we have in comprehending aspects of Melanesian life are not all a matter of difficulties with categories. When we address questions relating to origins we see further the extent of the gulf between our different preconceptions and approaches to problems. According to the Bogaia of the Muller Ranges, some of their kin groups originated as follows: Some kin groups 'came up' in Bogaialand, as people explain it. The kin groups called Iypaluwma, Imbuluw and Ayliy, for example, all descend from the snake–palm man called Wanaguw, who came to the Bogaia region from the headwaters of the Tekin River in the vicinity of Oksapmin. He was able to change his appearance from a young man to a yellow *sipera* snake to a black palm of the variety called *payliy*. When he arrived at the junction of the Bulago River with the Strickland River, at a place called Dogormiya, he found a house in which a woman called Mbaelmbaeliyma lived. She was asleep after eating a meal of grass shoots. Wanaguw waited until she awoke and came out to throw away the leaf waste. At first the strange changeling creature frightened and confused the woman, but they lived together from then on and she bore five sons called Iypaluwma, Imbuluw, Ayliy, Ngon, and Payliy. From the first three descended the present-day kin groups named after them, Ngon gave rise to a kin group which survives in the Oksapmin region, and Payliy featured in the founding of another kin group called Orsaengow. He came across a grass skirt one day at a place called Ilalimba, which is a large swampy hollow along the Bulago River upstream from Dogormiya. At the centre of the hollow there was once a wild screw-pine tree, surrounded by sedge of the kind used to make skirts. A woman had made and left a sedge skirt (which in Bogaia is called an *orsaengow*) at the base of the tree. The young man Payliy decided to lie in wait for the woman who had left it there. When she returned he took her for his wife, and she bore them a son they called Orsaengow, from whom the kin group so named descends. The Melanesian ethnographic record contains many accounts of the origins of different people in a similar vein. They seem to satisfy peoples' curiosity about their origins, mythical contents notwithstanding (see chapter 15), and we may treat them on some counts as oral histories, tolerably reliable accounts of past events. But they have limited historical depth. Answering questions of Melanesian origins requires archaeological evidence.

We customarily combine the evidence of physical anthropology and linguistics, outlined above, with that of archaeological investigations to answer questions relating to peoples' origins and ancestral lifeways. The ancient material remains unearthed by archaeological excavation give us fairly firm dates (using scientific techniques such as carbon-dating and thermoluminescence) by which to calibrate periods identified. Archaeological evidence on Melanesian populations, like that on the biology and languages is scanty and subject to constant revision as new material comes to light, but the broad outlines of their prehistory are now evident.

It is estimated that human beings first arrived in Melanesia 50,000 or more years ago, coming from South-East Asia during the Pleistocene era. This was the time of the Ice Ages, when seas were lower than they are today and landmasses consequently larger. Australia and New Guinea and many small islands of the South-West Pacific comprised one landmass that is called **Sahul**, and many of the islands of today's Indonesian archipelago were joined to the Asian mainland to produce a continent that is called **Sunda.** A stretch of sea with islands dotted about it that is called the **Wallacea** remained between them (marking today's Wallace line). It requires relatively little imagination to picture people leaving Sunda and island-hopping across to Sahul, the water between the two regions being considerably less extensive than it is today. We do not really know what these early arrivals were like or how they lived. The oldest site found so far in Melanesia is at a place called Kosipe in Papua New Guinea, which carbon remains date to 26,000 years BP. An excavation uncovered some interesting waisted axes, and similar axes have more recently been found in stream beds on the Huon Peninsula. We assume that these people lived by hunting and gathering. We envisage that they slowly trickled across the Wallacea and gradually spread from the west to the east, occupying Melanesia over several thousands of years.

The next archaeologically significant event with regard to immigrants is the arrival about 4,000 years ago, again from South-East Asia, of people who made pottery. The pottery they made is called Lapita ware (after a New Caledonian site). Fired at low temperatures, it is often fairly friable; it is usually plain, but the decorated sherds that occur are characteristically ornamented by dentate stamping (i.e. using toothed implements). The wares include globular cooking pots. Several pottery styles, some of them in use today, developed from this tradition. These more recent immigrants also built simple stone monuments. We assume that they were highly skilled seafarers, for we find their sites spread over a wide area, across scattered small islands and on the coasts of larger ones. They are thought to be of the same stock as those who went on to populate Polynesia and it is surmised that, like them, they were physically quite different from those who had arrived in Melanesia earlier, being lighter-skinned and more Mongoloid. Archaeologists have concluded that they were the Austronesians.

While we talk about these ancient population movements as migrations, they should not be thought of as sudden movements of large numbers of families, converging in flotillas of canoes on the Melanesian coastline. We are referring to a gradual movement of people over many hundreds, even thousands, of years which may have increased significantly in volume for a period when conditions were particularly propitious. These periodic booms may appear in the archaeological record as discrete migrations, each with its temporally discrete assemblage of artifacts, but whatever happened there was a constant blending of the new arrivals with the population already established in the region. Neighbours constantly interacted with and influenced one another, albeit to a limited extent geographically until Western foreigners intruded into their lives.

The important point to grasp from this brief review of Melanesia's prehistory because it conditions the contemporary ethnographic situation, which is our concern – is that we can clearly distinguish two migratory waves into the region: an ancient movement, extending over thousands of years, sometimes called the **Papuan**, and a more recent and briefer movement, the **Austronesian**. We need to have these clear in our minds, for they have given rise to the two great cultural traditions which we can distinguish in Melanesia today. The Papuans, or Non-Austronesians, are geographically and demographically the more prominent. The result is that accounts of them predominate in the literature on Melanesia, and this has led some writers to assume that they represent what might be thought of as characteristically Melanesian culture. The coming chapters also devote more space to the more numerous Papuans; the Austronesian minority is represented by the

Manus, Trobriand and Dobuan islanders. Although these two great cultural traditions are noteworthy, we should not forget that much mixing has occurred between them over the millennia, giving rise today to very considerable sociocultural variety. They do not exist as two separate monolithic cultural heritages; rather, they have contributed different traits to societies in varying proportions in different regions, one more markedly than the other at any given place.

Because many Melanesians used stone tools well into this century they are often considered backward, but in fact they were among the first people in the world to develop agriculture, contemporaneously with the occupants of the so-called Fertile Crescent in the Near East. Some have even suggested that the waisted axes found at Kosipe may have been used for clearing away natural vegetation to plant the soil (although this is only speculation, and we know that similar axes found in Australia were not so used). The first conclusive evidence of agriculture has been found in the Papua New Guinea highlands, where a series of ditches uncovered in the Wahgi Valley near Mount Hagen, the oldest dug 9,000 years ago, have been identified as designed to drain the swamps on the valley floor for agricultural purposes.

The arrival of new crops with the waves of immigrants from South-East Asia to supplement those that originated in the region would have been a significant factor. The region's indigenous crops include sago, sugarcane, breadfruit, screw-pine and varieties of green-leafed vegetables. Important introduced ones include yam, taro, bananas and sweet potato. The actual dates of arrival of these are unknown. Sweet potato is generally assumed to be a relatively recent arrival, although the date is hotly debated; the other crops had arrived in Melanesia by 5,000 years ago. The pig is another important food import from South-East Asia, and some finds in the highlands suggest that it may have arrived over 10,000 years ago. This ancient agricultural tradition remains alive in Melanesia, supplying the population with the greater part of its food requirements. The next two chapters take a closer look at it, reviewing subsistence practices.

FURTHER READING

Introductory texts dealing with Melanesia include:
P. Hastings, 1969 *New Guinea*. Melbourne: Cheshire.
F. M. Keesing, 1947 *Native peoples of the Pacific World*. New York: Macmillan.
M. J. Leahy and M. Crain, 1937 *The land that time forgot*. London: Hurst and
    Blackett.
J. Siers, 1984 *Papua New Guinea*. New York: St. Martin's.

Edited collections of papers include:

T. G. Harding and B. J. Wallace, 1970 *Cultures of the Pacific*. New York: Free Press.

L. L. Langness and J. C. Weschler, 1971 *Melanesia: Readings on a culture area*. Scranton: Chandler.

A. P. Vayda, 1968 *Peoples and cultures of the Pacific*. New York: Natural History Press.

On sociocultural anthropology see:

P. Brown, 1978 *Highland peoples of New Guinea*. Cambridge: Cambridge University Press.

A. Chowning, 1977 *An introduction to the peoples and cultures of Melanesia*. Menlo Park: Cummings.

I. Hogbin (ed.), 1973 *Anthropology in Papua New Guinea*. Melbourne: Melbourne University Press.

D. L. Oliver, 1989 *Oceania: the native cultures of Australia and the Pacific islands*. Honolulu: University Press of Hawaii.

On biological anthropology see:

R. D. Attenborough and M. P. Alpers (eds.), 1993 *Human population in Papua New Guinea*. Oxford: Oxford University Press.

W. Howells, 1973 *The Pacific Islanders*. London: Weidenfeld & Nicholson.

On archaeology see:

J. Allen and J. F. O'Connell (eds.), 1995 'Transitions: Pleistocene to Holocene in Australia and Papua New Guinea'. *Antiquity* vol. 69 special no. 69.

P. Bellwood, 1978 *Man's conquest of the Pacific*. London: Collins.

G. Irwin, 1992 *The prehistoric exploration and colonisation of the Pacific*. Cambridge: Cambridge University Press.

J. Terrell, 1986 *Prehistory in the Pacific islands*. Cambridge: Cambridge University Press.

On geography see:

H. C. Brookfield with D. Hart, 1971 *Melanesia*. London: Methuen.

D. Howlett, 1967 *A geography of Papua New Guinea*. Melbourne: Nelson.

FILMS

New Guinea: An island apart. British Broadcasting Corporation (The Natural World).

2 Food gathering, fishing and hunting in the Fly Estuary

People who depend directly upon their own efforts to meet their subsistence requirements live close to nature. Anthropologists regularly report that such people are able to identify several hundred, even upwards of a thousand, plants and other organisms that they encounter regularly in the course of their daily lives. This is ordinary, everyday knowledge familiar to all, not specialist lore restricted to a few experts. And these people may well be depending entirely upon their memories, having no floras or handbooks to consult.

Ethnoscience

A large body of information has been amassed over the years on the names given to plants and animals in other societies and the manner in which they are systematised into classificatory schemes. The elucidation of local taxonomies is thought to indicate the indigenous viewpoint and suggest how people manage relations with and exploitation of their environments. One of the current debates in this field of enquiry, called ethnoscience, concerns the universality or culture-specificity of principles used to classify natural phenomena and derives from the long-running anthropological dispute over the relationship between language and cognition known for the two writers who first formulated it in the 1930s as the Sapir–Whorf conundrum. It relates to what anthropologists call the 'emic' and 'etic' perspectives, the contrast between understanding indigenous explanations of phenomena and imposing Western intellectual theories on them. This problem regarding classification bears on chapter one's theme of defining categories in Melanesia. On the one hand, there are those who argue that because all human beings, regardless of culture, see the same objective discontinuities and organisms 'out there' (assuming that the world is not an imaginary creation existing only in our heads), it is irrelevant in postulating the existence of universal classificatory principles whether they have names for certain classes of phenomena. Even if some people in New Guinea, for example, have no word equivalent to our term 'marsupial', apparently not grouping together lexically all animals that rear their young in pouches, it is nonetheless valid to argue that they will be aware of the category because it is obvious 'out there'. On the other hand, there are those who argue that if people do not apparently group together some phenomena (lacking a term for such a category) they have a different conception of relationships in nature from the one they would have if they had a name for it, and that this different perception will inform their understanding of their environment and their approach to its exploitation. This latter position is closer to the post-modern critiques that are currently shaking anthropology to its foundations about the danger of imposing our worldview on others, questioning whether we can even comprehend, let alone aspire faithfully to represent, their view. This extreme relativist position not only privileges no discourse but also threatens to end all debate, for it makes us all prisoners of our own experiences and unique views. It is wisest perhaps to steer somewhere between these two extremes, accepting that there are facts 'out there' upon which we can agree but that our interpretation of these is subject to disagreement – that there may be no 'true' representation.

Another debate in ethnoscience centres on the extent to which peoples' naming and classification of species correlates with their importance to their livelihoods and, by extension, assists them in their exploitation of their resources by systematising their knowledge. Although there is some correlation on occasion between extent of classification and salience of species in peoples' lives, this is not an invariable relationship; there are many examples on record of complex classifications of phenomena that are relatively insignificant. Furthermore, the notion of cultural significance is woefully inadequate; many named plants and animals are important only in a secondary sense but nonetheless merit attention, having food-chain relations, for instance, with directly used, primarily significant species. It does seem reasonable to assume, however, that peoples' classifications of natural phenomena will inform their relations with nature and exploitation of its resources.

For our brief look at how people in Melanesia think about and exploit their natural environments we shall turn to the Fly Estuary region and the Gidra and Kiwai of the southern part of this enormous river's delta (some seventy-five kilometres wide at its mouth) (Map 2.1). It is where New Guinea comes closest to Australia. Its inhabitants have indirect connections with Queensland's Cape York Aborigines through their interaction with the people of the Torres Straits Islands (one of the first

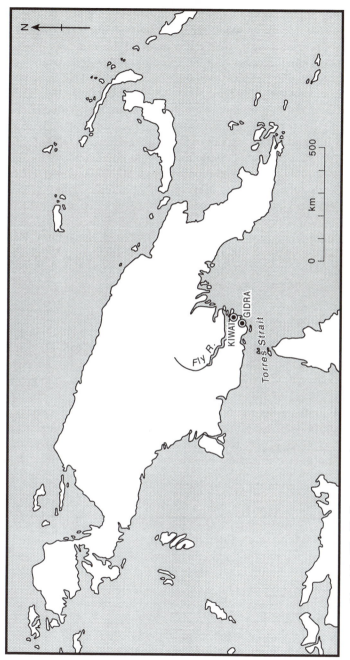

Map 2.1   The Fly Estuary peoples.

locations where anthropological fieldwork was conducted in Melanesia, by A. C. Haddon's Cambridge Expedition in 1898–99). It is a typical estuarine region – a low and relatively featureless plain, subject to seasonal inundation, with large areas of swamp criss-crossed by networks of small creeks.

In reviewing peoples' exploitation of their natural environments, this chapter concentrates on their use of wild resources through gathering, hunting and fishing strategies. Nowhere in Melanesia, contemporarily or in the recent past, are there any peoples that subsist entirely by hunting and gathering. Those who come nearest to it are perhaps the coastal inhabitants of some islands who barter fish with inland people for cultivated produce (e.g. on Manus Island [chapter 4]). Elsewhere, as in the eastern Fly Delta, wild food sources make up a significant part of peoples' diets, but even here horticulture plays a part in their subsistence arrangements; the Gidra and the Kiwai, for example, clear gardens during the dry season in which they cultivate yams, taros, bananas and sugarcane, among other crops. The mix of their subsistence activities raises some interesting questions of definition, relating again to the issue of categories and their contents in Melanesia.

Plants and subsistence

The Gidra identify eleven ecozones according to topographical location and associated vegetational community (Table 2.1); the Kiwai on the coast have additional marine ecozones, such as beach, lagoon, reef and open sea. The resources of these zones are well known to the local inhabitants, who structure their subsistence-related decisions accordingly; a Kiwai intending to make a dugong harpoon, for example, knows where he can expect to find a *túru* tree, the only straight-grained species of appropriate density. These ecozones offer different food-getting opportunities with their varying natural resources, which people exploit to achieve the returns they require. They not only know the conditions under which different plants flourish and where they prevail but also have an intimate awareness of the supply and maturity of various plants of interest to them in different locales.

The sago palm (*Metroxylon sagu* and *M. rumphii*), which the Kiwai call *doù* and the Gidra *sana*, illustrates the status of their knowledge and associated practices. This palm, the mainstay of their subsistence regime, thrives in the swampy conditions that characterise their estuarine region. A range of different swamp conditions occur here, from permanent to seasonally submerged locations, on plains and along margins of watercourses, and under various hydrophytic successions from sedge grasses

Table 2.1. *The vegetation communities identified by the Gidra. (After Ohtsuka 1983: 5.)*

Gidra Name	Vegetation Community	Dominant Species
bua	monsoon forest	Acasia, Flindersia, Hopea, Mangifera, Schizomeria, Parinari, Syzygium
kuur	savanna (heavily wooded)	Melaleuca, Imperata Pseudopogonatherum
yap	savanna (thinly wooded)	See kuur
tupi	grassland (large expanses)	Pseudoraphis, Schoenus, Eriachne
kuk	grassland (small areas)	See tupi
buayap	forest succeeding savanna	See bua and kuur
uotomibua	savanna succeeding grassland	See kuur and tupi.
posenibua	riverine forest (small creeks)	Terminalia, Barringtonia, Campnosperma, Syzygium
bojogbua	riverine forest (large creeks)	See posenibua
kulumbua	riverine forest (permanent rivers)	Rhizophora, Terminalia, Campnosperma, Syzygium
biit	swamp	Leersia, Phragmites

Table 2.2. *Gidra food consumption and percentage energy and protein intakes from different foodstuffs. (After Ohtsuka 1983:118–19.)*

Food Source	Average daily per-capita intake (g)	% Energy	% Protein
Sago	874	58.5	7.6
Coconuts	47	1.5	1.1
Garden crops	869	28.9	21.9
Wild plants	116	7.2	5.1
Meat	133	3.8	62.4
Fish	6	0.1	1.8

to water-tolerant trees. The sago palm may grow in any suitably wet location, but different varieties thrive under different conditions. The Gidra identify some twenty-three sago varieties and know well the conditions that best suit them and where these occur in their region. They are familiar with their growth requirements and habits and the length of time they take to reach maturity (from about ten years in permanent swamp to twenty years in seasonally flooded areas), and they are aware of the variations they can expect in their starch yields (from about 30 to 140 kg per palm).

Sago contributes significantly to the Fly peoples' diet, sago starch supplying 60 per cent of Gidra energy needs (Table 2.2). It is processed

Plate 2.1   Korowai women beating the pith of a sago palm in the extensive
swamps of south New Guinea, the Wildeman River region of Irian Jaya.

in a way common throughout Melanesia. Men fell the mature palms just
before flowering, when starch levels in the trunks are highest; the Kiwai
cut out the immature inflorescence some months before felling and so
prevent any starch transfer to the developing flower. After felling the
palm, men cut away the outer bark along the top half of the trunk to
reveal the starchy inner pith. Working in small groups, women grate this
with sago pounders, adze-like implements with concave, sharp-edged

ends. Then they transfer handfuls of the crushed pith to a trough made from a stout sago leaf sheath, using a fibrous coconut-spathe filter to catch woody pieces at the narrow end, above a palm-bark or palm-spathe receptacle (Plate 2.1). There they beat and knead it and rinse it repeatedly with water to flush out the starch, which is carried in suspension into the receptacle and sinks to the bottom as a fine white sediment (Plate 2.2). After draining off the orangey-brown water that fills the receptacle, they collect and dry the sago starch and store it in leaf-wrapped bundles.

Men claim ownership of individual sago palms and keep an eye on them, for example when hunting, or processing sago nearby. The palm, its flowering suppressed, depends on basal suckers to reproduce. These belong to the tree owner, who may dig them up and replant them elsewhere or leave them to self-propagate into dense stands. The growing palms require no attention until harvest. The horticultural status of these activities is equivocal, as is that of the activities associated with the coconut (*Cocos nucifera*), the sago palm's dryland equivalent. Although coconut is less prominent in the diet, the Gidra still distinguish eleven coconut cultivars with somewhat differing environmental demands. Coconut palms, which the Gidra generically call *gujo* and the Kiwai *ói*, are owned, like sago, by individual men who sometimes collect their fallen sprouting nuts and transplant them elsewhere and sometimes leave them to strike naturally. Like sago palms, coconuts demand no attention until they mature and bear nuts ten or fifteen years later, at which point youngsters climb them to harvest the nuts.

There is not much difference between these activities and those of nearby Australian Aborigines, customarily labelled hunter–gatherers, when, for example, they burn off grasses in limited areas to ensure a good yield of edible seeds next season or, when harvesting yams, they leave a proportion of tubers undisturbed in the soil at appropriate intervals to ensure adequate returns next time. They are engaging, like the Fly peoples, in limited management of plant resources, even exerting some human selective pressure on plant reproduction. They are to some degree practising horticulture with otherwise wild plant resources. The collection of food by the Gidra from certain other plants not cultivated in gardens might, in contrast, be called gathering. They collect galip nuts (*Canarium vitiense*) and tulip leaves and fruits (*Gnetum gnemon*), cycad seeds (*Cycas circinalis*), pandan nuts (*Pandanus brassii*), pangi nuts (*Pangium edule*), palm shoots (*Areca* sp., *Pinanga* sp. and others), wild yams (*Dioscorea pentaphylla*) and various other fruits (*Passiflora foetida*, *Citrus aurantifolia* and others). Their approach to the exploitation of these food sources is casual; for example, they fell galip trees randomly

Plate 2.2   A Korowai woman kneading grated sago pith in a palm-leaf-rib trough to release starch to be carried in suspension to a receptacle below.

around settlements to obtain their nuts, this abundant and rapidly growing tree requiring no apparent care at harvest to conserve stocks. The subsistence arrangements in the Fly region confuse the standard anthropological categories of 'hunter–gatherer', 'cultivator' and so on, by which we continue grossly to classify people. It is not only a question of determining at what point the management of plant resources moves these from the status of wild to farmed resources but also, as intimated, one of deciding how we are to categorise people who secure a proportion of their food needs from both gathering and cultivation. What proportion of their food supply do people need to cultivate to qualify as horticulturists? The Gidra obtain 71 per cent of their total energy requirements and 78 per cent of their protein intake from hunted and 'wild' resources, so they are perhaps more hunter–gatherers than farmers. But this designation implies that they engage in little horticulture, whereas garden produce supplies them with about one-quarter of their nutritional needs. The implication is that, as is often the case with anthropological terms, the categories 'hunter–gatherer', 'cultivator' and so on, are too imprecise for meaningful debate in Melanesia.

Subsistence and adaptation

Although sago supplies a substantial proportion of people's energy needs with its high carbohydrate content, it is deficient in many nutrients and demands supplementation to ensure an adequate and balanced diet. It often occurs as a swamp palm in regions with abundant fishable watercourses, and people commonly exploit these fish stocks for necessary protein. Dependence on fish varies from significant among the Kiwai, who live near or on the coast, to much less so among the Gidra, who live inland and extensively supplement their freshwater fish catch with hunted animals (Table 2.3). The complex exploitation of complementary food sources that characterises the food quest of sago eaters evidences their sophisticated adaptation to their environments. Adaptation is a central concept in evolutionary theory and relates to the adjustments that living things make in their dynamic interactions with their environments, the successful surviving under the relentless competition of natural selection. It has two aspects: one is biological and refers to the inheritable genetic changes in organisms which promote survival and hence reproductive success, and the other is cultural and refers to customary behavioural modifications or induced physiological changes that increase a population's chances of continuation.

These two sides to the idea of adaptation, biological and sociocultural, parallel a fundamental division in anthropology as a discipline between

Table 2.3. *Gidra and Kiwai ethnozoology and hunting returns.*
(After Ohtsuka 1983; Landtman 1927.)

Common Name	Gidra Name or No. Named Species	Scientific Name	Hunting Returns (No. animals & weight [kg])[1]
Pig	boma, worum	Sus scrofa	7 [308]
Grass wallaby	seba	Wallabia agilis	58 [720.6]
Bush wallaby	giur	Dorcopsis veterum	67 [296.8]
Scrub wallaby	suga	Thylogale sp.	
Bandicoot	ruei	Echymipera rufescens (?)	26 [45.5]
Bandicoot	girag	Echymipera sp.	
Cassowary	gigi, divare	Casuarius casuarius	4 [201]
Deer		Cervus timorensis	1 [58]
Possums and cuscuses	9	Pseudocheirus spp. Phalanger spp.	
Echidna			1 [2.7]
Rats	iare		1 [0.8]
Bats			12 [0.3]
Birds	ca. 100	Megapodius spp. Paradisea spp. etc.	26 [2]
Monitors	8	Varanus spp. etc.	3 [7.4]
Lizards	6	Egerina spp. Tiliqua sp. etc.	
Snakes	14	Liasis spp. Pseudechis sp. etc.	1 [20]
Crocodiles	hibara, sible	Crocodilus spp.	
Insects		Rhynchophorus sp. Oecophylla sp. etc.	
Turtles	gamo, waru, pamoa	Chelodina sp. Emydura sp.	
Dugong	momoro	Dugong dugon	
Fish	arimina (general name)	Sea and freshwater spp.	

[1] Survey of 80 days' hunting returns (Ohtsuka and Suzuki 1990).

biological (or physical) anthropology and cultural (or, more narrowly, social) anthropology. The former treats human beings as animals amenable to zoological study like any other species, covering issues such as biological evolution (both the fossil record and ethnological parallels with our nearest primate relatives), population genetics, disease patterns, physiological differences between people and so on. The latter, sociocultural side of the discipline treats human beings as unique culture-bearing creatures demanding sociological study and concerns the myriad manifestations of human society, encompassing such topics as economic organisation, political systems and ideologies, religious beliefs and practices, kinship arrangements, social change and history and such like. It is this perspective that largely informs this book's introduction to the mosaic of Melanesian societies. Some topics bridge the gap between these two sides of the discipline. Kinship practices and customs, for example, markedly influence population gene frequencies; beliefs about the cause and treatment of sickness relate to disease patterns; cultural devices interface between humans and their environments and influence ecological relationships and so on. Nutrition is another topic with both biological and sociological aspects. The human animal needs to take in a balance of nutritive elements within a certain range to survive biologically, but it is not only the foods locally available that influence the balance; cultural practices such as those relating to food preparation, food taboos and food procurement also have a noticeable impact on nutrition.

Sago processing combined with foraging appears to be a particularly successful adaptive response to swampland environments. The indications are that this subsistence combination is one of considerable antiquity. Sago is an ancient crop which probably originated in the swamps of Melanesia and, according to the sparse archaeological evidence currently available, the region's inhabitants have practised hunting and gathering for some tens of thousands of years. This suggests a markedly stable adaptation to swampy regions, which are not otherwise promising to human settlement. It ensures adequate nutritional intake under adverse ecological conditions for limited populations, but it is not one that allows for population expansion beyond certain modest levels – about 0.5 persons per square kilometre for the eastern Trans-Fly people. The natural resource base, both plant and animal, is inherently limited. The swampland environment favoured by sago is also unfavourable to human health, with several diseases, notably malaria, being prevalent there.

Hunting

The antiquity of the sago processing and hunting/fishing, food-getting arrangement corresponds with its intermediate status in relation to so-called foraging and farming subsistence regimes. Also noteworthy in this regard is the absence or relative unimportance of domesticated pig herds among the Fly Estuary populations (in striking contrast to nearly all other Melanesian societies), which reflects the comparatively limited development of a farming approach to subsistence in the region. The people here depend on hunting feral pigs more than herding domesticated ones to supply them with pork. They also hunt a wide range of other animals, including various marsupials (from wallabies to bandicoots), birds (from large flightless cassowaries to small, quick honeyeaters), reptiles (from crocodiles to lizards) and so on. Their hunting strategies range from individual stalking to group-organised drives. It is predominantly men who hunt, particularly larger game. We assume that the strategies that hunters employ utilise their natural knowledge to ensure the best returns for their efforts.

It is common for a man to go off to hunt alone, accompanied by a dog and armed with bow and arrows. He knows where to look for particular game – in the forest, for example, for shy bush-wallabies and on the savanna for easier-to-detect grass-wallabies. He will be on the lookout for evidence of recent feeding, looking under fruiting trees, for instance, to see if any animals have fed on the fallen fruits. He will search for tracks and droppings too. If he anticipates that an animal is likely to return to feed again, he may construct a leafy hide nearby overlooking the place. If the wait promises to be a long one he may erect a trap, especially if the spoor pattern suggests that the animal is repeatedly following the same approach to the food source. The Fly peoples commonly erect triggered deadfalls of heavy logs to fall on a pig, cassowary, or other animal that they think is in the vicinity. They bait the trap inside with sago pith, coconut kernel, or appropriate tree fruits and spread some of the bait along the path. The Kiwai also dig up one of the animal's footprints and place it walking into the trap: 'that mark . . . pig he go straight inside *di* [trap]'.

Sometimes a hunter will flush out an animal. He may spot a grass-wallaby for example, by the movement of grass around it as it feeds and give chase. He may try to stalk his quarry without disturbing it, beating on the ground to imitate the thump of the animal's tail as it hops along to suggest to it that a mate is in the vicinity. Dogs help hunters locate and run down their quarry, although these erstwhile canine partners may make off with the animal or, if it is large, be injured or killed by it. The Kiwai put great store by their hunting dogs and regularly feed them concoctions thought to improve their skill at flushing out and killing game. Among the ingredients believed to improve dogs' hunting skills are sticky grass burrs, *huhúomére* flies (which buzz irritatingly around people), leeches and *gópu* sucker-fish (which attach themselves to other marine animals), all of which they believe increase the tenacity with which dogs hang on to flushed game together with a white feather from the *gágome* wader (a bird that walks with a sideways movement of the head like a dog picking up the scent), a fragment of shark's tooth to promote ferocity and so on.

Communal hunting occurs less frequently. The Gidra arrange communal hunts in the dry season, when savanna grasses are dry. The party of ten or more men spreads out in a rough circle one to two kilometres across, enclosing an area where game returns are anticipated to be good, and lights a series of fires. The men, armed with bow and arrows, await animals fleeing from the fire; some animals are caught in the conflagration, and their charred bodies are searched for later. Another communal hunting strategy is for a group of men to surround a megapode's incubating mound and poke sticks into it to flush out any pythons lurking inside. The returns per participant in group hunting are somewhat less than those for individuals hunting alone; communal hunting is reported to yield 0.70 kg of game per hour, whereas bow-and-arrow-armed individuals may bag 1.01 kg per hour.

Fishing

The Fly peoples employ a range of techniques to catch fish. Sometimes they fish alone and on other occasions in groups, as they hunt. Men use bows and arrows and spears, particularly trident-pointed weapons, to fish both in the sea and on inland watercourses. They may wade in the sea, off the beach or out on a shallow reef, or they may use the same shooting/spearing technique while standing in a canoe. At other times they use hooks of turtle shell, gorgehooks of sharpened wood, or fish spines baited with sago grubs or other larvae and suspended from fine coconut-fibre lines. They may trail these baited lines from canoes or attach them to sago-midrib rods and cast them angling-fashion from the beach. Women use hoopnets to trawl for fish in both the sea and streams. They also gather shellfish and crustaceans, such as crabs and crayfish, in beach pools at low tide and in inland swamps and streams (Plates 2.3 and 2.4). They sometimes employ a conical fishtrap of basketwork, which they hold vertically, open end downwards, plunging it quickly over fish to trap them on the bottom; they secure their catch by squeezing the mouth of the trap together and flinging it up on the shore.

Other, larger conical traps are positioned in dams constructed across streams. Men fell trees across a creek and fill in holes with poles, palm fronds, and clay. The ebbing current on tidal creeks is so strong that it sweeps fish downstream into the traps. On some watercourses the tidal flow produces a turbulent torrent that carries all fish caught in it out to sea, and men standing along the banks can catch considerable numbers in the churning muddy water, spearing at random. Other waterways and swamp creeks are not tidal. If they dam these, men may beat *Derris* spp. shrubs in the water to poison the fish, spearing and shooting those which rise stupefied to the surface. Some streams develop ponds naturally in the dry season, their water levels falling to leave fish isolated in pools. Sometimes people bale these pools out further with palm-

Plate 2.3   A Korowai man making a basket-like container from a sago palm frond to serve as a fish trap.

Plate 2.4 Using a pole to submerge in a river the woven sago-leaf container, baited in the bottom with a broken-up ant's nest, to catch crayfish.

spathe scoops to catch the fish. They stage night fishing expeditions, holding flaming torches to attract the fish and shooting them as they swim curiously up to the surface.

Although fishing is a prominent subsistence pursuit for coastal people, contributing significantly to their diet, they prize the capture of dugong and turtle above all else. Men catch these animals out on the reefs. They use highly valued harpoons four metres long with detachable hardwood points attached to plaited lines. They harpoon from canoes, standing poised in the bows, or from platforms specially erected on the reef overlooking the seagrasses on which the dugong or seacow grazes. When a man strikes an animal, he throws himself into the sea to give the harpoon maximum thrust, putting the weight of his whole body behind it. Canoes pursue the wounded animal thrashing on the end of the line. Men dive into the sea to attach further lines to the stricken beast, which they haul to the canoe and lift in. They avoid further spearing of the animal and the spilling of blood in the sea. They place turtles on their backs in the bottoms of canoes and bludgeon dugong to death or drown them by holding them under water. The hunters announce their success as they approach the shore by blowing on conch shell trumpets, and a crowd comes to meet them. They distribute the flesh among their community, along kin lines, with careful regard to reciprocal obligations. The harpooner should keep only an insignificant cut for himself – a common practice among hunting people. By generously distributing the catch to others he enhances his social standing.

Environmental knowledge

According to the Fly peoples the catching of dugong and turtle depends not only on technical expertise but also on ritual management, as to a lesser extent do hunting and fishing generally. This aspect of subsistence behaviour embodies environmental lore augmenting that communicated in everyday contexts. The Fly peoples' ethnozoological classifications indisputably organise knowledge important to fishing and hunting success, codifying it and passing it on. A cursory review of the Kiwai ethnography, which attempts no systematic record, reveals some thirty names for fish, including *kairo* and *mavemave* (crayfish), *hamu* (stingray), *kurupu* (rock-fish), *peko* (blackfish), *búduru* (eel), *báidamu* and *kómuhóru* (sharks), *dúomu* (catfish), and *bíridáe* (flying fish). This knowledge may be organised in a way unfamiliar to us and may even lack systematic hierarchical structure. Among the Kiwai, for example, the nearest thing to our idea of 'animal' is *pómorona*, which includes pigs, wallabies, cuscus, rats, edible birds, iguana and carpet snakes but not birds of prey or any animals that live in swamps or water. The taxon *arimína*, which applies specifically to aquatic animals, includes not only fish but also anything edible. The definition of edibility varies, however, between persons depending on their totemic affiliation and associated taboo foods. In addition to passing on knowledge using exotically constituted classifications, these people transmit it in other ways even less accessible to us, such as in magical practices and ritual symbols.

The Fly peoples approach fishing and hunting not just as mundane subsistence activities but as enterprises hedged around with ritual observances that are necessary to ensure a favourable outcome. When a young Kiwai man harpoons his first dugong, for example, relatives mark the event to ensure future harpooning successes. When he beaches his canoe and disembarks, his father, mother's brother, or other senior relative meets him with a concoction comprising pieces of a hawk's eye and talon, a dog's tooth, a bone from a 'mysterious creature', and a *djábel* fish's tail. He ties it, wrapped up in a *mánabába*-leaf parcel, to the boy's bicep after making an incision with a *havaría* shell. The older man then stands astride the dugong on the beach, facing towards its head, and the young harpooner crawls through his legs along the dugong's back. When his head is above the dugong's, his mother puts some of the concoction in his mouth for him to swallow, and his straddling relative spits some that he has chewed onto his back. The next time the young man holds a harpoon he will feel his arm twitch in readiness to strike hard at the quarry.

Knowledge conveyed in such symbolic acts is alien to our scientific perspective and difficult to comprehend; we can only glimpse the imagery. The small *djábel* fish, for instance, is thought to pilot dugong to the harpoon platform on the reef; the dog is a valuable accomplice to hunters tracking and cornering game; and the sharp-eyed hawk with its powers of intense concentration and lightning reflexes, falls on prey and grabs it in powerful talons. But it would be a distortion simply to reduce these practices to cryptic communications of environmental knowledge facilitating exploitation of the natural world. They also reflect and promote a certain attitude of mind and approach to life. On one level it is possible to argue that the Fly peoples' knowledge of their natural environment is not enough to give them secure command of their food supply. In exploiting wild resources and catching unpredict-able fish and animals they confront the uncontrollable side of nature, and they may be expressing something about their perceptions of their relations with it. It may even provide them with a sense of psychological security in an unsure world to believe that ritual and magical manipula-tions give them some control over it. We should be wary of disparaging such ideas from the comfort of our more secure, supermarket-supported lives.

FURTHER READING

The ethnographic monographs upon which this review is based are:

B. M. Knauft, 1993 *South coast New Guinea cultures*. Cambridge: Cambridge University Press.

G. Landtman, 1927 *The Kiwai Papuans of British New Guinea*. London: Macmillan.

R. Ohtsuka, 1983 *Oriomo Papuans: Ecology of sago eaters in lowland Papua*. Tokyo: Tokyo University Press.

R. Ohtsuka and T. Suzuki (eds.), 1990 *Population ecology of human survival*. Tokyo: Tokyo University Press.

E. B. Riley, 1925 *Among Papuan headhunters*. London: Seeley.

On ethnoscience and ecological anthropology see:

B. Berlin, 1992 *Ethnobiological classification: Principles of classification of plants and animals in traditional societies*. Princeton: Princeton University Press.

R. Ellen, 1982 *Environment, subsistence and system*. Cambridge: Cambridge University Press.

C. Kocher Schmid, 1991 *Of plants and people: A botanical ethnography of Nokopo village, Madang and Morobe Provinces, Papua New Guinea*. Basler Beiträge zur Ethnologie 33.

I. S. Majnep and R. Bulmer, 1977 *Birds of my Kalam country*. Oxford: Oxford University Press.

P. Sillitoe, 1996 *A place against time: land and environment in the Papua New Guinea highlands*. Amsterdam: Harwood Academic Press.

On hunting and sago production elsewhere see:

P. D. Dwyer, 1985 'A hunt in New Guinea: Some difficulties for optional foraging theory.' *Man* 20: 243–53.

P. D. Dwyer, 1990 *The pigs that ate the garden*. Ann Arbor: University of Michigan Press.

R. L. Hide (ed.), 1984 *South Simbu: Studies in demography, nutrition, and subsistence*. Boroko: Institute of Applied Social and Economic Research.

P. K. Townsend, 1974 'Sago production in a New Guinea economy.' *Human Ecology* 2: 217–36.

FILMS

The Kiwai: Dugong hunters of Daru. Australian Broadcasting Commission.

The sharkcallers of Kontu. Institute of Papua New Guinea Studies Pacific Video-Cassette Series 4.

3 Swidden cultivation in the Bismarck Range

Although they grow a variety of crops, Melanesians customarily depend on one as their staple: the five major staples are sweet potato, taro, yams, sago and bananas. The crops they grow and the ones they depend upon as their staples vary from one place to another – the region's location, climate and so on, determining this to some extent.

Shifting cultivation

People are cultivators throughout Melanesia and have been, as we have seen, since ancient times. Horticulture features everywhere to some extent in the food quest, although dependence on cultivated vegetables and fruits varies from place to place – some relying more than others on hunting and fishing to supply them. Regardless of the crops grown and their proportions in the diet, we find that people cultivate them in a similar way across the Melanesian region. They all practise variations of the agricultural regime called shifting or swidden cultivation.

In this system of agriculture, people rotate the land they cultivate instead of the crops they grow on it. They restore the fertility of their soil in this manner by allowing it to rest and recover under natural vegetation. People periodically move or shift their gardens from one location to another under this land management, hence the name 'shifting cultivation'. They clear the natural vegetation from one site after another on the territory they occupy, and plant the clearings with crops one or more times. The burning of the vegetation cleared from the site – which is where the term 'swidden' comes from (it is old Norse for 'burning') – is an important step in this cultivation regime. The cultivators of sites abandon them before their crop yields decline unacceptably and allow them to lie fallow for many years, during which the surrounding natural vegetation recolonises the areas and restores their natural fertility.

In our study of Melanesian shifting cultivation we shall take a close look at the practices of the Maring, who live in the highlands of Papua

New Guinea, in the valleys of the Jimi and Simbai Rivers, which flow through the Bismarck Mountains (Map 3.1). They are typical high-landers, living in precipitous mountain country. They cultivate their swiddens on steep mountain slopes, depending on sweet potato as their staple and taro. They occupy squat houses, sometimes adjacent to gardens. Variably composed family groups make up homesteads. The Maring are fractious people and engage in periodic bouts of fighting with neighbours. They keep sizeable pig herds and kill animals at social and ritual events, often to appease the spirits of ancestors. They also place high regard on the exchange of these creatures and other valued objects such as sea-shell ornaments on prescribed social occasions.

Cultural ecology

The ethnography on Maring shifting cultivation presents it broadly in terms of cultural ecology, an apt paradigm for structuring a review of this agricultural regime. Cultural or human ecology borrows ideas from the biological discipline of ecology and applies them to human popula-tions. One approach to the study of ecology is to follow the flow of energy through biological communities. The ultimate source of this energy is the sun, the powerhouse of all life. Plants fix solar energy by photosynthesis; they also take up inorganic nutrients and water from the soil as they grow. Animals, unable to capture solar energy for them-selves, depend on plants, feeding on them either directly (herbivores) or indirectly (carnivores). The result is food chains or complex food webs in which different creatures feed on different plants and on one another to secure the energy and nutrients they require to live. In any region they are elaborately interlinked in an ecosystem. It is possible to measure the solar energy entering any ecosystem, flowing through it and maintaining life (the unit used in these measurements is the kilocalorie). Each time there is a transfer of energy in an ecosystem (animal eating plant or another animal), a substantial proportion is degraded and lost. Ecolo-gists sometimes convey this diminishing one-way flow of energy through ecosystems with trophic pyramids, shrinking towards their apices with decreasing available energy. Ecology is not synonymous with conserva-tion as many people think, although its study makes us acutely aware of how delicately balanced and interlinked natural systems are and engen-ders sympathy for conservation issues.

When studying human beings in an ecological framework, we are concerned with how they fit into and manipulate food webs. Applied to subsistence practices and behaviour, the ecological approach attempts to describe them in terms of a cost-accounting model relating human

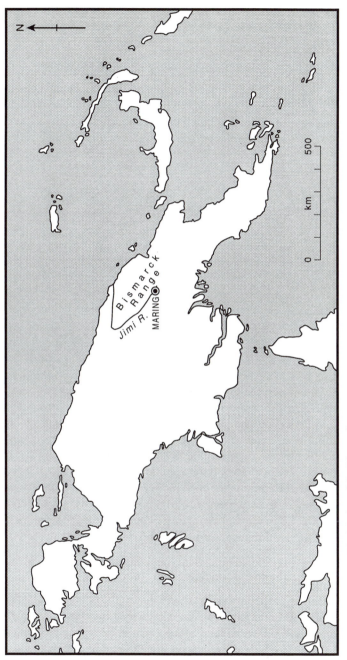

Map 3.1   The Maring of the Bismarcks.

Table 3.1. *A balance sheet of the energy transactions involved in Maring shifting cultivation.*

Debit Energy Expended in Gardening (kcal per acre)		Credit Energy Obtained from Crops (kcal per acre)	
Clearing vegetation	39,639	Tubers	4,005,785
Fencing in area	17,082	Greens	120,263
Burning dry vegetation and preparing plots	16,722	Pulses	14,894
Planting crops	16,553	Cucurbits	73,484
Weeding and garden maintenance	104,668	Shoots	33,394
Harvesting crops	42,567	Maize	33,336
Carrying crops home	59,882	Bananas	304,048
		Sugar cane	304,609
Total	297,113	Total	4,889,849

Rate of energy return (debit/credit ratio) = 1:16.5 kcal

For detailed figures see Rappaport (1984: tables 3, 4, and 5). He distinguishes between two kinds of gardens: predominantly sweet potato at higher altitudes and taro-yam lower down; the yields from different crops vary between them, as does the energy expended in harvesting from them and carrying their produce home. The data relating to both kinds of gardens are combined in this table.

food-getting activities to the natural environment exploited. Human ecology tries to document the energy people expend in pursuing their subsistence activities and compares this with the energy they obtain in return, from the food secured, to fuel their biological survival. The ecosystems perspective uses a balance-sheet approach with energy expended in subsistence activities on the cost side and that gained from food obtained on the income side. Physiological tests with equipment that measures rates at which individuals respire and consume oxygen (which is biologically speaking the way in which we burn energy) tell us how many kilocalories they use in various activities, and chemical analysis of the food they consume tell us how many kilocalories human beings obtain from what they eat. The major agricultural activities and crops of the Maring are arranged as a balance sheet detailing the energy they expend and that repaid in the crops harvested in Table 3.1.

Establishing gardens

The Maring gardener has first to select a site for a new garden. A range of factors will influence his choice, including rights to land as determined by the kin-based land tenure system of his society, which restricts men to tracts where others recognise their rights to claim land through

kin connections. Physical considerations such as site topography, vegetation cover, altitude, aspect and nearness to other gardens and homesteads will also influence his decision. Once a man has decided on an
area for a new garden he has first to clear it of natural vegetation. The
vegetation will usually comprise secondary regrowth of soft-wooded
trees and occasionally grass; the Maring commonly clear areas that have
been cultivated previously and left fallow, often by their fathers many
years before. Sometimes they clear virgin rain forest, but the trees here
are considerably larger and harder, and such sites are usually further
from settled areas, increasing the work demanded to establish and
manage them. Men prefer secondary forest for gardens because it is
easier to clear and maintain.

Initially, men and women work together to cut down the understorey
vegetation of small plants and saplings, leaving the large trees standing
across the site. After a couple of weeks or so, when the cut vegetation
has dried somewhat and fallen back, men proceed to fell the trees and
lop off their branches, scattering the smaller wood about the already cut
undergrowth to dry. They climb and pollard the largest trees, not felling
them because they would be difficult to clear off the site. Previously,
working with stone tools, site clearance was somewhat harder work than
it is today using introduced steel axes and bush knives (see chapter 7).
In the new steel tool era, the Maring expend a calculated 39,639
kilocalories clearing one acre.

Once they have cleared a plot of vegetation, the next task facing
swidden agriculturalists is to enclose it. The Maring, like other highlanders, have to enclose their swiddens to prevent the depredations of
pigs. They construct fences by driving in stakes at roughly three-metre
intervals and lashing between them logs laid horizontally on top of one
another (in other parts of Melanesia people construct other types of
barrier; some drive in stakes closer together and omit the horizontal
logs, lashing a sapling along the top edge to give strength, others arrange
barriers of tree trunks, some dig ditches and ramparts, and so on). The
heavy work of enclosing a plot falls to men (Plate 3.1). It is strenuous,
entailing the splitting and dressing of stakes and logs and frequent trips
into the forest to collect vines for binding the logs in position. The
amount of fencing erected around gardens varies because men cluster
their gardens together and share fence lines where possible. Fencing
entails the expenditure of an estimated 17,082 kilocalories per acre.

The next stage in the swiddening cycle involves the burning of all the
vegetation cut down on the site once it has dried out. This is important
not only because it disposes of the vegetational litter, thus exposing the
soil for planting, but also because it releases the mineral nutrients locked

Plate 3.1   Establishing a garden: a man, surrounded by the vegetational debris of clearance, uses a club to hammer wedges into a tree trunk to split it for fence stakes.

up in the natural vegetation, making them available to the future crop. This stage is crucial to the fertility of the site for the cropping interval and its yields. When we consider that the layer of fertile topsoil suitable for cultivation is rarely more than a few inches deep in the Maring region – a common situation in tropical forested areas – and is therefore soon depleted of nutrients under cultivation, we can appreciate that the releasing of nutrients through burning is beneficial if not critical to the growth of the crops subsequently planted on the site. Furthermore, a tropical forest ecosystem stores a substantial part of its nutrient capital in its standing vegetation as an adaptation to the low nutrient-holding potential of many soils: 'The tropical rain forest lives not on the soil beneath it but on itself' (Hastings 1969: 8), new growth depending on humus for a goodly proportion of its nutritional requirements. Shifting cultivators must consequently reduce the vegetation to ash, thus making nutrients quickly available to their crops, for they cannot rely on the soil's store alone.

The Maring begin to burn the vegetation they have cut down between one and four months after starting on a garden, depending on the weather, the rate at which the vegetation dries out and on the pace at which they work. They light fires on a number of days, for one burning is not sufficient to incinerate all the litter. This is not particularly onerous work. At the same time they weed the area of wild herbs that have established themselves in the interval spent fencing the site. They further prepare the plots for planting by marking out individuals' areas with logs and laying other logs across the grade of the slope to retain the soil and reduce erosion losses. All this work uses an estimated 16,722 kilocalories per acre.

The plot is ready for planting once they have cleared all the natural debris. The Maring raise the majority of their crops from vegetative cuttings, including sweet potato, taro, yams, sugarcane and *Setaria* grass; the seed-propagated exceptions include the pulses and maize and some of the greens and cucurbits. When they are ready, gardeners first collect together their planting stock, mainly fresh cuttings from established gardens, plus any fireplace-stored seeds. They plant their cuttings in dibble holes which they punch with heavy pointed digging sticks into the otherwise untilled soil; seeds are either planted individually in thumb-made depressions or scattered on the soil surface (Plate 3.2). Women plant, and are responsible for, some crops and men tend others, reflecting the strict sexual division of labour that generally orders agricultural work. They expend an estimated 16,553 kilocalories of energy planting an acre of garden.

Once planted, a garden demands some attention while the crops

Plate 3.2   Planting a garden: a woman, surrounded by newly dibbed areas,
firms sweet potato slips into the recently cleared and cleaned soil.

grow. This consists primarily in weeding out herbaceous competitors
that seed themselves within the swidden, a task which in a few months
becomes virtually continuous. Weeding demands the expenditure of
more energy than all the work put in previously to establish a garden,
some 104,668 kilocalories per acre. This high expenditure figure
includes energy used in other maintenance work undertaken during this
period, such as tying sugarcane to supports, propping up plants heavy
with produce (e.g. bananas), and so on.

The Maring do not practise clean weeding but are careful to leave any
newly seeded tree saplings untouched. They call these the 'mother of
gardens', a reference to their coming fertility-restoring role when the
plot has been abandoned. A garden takes goodness out of a site to
sustain the human population. The secondary regrowth which these
trees portend will naturally restore the site's fertility during the fallow
period. Hence the Maring nurture them, even though they compete
with the crops they have planted. Indeed, when they are robust saplings

these trees will induce gardeners to abandon sites before they have harvested all of their crops; by rendering harvesting more laborious as it becomes less rewarding, they help prevent people from seriously depleting the soil. These young trees also provide a web of roots penetrating deeper than the roots of crops which serves to protect the soil against tropical downpours and the leaching of nutrients during the cropping period; their developing leaf canopy later serves the same purpose.

Harvesting gardens

The Maring start to harvest crops from a garden about two months after planting it and continue to do so without a break until they abandon it some one and a half to two years later. By this time another garden subsequently established will have started to yield. The agricultural regime is a continuous cycle of shifting but overlapping gardens. The people of the Jimi Valley cultivate areas briefly and move on to new swiddens relatively quickly; in the Central Highlands in contrast, people have evolved a highly efficient soil management strategy involving periodic short grassy fallows which allows them to keep some gardens under more or less continuous cultivation for many years.

Harvesting is an almost daily task, for the crops cultivated here (unlike some Melanesian staples, such as yams and sago) do not lend themselves to storage. A garden is analogous to a living pantry. The Maring approach to harvesting is not to damage crop plants but to take a little from them at intervals, thus allowing them to recover and continue yielding (they pluck a few leaves at a time from spinach plants, for instance, until they are old, when they may uproot them). There are some plants, however, such as taro, for which this strategy is inappropriate, and these they have to harvest all at once.

The daily chore of harvesting, which falls largely to women, is not onerous, but the energy expended on this work in the course of a garden's life is considerable, an estimated 42,567 kilocalories per acre. While harvesting women also engage in some weeding nearby. The Maring also expend considerable energy in transporting their harvested produce back to their homes; it is estimated that, after weeding, this is the most demanding gardening task. When they have trudged home with their produce, the Maring cook and eat it – that is, they take in energy to replace both that which they have expended on the above activities and on the others that characterise their life. We now move from the debit side of our balance sheet to the credit.

The Maring diet is predominantly tuberiferous; tubers make up five-

Table 3.2. *The crops cultivated by the Maring. (After Rappaport 1984: 44–46; Clarke 1971: 225–40.)*

Crop	Maring Name	Identification	No. of Cultivars
Bananas	*yobai*	*Musa*	28
Beans	*bar*	*Psophocarpus tetragonulobus,*	4
		Dolichos lablab	
Cucumbers	*pika*	*Cucumis sativus*	1
	mop		1
Ginger	*ranggo*	*Zingiber*	1
Gourds	*yibona*	*Lagenaria siceraria*	1
Greens	*chengmba*	*Rungia klossi*	5
	rampmañe	*Commelina*	1
	gonebi	*Brassica juncea*	1
	rumba	*Cucurbitaceae*	1
	kumerik	*Pollia*	2
	kiñkiñmai	*Hemigraphis*	2
Hibiscus	*chem*	*Hibiscus manihot*	17
Maize	*konapa*	*Zea mays*	2
Manioc	*baundi*	*Manihoc esculenta*	1
Parsley	*kiñipo*	*Oenanthe javanica*	1
Pawpaw	*paipai*	*Carica papaya*	1
Pitpit	*mangap*	*Saccharum edule*	16
	kwiai	*Setaria palmifolia*	7
Pumpkin	*ira*	*Cucurbita pepo*	1
Screw pine	*komba*	*Pandanus conoideus*	34
Sugarcane	*bo*	*Saccharum officinarum*	27
Sweet potato	*ñogai*	*Ipomoea batatas*	24
Tannia	*kong*	*Xanthosoma sagittifolium*	1
Taro	*dang*	*Colocasia esculenta*	27
Tobacco	*yur*	*Nicotiana tabacum*	1
Tree ferns	*bep*	*Cyathea*	3
Watercress	*ningk gonebi*	*Nasturtium officinale*	1
Yams	*wan*	*Dioscorea alata*	32
	man	*Dioscorea bulbifera*	4
	dingga	*Dioscorea pentaphylla*	1
	ruka	*Dioscorea esculenta*	1

sixths of the total energy produced. The tuber crops include the two staples, sweet potato and taro, plus yams and cassava. Besides these crops, the Maring cultivate varieties of green leaf-yielding plants, such as parsley, hibiscus, watercress and ferns; pulses, including winged and hyacinth beans; cucurbits, including pumpkins, cucumbers and gourds; shoots harvested from domesticated grasses; maize, bananas and sugarcane; and screw pines from which they obtain oil-rich fruits – thirty-two species of plants all told (Table 3.2), with more than 200 varieties. As do

Plate 3.3   A young man, standing in a thick carpet of sweet potato vines, harvests beans from a vine trained up a pole standing in the centre of a clump of edible *Setaria* shoots.

many other shifting cultivators, they grow these crops intermingled with one another in the same gardens. A mature garden is a stratified stand of vegetation with creeping foliage (such as that of sweet potato) on the surface, low-standing herbs (some greens), plants of middling height (such as taro), taller plants (e.g. sugarcane), and finally the tallest crops (notably bananas) spreading out over all (Plate 3.3). To enter a Maring garden 'is to wade into a green sea. To walk is to push through irregular waves of taro and *Xanthsoma* and to step calf-deep in the cover of sweet potato vines. Overhead, manioc, bananas, sugar cane and *Saccharum edule* provide scattered shade. Rising above the flood of crops are remnants of the forest which was there before clearing' (Clarke 1971: 76).

This intermingling of crops is a highly efficient cultivation strategy. It uses space effectively, achieving a high photosynthetic rate for a given area, and roots replicate the efficiency of the foliage above by tapping all zones for nutrients. Intercropping discourages the spread of plant-specific insect pests; they cannot pass casually from plant to neighbouring plant. It also offers maximum protection to the thin tropical soil. In this regard the structure of swidden plots has been likened to that of the forest they replace, but in other regards it is very different. The crop plants do not lock up the greater part of a plot's mineral nutrients when under cultivation; they only temporarily tap a fraction of its nutrient store for consumption by the human population and their animals, to be replaced naturally over many years under the secondary vegetation that recolonises the site after its abandonment. This natural vegetation cover also takes up again many of the nutrients temporarily released into the soil by burning, so that they may be released a generation or more later when the site is again cleared and burned.

Regarding the energy that Maring gardeners secure in return for their labour, the balance sheet speaks for itself. For every kilocalorie they expend, the Maring obtain in return more than sixteen. Furthermore when the data upon which these calculations are based were collected the Maring were not living near their gardens, as is their usual practice, but clustered around a dance ground in anticipation of a large festival involving the slaughter of many pigs. This increased considerably the work involved in carrying produce home from gardens. The return on energy expended on gardening in normal times would probably be nearer twenty to one. Whatever the actual rate of return on their investments, it supplied Maring adults with an excess of 2,000 kilocalories each daily, an adequate nutritional intake for them to lead healthy and active lives – to establish more gardens and have a surplus of energy for pursuing the other activities that make up their social round.

On the basis of these kinds of energetic data we can compile sophisticated graphic models to depict and compare subsistence systems (Figure 3.1).

Energy accounting alone, however, produces a lopsided view of the results of subsistence activities. Energy intake, largely carbohydrate-fuelled, is only one aspect of nutrition, which also concerns the balanced consumption of a range of essential minerals and vitamins to ensure adequate bodily function (cell maintenance, co-enzyme synthesis, tissue growth and so forth). The other elements essential to life are continually cycling, and it is difficult to track their flow. Furthermore, authorities dispute what levels of intake are adequate for a healthy life; inappropriate Western diet standards have been applied to other cultures. And finally, even highly sophisticated nutritional studies, unless they reveal serious deficiencies that demand rectifying, only demonstrate what is already evident – how peoples' diets allow them to lead healthy active lives. Nonetheless, the source and flow of nutritional components can serve to place other issues of importance in context. Regarding the Maring, the energy budget approach underlines the inordinate amount of effort they expend in keeping pigs.

Pig keeping and energy

The Maring garden not only to support themselves but also to raise and maintain sizeable herds of domestic pigs. They produce a considerable surplus of plant food for this purpose; they feed some 37 per cent (measured in kilocalories) of their produce to their pigs, largely as sweet potato, of which 54 per cent (by weight) is so used. This rate of feeding tubers to pigs is quite usual throughout the highlands; the Wola feed almost 50 per cent and the Enga 64 per cent of their sweet potato crops to pigs. The highlanders are somewhat atypical in their intensive keeping of sizeable pig herds. Other Melanesians practice more extensive pig herding, leaving their creatures more to forage and root for themselves. The differences in breeding strategies epitomise the contrasting approaches. There are few wild pigs in the densely settled highlands, and people service sows with young domestic boars, whereas elsewhere in Melanesia people tend to leave impregnation to feral boars in the forest. This somewhat hit-or-miss approach typifies the unsupervised nature of pig herding in many regions, to the point that it is sometimes difficult to decide whether a group preys on wild pigs or herds semi-domesticated ones.

Throughout Melanesia, however, people 'keep' pigs or at least keep an eye on them. Pig herding is largely women's work. The Maring,

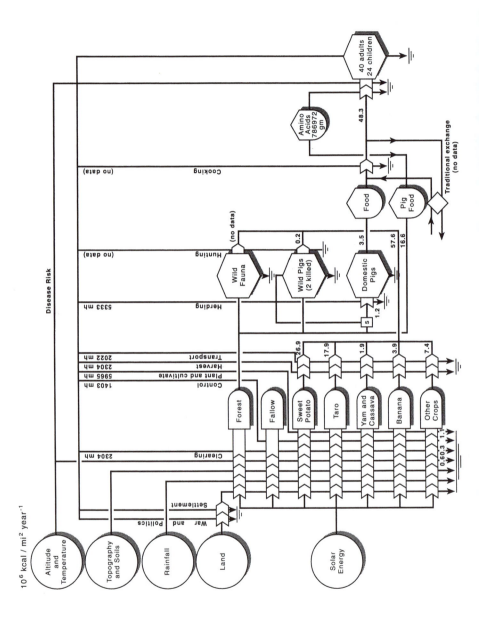

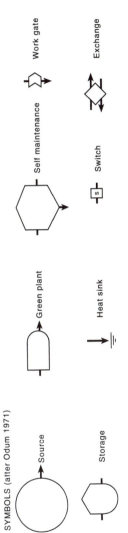

SYMBOLS (after Odum 1971)

Source

Green plant

Self maintenance

Work gate

Storage

Heat sink

Switch

Exchange

Figure 3.1   The flow of energy through the Maring subsistence system. Energy transactions are expressed in millions of kilocalories per square mile per annum and time expenditure in man-hours, for community of sixty-four persons. (After Mörren in Bayliss-Smith and Feacham 1977: 300.)

Plate 3.4   A prized pig (*Sus scrofa papuensis*) stares out from the entrance
of the stall in which it is tethered.

illustrating the intensive Melanesian extreme, treat piglets as pets, taking them with them when they go to their gardens each day, either on a leash attached to a forefoot or freely following at their heels. They pet, talk to and feed choice morsels to young pigs, and they give animals that survive past infancy personal names; these animals become in some regards members of the family. When four or five months old pigs no longer accompany women to the gardens but are turned loose in the morning to forage and root for themselves untended in the surrounding neighbourhood and forest. In the evening they return home, sometimes at the call of the woman who herds them, to be fed, mainly on sweet potato and vegetable waste such as discarded cabbage leaves. The Maring do not house their pigs in separate sties; the animals occupy stalls in the houses of the women who herd them (Plate 3.4). (Men, as they often do throughout Melanesia, occupy separate men's houses.) An adult pig is 'separated from the living quarters only by a rail fence through which the animal can thrust its snout for scratching or for morsels of food' (Rappaport 1984: 58). Small pigs live in the main part of the house, amongst the women.

The work involved in herding pigs centres largely on supplying them with their food; otherwise they demand relatively little time and energy to keep. But supplying them with food requires a good deal of work. Before a large festival and pig slaughter, when pig herds reach their peak size, one-third of the garden area established by the Maring supports crops fed to pigs, and hence one-third of the energy they expend gardening goes during this period towards keeping them. An adult pig, for example, consumes (by weight) about the same amount as a Maring adult. A woman with six large pigs to care for (the norm prior to a festival slaughter) is therefore feeding the equivalent of six more adults, which uses up nearly 50 per cent of the total daily energy a healthy Maring woman has to expend. Keeping one pig demands the expenditure of an estimated 45,000 kilocalories per year. When we consider this in terms of energy transfer up the trophic pyramid, we find an enormous loss of energy. The Maring lose 90 per cent of their crops' energy by feeding them to pigs and converting them to meat. If they consumed the plants directly this energy would be theirs, for although pork is rich in protein its production is energetically extravagant. And the Maring and other highlanders exacerbate this drain on their energy by not slaughtering their pigs as soon as they are fully grown but keeping them for up to ten years. It is clear that we are not considering here an agricultural regime geared simply to production for food. Why do these people and other highlanders feed such staggering proportions of their crops to pigs? We shall address this question in coming chapters.

FURTHER READING

The ethnographic monographs on which this review is based are:

T. P. Bayliss-Smith and R. G. Feacham (eds.), 1977 *Subsistence and survival: Rural ecology in the Pacific*. London: Academic Press.

W. C. Clarke, 1971 *Place and people: An ecology of a New Guinea community*. Berkeley: University of California Press.

P. Hastings, 1969 *New Guinea*. Melbourne: Cheshire.

C. Healey, 1990 *Maring hunters and traders*. Berkeley: University of California Press.

E. Lipuma, 1988 *The gift of kinship*. Cambridge: Cambridge University Press.

R. Rappaport, 1984 *Pigs for the ancestors: Ritual in the ecology of a New Guinea people*. New Haven: Yale University Press.

On energy flow within ecosystems see:

M. Began, J. L. Harper and C. R. Townsend, 1990 *Ecology: individuals, populations & communities*. Oxford: Blackwell.

E. P. Odum, 1975 *Ecology: The link between the natural and social sciences*. New York: Holt, Rinehart and Winston.

H. T. Odum, 1971 *Environment, power and society*. New York: Wiley.

On agricultural practices elsewhere in Melanesia see:

H. C. Brookfield and P. Brown, 1963 *Struggle for land*. Oxford: Oxford University Press.

B. Malinowski, 1935 *Coral gardens and their magic*. (2 vols) London: Allen and Unwin.

P. Sillitoe, 1983 *Roots of the earth*. Manchester: Manchester University Press.

A. Steensberg, 1980 *New Guinea gardens*. London: Academic Press.

E. Waddell, 1972 *The mound builders*. Seattle: University of Washington Press.

B. Weightman, 1989 *Agriculture in Vanuatu*. Cheam: British Friends of Vanuatu.

4   Socialisation in the Admiralty Islands

When does a helpless human baby become a social human being? In several Melanesian societies it is not until the child is given a name, perhaps some months after birth. Before this the child is 'outside' society, the concern of its mother; the father may not have seen it or acknowledged its existence. This behaviour is more understandable when we remember the traditionally very high rates of infant mortality in these societies; the relatives of the newborn adopt a pragmatic stance in the face of this brutal fact. The naming of a baby may be a social event marked by an exchange of wealth between paternal and maternal relatives. It signals the beginning of the conversion of an incapable, asocial little creature into an independent and fully cognisant member of society.

Socialisation

Social scientists refer to the process whereby an immature human being becomes a full member of society as socialisation or enculturation (some writers distinguish between these terms, applying the former to the learning of social roles and the latter to cultural traditions; here I use them interchangeably). Socialisation is synonymous with growing up. It covers the early formative years of human life when children learn the norms, expectations and values of their society. It may feature some formal learning, although more often in Melanesian societies it takes place in informal everyday contexts, as children observe and interact with others. It may involve both positive reinforcement, such as approval, esteem and reward for culturally appropriate, 'good' behaviour, and negative sanctions, such as disapproval, disdain, and punishment for 'bad' behaviour. The experiences of socialisation – the behavioural responses encountered while growing up – contribute significantly to the personality of the adult.

Socialisation and personality development are very complex processes, our understanding of which remains very incomplete. They are now widely recognised to involve the interplay of several factors: the sociocultural environment (instillation of attitudes, assumptions and so on), the individual's genetic inheritance (biochemical processes within the organism which determine behavioural responses to stimuli), and idiosyncratic life experiences which influence expectations. An old controversy in anthropology called the **nature:nurture** debate pitted the sociocultural factors against the biological ones in a premature attempt to assess the relative contributions of each in determining human personality. The debate has more recently been recast as the **nature:culture** issue, although here it more concerns the purported universal existence of cerebral binary structures, of which this is a primary opposition (reflected in such opposites as wild and tame, hot and cold and so forth [see Chapter 15]).

Sociocultural anthropologists, as opposed to biological anthropologists, have tended to place emphasis on cultural influences – on the transmission of cultural mores during the process of socialisation – in shaping human personality. The culture-and-personality approach, which has been particularly influential in the United States, has even referred to national character types, citing stereotypic personalities from different parts of the world as evidence. Some have even argued that what many assume to be largely biologically determined differences are largely socioculturally conditioned – that our ideas about male and female behaviour, for example, result from our particular cultural and historical circumstances rather than any innate biological difference between the sexes, personality traits labelled masculine or feminine being no more substantial than the clothing or headgear socially assigned to either sex at any given time. Although the majority of anthropologists would agree that culturally specific social conditioning informs our perceptions of gender, few would agree that we can rule out biological considerations.

In our review of issues relating to socialisation in Melanesia we shall turn to the small island of Manus in the Bismarck Sea (Map 4.1). It is one of the Admiralty Islands, an archipelago some 300 kilometres north of New Guinea. The population is largely coastal-dwelling, occupying pile houses in villages stretching pier-like out into lagoons. They include Austronesian-speakers of the Titan language. These seafaring people subsist largely by fishing, bartering some of their catch for food crops such as taro and yams with small interior populations with which they have customary arrangements. They not only exchange subsistence products but they also exchange wealth objects including earthenware pots, strings of small white shell discs and ornaments of dogs' teeth, in sociopolitical distributions marking important social events.

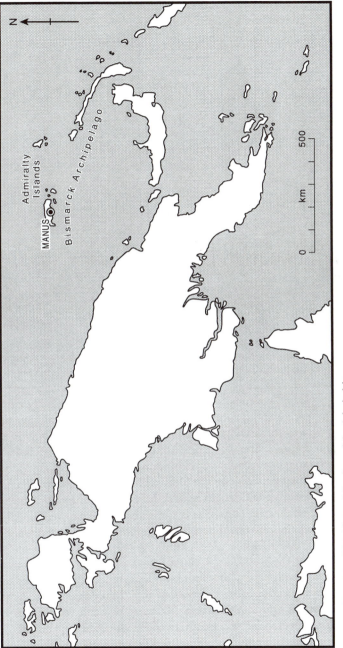

Map 4.1   The Manus Islanders of the Admiralties.

Plate 4.1   A bride decorated in finery and standing on a carved platform (part of the wealth featuring in the marriage exchange), in a canoe with her kin as they prepare to transport her to her new husband's house.

The early Manus ethnography deals with the upbringing of children with a view to throwing light on contemporary problems in education in the United States in the 1930s. The contrasts fell in with the ethnographer's agenda of relating her work to her own society and commenting provocatively which, while it helped to popularise anthropology greatly, also led Margaret Mead, according to some critics, to misrepresent the ethnography in order to put across her points regarding the cultural relativity of socialisation practices and pains of growing up. Reading this ethnography, while bearing in mind the context of the intellectual climate that prevailed when it was written, illustrates well how contemporary Western social issues may inform our understanding of other cultures. It is salutary regarding the purported authority of ethnographic texts, it being difficult to see at the time – a different period, as the historians say, is a different culture, throwing these issues into relief.

Infancy on Manus

According to psychologists the first few years of life are critical regarding the imprint of culture on nature, supplementing instinctive behaviour with socially conditioned responses. The first year of a Manus child's life is spent secure and warm, close to its mother. The two remain in seclusion behind a mat curtain for the first month or so after the birth. They emerge only when the mother's relatives have amassed enough sago, pots, shell and dogs' teeth wealth to mount a feast and an exchange marking the child's arrival. The event comprises a canoe flotilla laden with the exchange goods, heralded by slit-gong calls. The mother is uncomfortably weighed down with some of the fine wealth, which she is expected to wear in the prestation to her husband's kin. Mother and child remain largely housebound for the first year or so, the child being breast-fed on demand. Adults keep a watchful eye on the crawling infant, although they do not cosset it. Indeed, the emphasis is on encouraging some independence early in life, and children quickly develop the considerable physical agility which their waterborne life demands. Parents introduce toddlers to the sea and encourage them to splash about around the piles of their homes at low tide; children learn to swim at an early age, almost simultaneously with learning to walk. Sometimes their introduction to the sea comes very young when they fall through the slat floors of their elevated homes or, shoulder-riding on parents, take a rude ducking when canoes capsize. Infants learn to hold tightly to their parents' necks as they are carried around, not releasing their grip even when doused in salty, eye-smarting sea water (Plate 4.2).

As children become more independent, their fathers begin to play a more prominent part in their lives. The father is an indulgent figure who plays with his children and takes them on interesting trips to trade, fish and so on. The mother spends increasing periods of time engaged in subsistence activities unsuitable for child participation such as shell fishing and sago processing and leaves children in their father's company. Relations between husband and wife are portrayed as distant and shame-ridden, occasionally even violent, and children soon learn to take advantage of this situation to get their own way. They realise that the father is the important figure in their house, which is situated among the dwellings of his kin, and his relatives continually emphasise his relation to his children in behaviour and speech and belittle his wife's claims to parental regard. The image is vividly conveyed by three-year-olds who frequently leave their father's arms to satisfy themselves at their mother's breast only to return swaggeringly to their tractable fathers, grinning insolently at their mothers. At some time during this

Plate 4.2   A Manus woman disembarking from a canoe into her pile house in
Peri village carrying a young child on her back. Children are taught early to
cling to their mother's back in order to leave the mother's hands free.

period the mother is likely to become pregnant again and will start to
wean the child. It is a slow process. The child is used to having its own
way and being fed on demand. The mother may tie bundles of hair to
her nipples to repel the child, who resents her withdrawal and turns
increasingly to the father for comfort.

Weaning is one of the early experiences which psychologists consider
significant in the development of personality. Suckling characterises the
first Freudian 'oral' stage of libido or psychosexual development. The
second stage is the 'anal' one, focusing on sphincter control and
excretion, and is marked by the emergence of either a sense of autonomy
or feelings of shame and doubt. Young Manus boys learn at about three
that a certain lee place on the island, never visited by females, serves as a
latrine. No severe stress is placed on relieving oneself at the appropriate
place at a young age, but children do begin to become aware of a certain
adult prudishness. Relations between the sexes on Manus, particularly
between those eligible to marry and their respective kin, are severely
constrained. Children notice the shame that attaches to relations

between the sexes as they pass through the third 'phallic' stage of libido development, when pleasurable sensations centre on the genitals, individuality develops, and they may experience feelings of guilt. Adults communicate their sense of shame not by chastisement but by the repugnance they display towards acts of carelessness, such as being uncovered before others, although they allow children to run around naked for the first ten years or so of their lives.

Gender relations

Children learn that there are supernatural sanctions behind the tense relations between members of the opposite sexes. On Manus people believe that the spirits of their ancestors watch over them, and they keep the skulls and finger bones of their deceased relatives in carved bowls suspended in the roof spaces of their houses. They think that these ancestral spirits help them in fishing and protect them, particularly from attack by malicious spirit forces, but in return expect their charges to lead chaste and virtuous lives. When people become ill or die, the Manus expect all their relatives to search their consciences for any sexual improprieties that could have angered the ghosts and to confess and so allow appropriate ritual action to appease the angered ancestors. The offence need not be serious, ancestral ghosts punish not only illicit intercourse but also the breaking of any of the taboos that hedge around relations between the sexes, such as breaking in-law avoidance requirements, improper physical contacts, and even suggestive jests. The Manus feel unworthy only when others find out about their wrongdoing but reveal behavioural violations when they experience remorse with believed supernatural discovery (i.e. they are both shame- and guilt-oriented). Sickness is common on Manus, and children live in an atmosphere of constant suspicion and supernatural sanction.

The sullen, stifling and shame-ridden life depicted on Manus seems to apply more to women than to men. It is common throughout Melanesia for women's and men's social obligations and responsibilities, even to some extent their cultural worlds, to be sharply separated, and we can detect this separation early in the socialisation of children. On Manus, as elsewhere, girls are obliged to wear skirts and cover themselves sooner than boys and to pay considerable attention to decorum. They are taught to take great care when they are menstruating in particular and to avoid others at this time. This is a common avoidance throughout Melanesia, where people regularly regard menstrual blood with abhorrence, men frequently equating it with poison. The tedium of in-law avoidance also falls more heavily on women than on men. They regularly have to carry a cloak with them under which they can cower if they come near tabooed relatives, sometimes huddled for lengthy periods in uncomfortable places such as the stifling hull of a canoe under a hot sun on a rolling sea. Females also have to take up the onerous duties of adulthood in their early teens, several years before their male counterparts, who are unlikely to assume adult responsibilities before their early twenties. And girls have to endure antagonistic marital relations, with little affection and perhaps some brutality among their husbands' kin, sexual relations are perfunctory and aggressive.

The prudery and sense of shame that characterise life on Manus are strangely mixed with shows of sexual prowess by men, making Western-derived psychoanalytic theories of personality development and behaviour seem out of place. When engaged in hostilities with other communities, for example, if warriors captured a woman in a raid, they would brutally gang rape her in public and engage in lewd behaviour unheard of in their villages. And during some large exchange events men engage in a salacious dance in which they swing their sea-shell-sheathed penises violently to and fro, catching them between their thighs and vigorously flinging them upwards, while taunting the recipients of the presentation with conventional insults about matching the gifts when the time comes to repay them (Plate 4.3). Adults applaud little boys who master the dance (Plate 4.4).

Childhood on Manus

Besides an ability physically to fend for themselves (an awareness of the danger of fire, competence in their watery world and so on) and an awareness of the shame that attaches to genitalia, the only other expectation of young children is that they show respect for property, particularly a regard for wealth objects such as traded pots and dogs'-teeth ornaments. This amounts to uncharacteristic restraint on their behaviour, because any child who trifles with these things will be severely reprimanded, particularly if any damage occurs. We might suppose that this curbing of youthful curiosity derives from the central importance of wealth exchange on prescribed social occasions in Manus society – as in Melanesian society generally. Although children are unaware of the complexities of the exchange networks in which their adult relatives are enmeshed and the onerous obligations on them to meet their transactional commitments at requisite social events, they are nonetheless imbued with awe of these activities. The large sociopolitical distributions which they witness are impressive events, even from the fringes, punctuated as they are by the thunderous beating of slit-gongs

Plate 4.3 Men performing the penis-swinging dance sheathed with *Ovalis* sea shells in a conventional challenge gesture at large wealth exchanges and warfare preparations.

Plate 4.4   A boy at play, mimicking adult behaviour and practising the penis-swinging dance.

and heated speeches, parades and dancing of colourfully decorated men. Youngsters are largely uninterested in the transactional details of this aspect of adult life, but exchange is clearly an important business and one that they learn to respect early.

Otherwise childhood is a period of relative freedom. Children play where, what, when and with whom they like. They may eat and sleep when they wish. They show little deference to either their parents or other adults. Indeed, their indulgent upbringing makes children offhand and inconsiderate of grown-ups' wishes. They may scramble up the ladder to their mother's cooking fire at any time and request feeding, however inconvenient the demand. Play groups are loose associations, older children sometimes trying to exert some leadership and direction over others. Youngsters may play on the sheltered lagoon in their own child-sized canoes, chasing each other, spear fishing and swimming, or they may run about throwing reeds in mock battles, erecting swings, building playhouses and so on. They master through play, not formal instruction, the skills required in adult life. They learn about their region's resources and how to exploit and manipulate them; they develop alertness and physical resourcefulness, initiative and inventiveness.

The emphasis in childhood play is on practical activities, as in adult life. Youngsters do not indulge much in intellectual play and figurative games, not apparently allowing their imaginations to roam, invent and embellish on life in stories and fantasies; their culture has few elaborate childhood myths and legends. They learn about their world largely through experience, developing knowledge and skills through practice rather than didactic discussion and extensive spoken instruction. Consequently, much of their knowledge is experiential, not readily put into words. We might anticipate that asking a Manus fisherman why he has canoed to a particular reef location and is using a certain tackle arrangement would bring forth expressions of incomprehension; no one needs to explain – everyone knows – that when the tide is running this way at this time of the month and year and under these wind conditions shoals of snapper congregate here and are attracted by appropriate spinning lures.

The marked freedom of Manus childhood is an issue that deserves emphasis. It is a widespread characteristic of Melanesian upbringing, producing an autonomous spirit that prepares children to take their places in their society's egalitarian political order. No one has the right to dominate anyone else – not even a husband his wife, regardless of their shame-conditioned and strained relations, for each has rights which the other cannot violate without sanction. If a man oversteps the culturally recognised mark regarding his attitude and expectations of his wife, she may leave him and take refuge with her kin until he mends his ways. The village is a loose democracy; families are bound together by ramifying exchange obligations, with fear of ancestral spirit sanction enforcing, if necessary, observance of proper conduct. The freedom extended to children reflects the egalitarian ethos of this acephalous (headless) society, conditioning them not to tolerate domineering behaviour on the part of others. From childhood onwards, no one has the power to control the actions of others or the right to force from them anything that they are unwilling to concede.

Individual personality development

Although the process of socialisation on Manus inculcates a common core of cultural values and behavioural expectations, differences in the treatment of children during their formative years predictably result in the development of various contrasting individual personalities. Idiosyncrasies in speech, manners and gestures become evident early in life. They reflect the differential evolution of personality traits such as aggression, compliance, egocentricity and so on. Play group interaction does not have a levelling effect on personalities because of children's strong identification with certain adults, notably their fathers. The identification is so strong and has such a marked effect on children's personalities, that 'it is possible to watch a group of children for half an hour and then guess at the age or status and general demeanour of their parents, particularly of their fathers' (Mead 1963: 106). The offspring of strong-willed and overbearing men are aggressive and noisily confident; even as babies they stamp their feet and shout for attention, and when older they tear around loudly trying to get their own way. Children of quieter men who have less celebrated wealth-exchange records are more timid, less garrulous and tend to keep their own counsel more; they are less demanding and more subdued. According to Mead inbreeding occurs on Manus, the prescribed cousin marriage rule reinforcing the small-population effect, such that the island's genetic make-up is more uniform than that of many others. The personality differences manifest are thus evidence of the stamp of social conditioning and interaction. The personalities of young children even purportedly change if they are adopted to reflect the demeanour of the adopted parent with whom they identify. This is to argue with a vengeance for the imprint of idiosyncratic experience on the genetic and culturally forged template of individual personality. Some brief impressionistic and anecdotal case histories are given as evidence for these sweeping assertions: Pwakaton, a good-humoured man of mild disposition, was an excellent slit-gong drummer and a fair fisherman, but he was unable to manage his sociopolitical exchange obligations effectively and as a result was of little social consequence. His daughter was likewise an unsure and quiet girl. Talikai, a more successful and respected older man who loudly and histrionically proclaimed his intentions, had adopted a younger child of Pwakaton's and at two years of age this child copied his foster father's noisy and demanding behaviour, even to the point, on one occasion, of wrenching the man's attention from a public ceremony in which he was playing a central part. Another adopted son of his, an adolescent whose natural father was likewise quiet and unassuming, was regularly to be seen trying to dominate play groups.

Whatever the relative contributions of biological endowment, cultural conditioning and individual experience to individuals' personalities, it is obvious that Manus society, for all its relatively limited gene pool and small-scale cultural homogeneity, does not produce a series of similar personalities. Consequently, when we talk about egalitarianism in Melanesian society we are not implying that everyone is of equal endowment. Nowhere are those who comprise a society the same in terms of personality, aptitude, skill, ability and so on. Some will be better than others at some activities and those who excel at the activities valued by their culture because of their genetic and cultural inheritance and life histories will receive the admiration of others. The important point is that in Melanesian societies neither these people, nor those who are of aggressive, domineering or duplicitous personality, can aspire to political power over the lives of others.

Social cycles

Growing up is the first stage in the human **life cycle**, which starts with the birth and ends with the death of the individual and includes marriage, parenthood, grandparenthood and so on. In Melanesian society, sociopolitical exchanges of wealth often mark these milestones on the individual's journey through life. The exchange associated with birth on Manus has already been mentioned; other sociopolitical transactions, collectively called *kawas*, occur at puberty and betrothal, marriage and pregnancy, and later between the couple's kin when they are grandparents and upon death and at burial.

Another analogous social cycle recognised by anthropologists is the **developmental cycle**. This follows changes in the constitution of domestic groups over time, paralleling their members' life cycles. In the most straightforward case young people establish a new household at marriage which expands as they have children, contracts as the offspring depart to establish their own households, and may incorporate both parents or one widowed one in their old age. On Manus the developmental cycle can be considerably more complicated as the composition of households is variable and the dynamics of their change complex. Some domestic groups comprise a nuclear family and potentially follow the above simple developmental cycle, although relationships may be complicated by the husband's being polygynous, with two or more wives, perhaps of widely differing ages, living in the household together with their children. Domestic groups are usually even more tangled, however, and follow more complicated developmental cycles, with two or more nuclear families at about the same or at different developmental stages living together. Two parallel cousins and their families may reside, for example, in the same pile house (parallel cousins have parents who are siblings of the same sex), or a couple and their children together with their married daughter's family. The dependence of younger men on older relatives to assist them in meeting their socio-political exchange obligations often results in their living together in the same house, ensuring the existence of extended family groups at some point in the developmental cycle, until the younger party is independent enough to establish his own household. On top of this is the complication introduced by the frequent adoption of children. A common interest in a child will unite the two households involved, as does the ramifying kinship web that runs through the community. Indeed, many of the pile houses are interconnected, their residents moving freely among them.

All this relates to, and to some extent is structured by, kinship relations, another topic to which anthropologists devote considerable attention because of its prominence in the lives of people living in small-scale societies. The localised, exogamous, named patrilineal clans identified by Manus Islanders have relatively little formal influence on domestic group composition. The kinship system is bilateral in practice but these patrilines, as kin-constituted groups, nonetheless give some structure to the direction of certain exchange payments. It is these transactions which give more form to household composition, because, as has been mentioned, younger men often depend on older relatives to help them meet their obligations (notably, to finance their marriages) and are drawn to them early in their adult lives, giving them assistance and contributing to their households until they can establish their own homes.

Domestic life on Manus is tense. The strictly observed rules of in-law avoidance make household interaction awkward where, as frequently happens, affines reside together. It is usual at marriage for a woman to move in with her husband's relatives and occupy a mat-partitioned area at the rear of the house. She must ensure that her father-in-law does not see her, covering her head with a cloak as necessary, and cannot mention his name. Although life becomes easier when her husband is able to establish his own household, feelings of hostility and shame remain between spouses. Betrothed to one another as children, they rarely establish a close relationship. A man has a warmer relationship with his sisters, towards whom he feels a sense of obligation, supporting them in exchange contexts even though they live elsewhere. His wife conducts herself with reserve towards them, seeing them as competitors for his allegiance in the all-important formal transactions of social life. Siblings of the opposite sex cannot entertain any sexual innuendo, but cross cousins enjoy a joking relationship which permits a certain degree of breast-fondling intimacy.

The effect of these various kin-structured normative relationships on marriage and the household are reportedly sombre. A man identifies closely with his father or brother and is dependent upon him for help in the transactions of social life. His wife is obliged to avoid this senior figure, though in all probability they occupy the same house. A man feels affection and a sense of duty to his sister, whose household he supports as appropriate in exchange contexts. Relations between sisters-in-law are constrained even though they live apart. Towards female cross cousins a man acts playfully and intimately (cross cousins have parents who are siblings of a different sex), which diverts this warm behaviour away from his wife. And towards his children he extends tender care and entertains amicable feelings, spoiling them and setting them against their mother. Western notions of romantic love and tender intimacy are clearly out of place in the Manus household, as they are in Melanesia generally. Before we despair or respond in indignant rage at the Manus woman's lot, however, we should remember that she will be not only a wife to one man but also a daughter, sister, cross cousin and mother to others, taking various parts during her life cycle in the cultural strata-gems that characterise family life. The family appears to meet Manus children's needs well enough, as an institution central to their socialisa-tion, albeit reproducing in the next generation what to an outsider's mind is a stressful house on stilts.

FURTHER READING

The ethnographic monographs upon which the review is based are:

M. Mead, 1930 *Growing up in New Guinea*, New York: William Morrow (reprinted, 1963 by Penguin Books).

M. Mead, 1930 'Melanesian middlemen'. *Natural History* 30: 115–30.

M. Mead, 1934 *Kinship in the Admiralty Islands*. Anthropological Papers of the American Museum of Natural History 34 Part 2.

M. Mead, 1956 *New lives for old*. London: Gollancz.

B. Gustafsson, 1992 *Houses and ancestors: Continuities and discontinuities in leadership among the Manus*. Gothenburg: Gothenburg University Institute for Advanced Studies in Social Anthropology.

A. H. Carrier and J. G. Carrier, 1991 *Structure and process in a Melanesian society*. Amsterdam: Harwood Academic Press.

R. Fortune, 1935 *Manus religion*. Philadelphia: American Philosophical Society.

L. Romanucci-Ross, 1985 *Mead's other Manus*. South Hedley: Bergin and Garvey.

See also:

D. Kulick, 1992 *Language shift and cultural reproduction: Socialization, self, and syncretism in a Papua New Guinea village*. Cambridge: Cambridge University Press.

M. Mead, 1935 *Sex and temperament in three primitive societies*. New York: William Morrow.

B. B. Schieffelin, 1990 *The give and take of everyday life: language socialization of Kaluli children*. Cambridge: Cambridge University Press.

E. L. Schieffelin, 1976 The sorrow of the lonely and the burning of the dancers. New York: St. Martin's Press.

On personality and socialisation see:

F. L. K. Hsu, 1995 *Psychological anthropology: Approaches to culture and personality*. Ann Arbor: U.M.I.

G. Jahoda, 1982 *Psychology and anthropology*. London: Academic Press

FILMS

Coming of Age, Margaret Mead, 1901–1978 Central Independent Television Series S*trangers Abroad* Programme 5.

5   Exchange cycles in the Massim Archipelago

In the light of our review of foraging and fishing practices and the slash-and-burn horticultural traditions of Melanesia (chapters 2 and 3), is it possible that there are societies in which the resources, labour and skills necessary to produce what people need fully to satisfy their material needs are not scarce and hence there is no need for market transactions and associated economising behaviour? There is a school of anthropological thought which maintains that Western economic theory, which by definition assumes maximising between scarce ends, is inapplicable to societies in which resources and means may be scarce but needs and wants in relation to them are modest. The debate over the relevance of formal economic theory to other societies is a classic illustration of how theoretical conflicts that characterise different intellectual periods can compromise our interpretation of ethnography, and call into question the status of anthropologists' writings on other cultures. The formalists believe that the assumptions of economists – such as the supply of natural and human resources used in the production of goods and services desired by humans is finite every-where and all people have to make choices between alternative uses for resources and manoeuvre for power to control their allocation – are so general that economic theory must be relevant to every society regard-less of place and time. The substantivists, while not denying that resources are ultimately finite everywhere, believe that other people's perceptions of these limitations differ profoundly from our own – that these people perceive no scarcity and therefore recognise no need to economise.

We see revealed in this debate the tugging of the paradoxically opposed forces that are central to the entire methodology and episte-mology of anthropology, where we inevitably use some of our own culture's concepts and assumptions to make sense of others' behaviour and convey what we think we have observed and heard to other members of our society (= 'formalism'), but not without rearranging and modifying them to allow for their being conditioned differently by other cultural contexts (= 'substantivism'). We necessarily work in this split-minded and sometimes contradictory way because otherwise what we think we hear and observe in other societies would be beyond expression. The uncritical use of words and concepts from our culture such as 'money', 'credit', 'market' and so on, to relay what we think is happening in other societies has in part fuelled the debate. This is the high road to distortion and error, and we have to guard against it at all times. But this is a perennial anthropological problem, one that faces us whenever we translate the customs and practices of others into our language. It lies at the very heart of the veracity of the discipline. We have to be careful how we play with language and translation if we are to avoid defeating our purpose as anthropologists – to make foreign cultures understandable.

One of the first anthropologists to strike a blow in the battle over the relevance of Western economic theory to the study of non-industrialised societies was Bronislaw Malinowski in his study of the Trobriand Islanders, a matrilineally organised Austronesian-speaking people of the Massim Archipelago (Map 5.1). In the context of his investigation of the *kula*, an exchange institution which has some appearances of an economic activity, he came out strongly for the view that Western theory has little relevance. In particular he challenged the appropriateness for Trobriand Island society of the concepts of 'Economic Man', an imaginary person prompted in all his actions by self-interest and seeking to achieve his aims with the least possible effort.

If anthropologists continue to consider Malinowski's work relevant today despite its more than passing resemblance to the Victorian travelogues that preceded it, it is partly because the *kula* continues to intrigue them. It is one of several such institutions in Melanesia involving startling numbers of people spread out over vast geographical regions (others include the *moka* and *tee* exchange cycles of the Central Highlands of Papua New Guinea). Another reason for the enduring appeal of Malinowski's work is that it is one of the first ethnographies to be based on intensive fieldwork – even by today's standards a superb account of an exotic way.

The *kula*

The *kula* is a ceremonial exchange system involving the inhabitants of several islands whose archipelago approximates to a circle, resulting in a closed transactional circuit which Malinowski called the *kula* ring (Map 5.2). Around this circuit two kinds of highly valued articles constantly travel in opposite directions. Clockwise we find long neck-

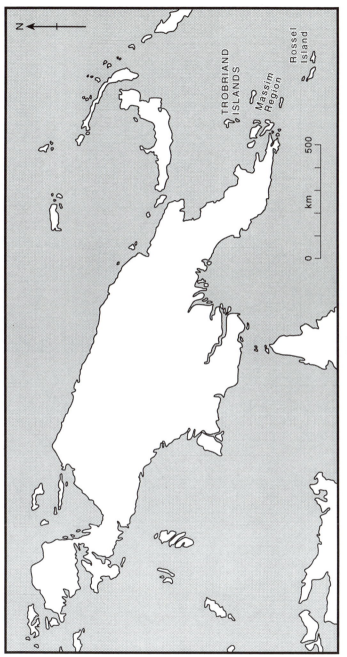

Map 5.1   The Trobriand Islanders of the Massim Archipelago.

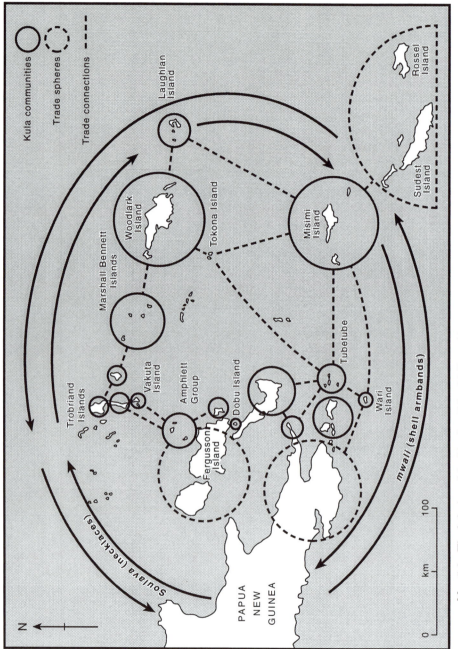

Map 5.2 The *kula* ring of the Massim. (After Malinowski 1922.)

Kula communities
Trade spheres
Trade connections

Rossel Island
Laughlan Island
Sudest Island
Woodlark Island
Marshall Bennett Islands
Tokona Island
Misimi Island
Trobriand Islands
Vakuta Island
Amphlett Group
Dobu Island
Fergusson Island
Tubetube
Wari Island
mwali (shell armbands)
soulava (necklaces)
PAPUA NEW GUINEA
N
km 0 100

laces made of red *Charma* shell discs (called *soulava*), counter-clockwise armbands made from polished white *Conus* shells (called *mwali*). These two kinds of objects are, in a 'utilitarian' sense, ornaments, but they are worn only infrequently (if at all), for dances, feasts and other large ceremonial occasions, and are not pursued for the privilege of wearing them; successful men may possess at any time more armbands and necklaces than they could wear and sometimes lend them to relatives and friends. The object of coming by an armband or a necklace is to give it away again. On every island and in every village there are several men actively engaged in the *kula* – receiving these valuables from partners, holding onto them for a period, and then handing them on again to others from whom they receive the opposite article in exchange (i.e. a necklace for an armband). Each of these objects, as it travels unidirectionally around the closed circuit, continually passes articles of the other kind, against which it is constantly exchanged, and no one ever holds onto any of the things for any length of time. One transaction is not the end of the *kula* relationship; the rule is 'once in the *kula*, always in the *kula*'; and each relationship between two men is for life. All *mwali* and *soulava* can be found constantly travelling and changing hands; there is no suggestion of their ever remaining permanently in one man's possession, and thus the maxim 'once in the *kula*, always in the *kula*' applies equally to the valuables as to the men handling them.

A set of conventions regulates the movement of *kula* valuables, and elaborate magical ritual to ensure success accompanies some *kula* transactions and other public ceremonies. Men do not freely exchange valuables in the *kula* when the opportunity arises and wherever they like. It is subject to clear expectations and limitations. Only partners can engage in *kula* transactions and a partnership is a formal institution that is entered in a prescribed way. The most successful men may have tens of partners, while less able manipulators of wealth have only a few.

Any two partners are obliged to *kula* with one another. They behave as friends and recognise a number of mutual duties and obligations which vary with the distance between their villages and their relationship. There are basically two categories of *kula* partner. There are those who live nearby, perhaps in the same village or a neighbouring one, with whom a man will regularly interact and with whom he will be on close and friendly terms. And there are those who live further away, usually overseas on other islands, whom he will visit only irregularly, by canoe in the exciting seaborne expeditions that characterise the *kula* (Plate 5.1). The overseas partner is a host and friend in a foreign place of potential danger, providing food in addition to physical security. The institution of *kula* partnership provides a man with both a number of friends

Plate 5.1   Visitors viewing canoes in their hangars on Kaulukuba beach at the *vayola* display before the sailing of a *kula* fleet.

nearby and a few allies in far-off regions. These are the only persons with whom he may *kula*, but he is at liberty to choose from among them to whom he will offer which of the valuables that come his way.

The *kula* ring is a vast network of relationships linking islanders separated sometimes by hundreds of miles of sea who sail periodically to exchange with one another and on occasion meet at large inter-island gatherings. It is an enormous institution, comprising thousands of men united by a common passion for exchanging valuables. The *kula* rule that no one can keep a valuable longer than a year or two is of the utmost significance. A man who holds something for longer will earn a reputation as niggardly. His temporary custodianship affords him an opportunity to bolster his renown, to display the valuable and recount how he received it, and to negotiate with the partner to whom he intends to give it. This is one of the most popular topics of Trobriander conversation. Every valuable moves in one direction only, never stopping permanently, and takes an estimated two to ten years to complete a circuit of the island ring.

The central principle underpinning *kula* exchanges is that the receiver of a ceremonial gift is obliged to repay it with an equivalent countergift sometime later (which may be within a few hours, although it is more usual for several months or even a year or so to elapse before repayment). This delayed reciprocity is crucial. Another significant point is that partners never discuss the equivalence of the valuables which they exchange or calculate their relative values and bargain about them. Here there is a very clear distinction between the *kula* and trade transactions for utilitarian objects (in which they may bargain). Another important principle of the *kula* is that the giver calculates the equivalence of the return gift. The receiver cannot express his opinion – indeed, doing so would be extremely ill-mannered. The expectation is that a partner who has received a *kula* gift will make a return gift of equal value – for instance, give as good a necklace in return for any armband he receives. He must *not* substitute several minor ones, although he may give these as intermediate gifts to mark time before he makes the real repayment. The Trobrianders carefully distinguish between these different types of gift.

The receiver of a fine piece will be anxious to lay his hands on a suitable complementary object of equivalent value to make an adequate repayment, because a man who takes a long time to do so (or worse, fails altogether) loses respect and earns the reputation of a failure. A man may try to lobby for a valuable he knows to be in the possession of one of his partners by giving 'solicitory gifts', of which there are several kinds. When someone comes into the possession of an outstanding valuable the news spreads throughout the area, and all the partners of the recipient who are on the right side of him in the ring, so to speak, to receive it, compete for this honour and favour.

Kula and trade

Some writers of the formalist persuasion think that the *kula* fulfils a straightforward economic role. Their interpretation relates to another form of exchange which the Trobrianders call *gimwali* 'trade', the only transaction they engage in that is unambiguously economic. *Gimwali* covers exchanges of consumable and utilitarian objects in which we can detect the operation of a Western market-like principle. In contrast to the formal behaviour of *kula* exchanges, in *gimwali* we find the haggling of the marketplace, persons dealing freely with anyone they please. If they are related, for instance, the parties will behave differently and may settle at a different rate of exchange than they would if they were strangers, and if one of them desperately needs what the other has, the latter may be able to drive a harder bargain in the highly imperfect market that prevails.

When on an overseas *kula* expedition men also engage in *gimwali* for utilitarian objects and food, but they do not do so with their *kula* partners, for the bargaining would be antithetical to the generosity and decorum expected in *kula* transactions. Some observers have seized on this fact to account for the existence of the *kula*, noting, for instance, that we 'learn only incidentally, never in detail, that the whimsical voyagers circulate not only armbands and necklaces but coconuts, sago, fish, vegetables, baskets, mats, sword clubs, green stone (formerly essential for tools), mussel shells (for knives), and creepers (essential for lashings)' (Harris 1968:563). Focusing on these latter utilitarian objects, they interpret the *kula* as a supportive mechanism facilitating their trade, providing a network of meaningful personal relationships through which the exchange of these strategic subsistence materials can take place. Thoroughly documented arguments along these lines have been advanced: 'We have here a regional trading system facilitating considerable specialisation in production; the economic role of the clockwise and anti-clockwise circulation of valuables was to integrate the system ... Without the valuables there would be little incentive for regular transfer, and hence for the continuity of long-distance trade on which the scale of specialisation in other parts of the ring depended' (Brookfield and Hart 1971:327).

This explanation seems plausible to us in the light of our own Western economic experience, but it hardly accounts for the evolution and continued existence of the *kula*. It is indisputable that *one effect* of the *kula* is to promote the movement in trade of utilitarian objects around the ring, but it is quite another to argue that this is the reason for it. Indeed, on occasion people enter into *gimwali* outside *kula* contexts, and island and mainland New Guinea communities that do not participate in the *kula* trade for specialised utilitarian objects that originate elsewhere (such as pots and stone axes). The *kula* is not essential, then, for the diffusion of resources and material objects. Moreover, we find *kula* exchanges regularly taking place between persons living on the same island, who, by and large, have access to the same resources and utilitarian objects.

Other evidence against the utility-founded trade explanation is that the Trobrianders and other islanders in the Massim region continue with the *kula* to this day. Access to trade stores and the superior technical products of the industrialised world has made stone axes, creepers, clubs, shell knives and several of the other articles that used to figure in *gimwali* unimportant, but the *kula* goes on. Similarly, regarding the assumption that the formal exchange of valuables ensured the traders' safety from erstwhile enemies on the next island who might kill them; the British colonial administration had stopped all tribal warfare long before Malinowski arrived in the region, but the *kula* continued. One could argue, I suppose, that the people in this region still use some of the objects traded in *gimwali* (such as taro, sago and pots) that come from certain islands only, and still fear violence in the form of sorcery, and it is these that prompt the continued existence of the *kula*. (Or worse, that without *gimwali* the *kula* is a sort of cultural relic that will eventually fade away.) But these arguments amount to a weak and unconvincing last-ditch stand.

Social and economic contexts

The *kula*-for-trade argument pushes this institution into the inappropriate context of a market-like economy. Insensitive attempts like this to apply formal Western economic concepts to exotic 'economies' bring this entire theory into disrepute with some anthropologists. But are formal economic concepts like scarcity, choice, maximisation and so on, which relate to access to material goods and services, entirely inappropriate to the *kula* institution, and can the handling of material objects to acquire social standing be ruled completely out of the economic domain? After all, someone has to produce the shell objects exchanged in the first place, and on occasion people use these objects in purchase-like transactions.

On the Trobriand Islands people may give the same valuables in either an economic or a social transaction, the latter overwhelmingly predominating. It is important to attend to the *context*. If one man gives another a *soulava* necklace, for example, in a *kula* transaction and the receiver, after holding the valuable for a few months, hands it on to another partner in a *kula* exchange, then we must say that we have witnessed a gift transaction involving a materially useless item. The vast majority of transactions with these non-utilitarian wealth items among the Trobrianders are of this social kind; they circulate largely in gift and not commodity transactions. Nevertheless, Trobrianders sometimes make purchase-like calculations when using valuables. On occasion they exchange necklaces and armbands for pigs, tubers and other

Plate 5.2   The ceremonial filling of yamstores with tubers during an *urigubu* harvest prestation.

garden produce, which commodities they may intend to consume. These are transactions of a different order called *laga*. Suppose a man gives a *soulava* necklace to someone for a pile of yams which he has worked hard to grow in his garden. If he goes away and eats the yams with his family, then we shall call the transaction commodity exchange, but if he presents them to his sister's husband in an *urigubu* exchange (Plate 5.2) we shall call them a gift. If the gardener in turn gives the necklace to a partner in a *kula* transaction (which is more likely than his spending it on a consumable) the transaction is a gift, but he has in effect 'earned' the wealth with the hard work that he has put in on his garden to grow the yams and hence received it in an economic context. Nonetheless, the parallels with formal economics are limited. There is no regular or orderly market in which men can bargain for subsistence produce with valuables, they do so only occasionally, and when they in turn give that produce in a gift exchange or feast (as often happens) it never becomes a consumable commodity for them. Conversely, men cannot increase their production of consumable items with a view to selling them for and so earning *kula* wealth.

This brings us to the issue of the manufacture of valuables, which might be assumed to fall into the category of economic behaviour but does not, strictly speaking, do so. If handling these objects earns a man renown, then we should expect to hear that Trobrianders are busy making them, but the reverse is the case. The fact that no one can control the production of *kula* wealth is of profound significance with regard to political power in these societies (see chapter 8). The *Conus* shells used to make armbands occur in the Trobriand Island lagoon and men sometimes find particularly fine specimens. They do not, however, at once set to work to produce armbands. Instead they give the shells to someone else in an exchange context, for instance, a brother-in-law as a return gift in the *urigubu* yam prestation sequence. The brother-in-law may then cut the end off the shell, thus giving it an armband shape, and present it to a *kula* partner. The partner who receives the shell may then clean some of the accretions off it and pass it on again in another exchange to someone who will start to polish it. This handing on and polishing process will go on through several other partners. Then someone will start to decorate the armband with beads and smaller shells such as cowries, and the creation of the valuable's myth, recounting who has handled it and in what contexts, begins. Somewhere along the way someone will also give it a name. The important point is that the 'manufacture' of valuables continues as they move around the ring. No one man could ever make an entire article from start to finish; it requires transactional use and social sanction. This points to the importance of giving and receiving these items in social contexts like the *kula*, not any economic connotations that we might try to attach to them because of their manufacture or use in what we might call economic contexts.

The profound differences between the material behaviour studied by Western economists and the Trobrianders' behaviour have led some writers to rule the *kula* out of the economic sphere altogether. The two items exchanged have symbolic, not economic value, and since they have no practical use we cannot think that the Trobrianders exchange them under duress of any material need. Nor are they currency or money, although they may infrequently feature in purchase-like transactions. We are not concerned here with marketplace transactions in

Plate 5.3   A mortuary ceremonial exchange with a display of *lisala dabu* –
the things that women exchange.

which people deal with the highest bidders, for participants are tied to
lifelong partners, nor are the exchanges diplomatic cover for trade. In
the light of these differences we make a significant distinction between
economic exchange and *social exchange*, sometimes called 'ceremonial
exchange' and here sociopolitical exchange. It is defined as a public
event performed according to conventions and carrying with it social or
religious obligations. This is a distinction attributed to the Trobrianders
themselves, and we find that many Melanesians make a similar discrimination. It is not a matter of two systems but one of different transactional contexts with the same articles featuring in both.

Plate 5.4 A *peumkwala* 'challenge gift' made competitively between men to validate their exchange standing and renown; notice the stooped posture of the man in the foreground, the traditional mark of respect before those of higher status.

This distinction between social and economic exchange moves us to a new explanatory front that is sociological rather than strictly economic. According to the ethnography, what is critical to the *kula* is the 'fundamental human impulse to display, to share, to bestow [and] the deep tendency to create social ties through exchange of gifts. Apart from any consideration as to whether the gifts are necessary or even useful, giving for the sake of giving is one of the most important features of Trobriand sociology' (Malinowski 1922: 175). We have here a large and complex institution, both in its geographical extent and in its socio-logical spread, involving large numbers of people and communities. It embraces a vast complex of interconnected activities that play one into another, for the *kula* is not the only ceremonial exchange occurring in Trobriand society. These people, like other Melanesians, engage in a host of similar transactions (Plates 5.3 and 5.4). The *kula* is tied in with these other exchanges as part of a complex interrelated system, and cannot be properly understood apart from them – which is to reiterate one of the truisms of Malinowski's favoured functionalist theory, that we must consider any society as an integrated whole.

The upshot is that the concepts of formal economic theory may have some limited relevance to an understanding of Trobriand society but that we need to deploy them sensitively and modify them as necessary to fit a radically different sociocultural context. We are left, however, with the problem of explaining why the Massim peoples invest such inordinate time and effort in this activity. This behaviour brings to mind the pig herding practices of the Maring and other highlanders (see chapter 3); the Trobrianders keep pigs too. We can understand economic motives – they relate to the exploitation, distribution, and consumption of material resources – explaining social ones in terms of some deep impulse for sociability seems to us inadequate. Why should sociability prompt such extravagant gift-giving activity among Melanesians and not among us?

FURTHER READING

The ethnographies on which this review is based are:

F. H. Damon, 1990 *From Muyuw to the Trobriands*. Tucson: University of Arizona Press.

F. H. Damon and R. Wagner (eds.), 1989 *Death rituals and life in the societies of the kula ring*. Dekalb: Northern Illinois University Press.

J. Leach and E. Leach (eds.), 1983 *The Kula: new perspectives on Massim exchange*. Cambridge: Cambridge University Press.

B. Malinowski, 1922 *Argonauts of the Western Pacific*. London: Routledge and Kegan Paul.

B. Malinowski, 1926 *Crime and custom in savage society*. London: Routledge and Kegan Paul.

N. D. Munn, 1986 *The fame of Gawa*. Cambridge: Cambridge University Press.

J. P. Singh Uberoi, 1962 *Politics of the kula ring*. Manchester: Manchester University Press.

A. Weiner, 1976 *Women of value, men of renown*. Austin: University of Texas Press.

A. Weiner, 1988 *The Trobrianders of Papua New Guinea*. New York: Holt, Rinehart and Winston.

M. Young (ed.), 1979 *The ethnography of Malinowski*. London: Routledge and Kegan Paul.

On economics and anthropology see:

S. Gudeman, 1986 *Economics as culture*. London: Routledge.

E. E. Le Clair and H. K. Schneider (eds.), 1968 *Economic anthropology: Readings in theory and analysis*. New York: Holt, Rinehart and Winston.

S. Plattner (ed.), 1989 *Economic anthropology*. Stanford: Stanford University Press.

Also referred to are:

H. C. Brookfield with D. Hart, 1971 *Melanesia*. London: Methuen.

M. Harris, 1968 *The rise of anthropological theory*. London: Routledge and Kegan Paul.

FILMS

Kula: Argonauts of the Western Pacific. Nippon A-V, Shinjuku, Tokyo.

Off the verandah, Bronislaw Malinowski 1884–1942. Central Independent Television Series *Strangers Abroad*. Programme 4.

Trobriand cricket: An indigenous response to colonialism. Jerry Leach and Gary Kildea.

The Trobriand Islanders. Harry Powell, Royal Anthropological Institute International Video.

The Trobriand Islanders of Papua New Guinea. Granada TV Disappearing World Series.

6   Sociopolitical exchange in the Southern Highlands

What is it that makes human beings, as social creatures, behave themselves? We may do so out of fear of the consequences of police action, courts and prison but what about societies that do not have these institutions? Attempts to answer this question have featured prominently in anthropological thinking. They relate to what we call the maintenance of the social order, and this goes to the heart of the issues just identified in connection with Melanesian pig raising and the *kula*. In order to see the connection we need to return to the institution of sociopolitical exchange.

Sociopolitical exchange

Ceremonial exchange institutions are central to the ordering of relations among human beings in Melanesian society. We find them throughout Melanesia; they lie at the very core of social life. The term 'ceremonial exchange', although widely used in the Melanesian literature, is somewhat inappropriate for this activity. It returns us to the issue of how our terms, reflecting our intellectual concerns at any time, condition in some regards what we think we understand of others' behaviour. Many transactions involve little if any ceremony, being carried out informally or even offhandedly. The term 'gift-giving economy' has been coined to cover these transactions, but this seems equally inappropriate; people present things not as gifts but in anticipation of agreed-upon returns, commonly in normatively regulated transactions and sometimes during highly structured events. I suggest replacing these terms with 'sociopolitical exchange' a term that enables us to consider a wider class of activities and because of its novelty has the merit of some neutrality. Sociopolitical exchange is the giving and receiving of wealth, frequently between kin, on prescribed social occasions. The events at which Melanesians exchange valuables vary from one place to another; some of the commoner ones are important life-cycle events such as birth, marriage and death, and important cultural events such as rituals, festivals and peace ceremonies. They are governed by a code of rules to which all participants subscribe, rules specifying who should give and receive what from whom and when.

We cannot equate these exchanges with economic transactions involving material goods in Western society (chapter 5). They are of an entirely different genre, being social and political rather than economic in nature. A crucial point of difference between Melanesian societies and our own is that we all derive our living from exchanging something on the market. In other words, we are specialised according to occupation and have to sell the goods or services that we specialise in to buy the many things that we do not produce but are nonetheless essential to our well-being. This specialisation makes it necessary for us to have some way of comparing and valuing each other's disparate goods and services, a commonly transactable medium to facilitate our exchange of them, namely, money. The vast majority of our economic transactions involve the use of money, because in a market-organised economy all labour, raw materials and finished goods must carry price tags so that sellers and buyers can exchange them. Microeconomic theory emerged from the attempt to understand the transactional forces which determine prices in an industrial market economy, concentrating on these mechanisms because of their crucial integrative role in determining supply and demand, outputs and incomes.

This contrasts directly with the situation in traditional Melanesian societies, where individuals and their families produce enough for their own subsistence and there is little or no specialisation by occupation. On a subsistence level, therefore, there is little call in Melanesian societies for elaborate distribution networks such as we find linking specialists under market regimes. Whereas we must exchange to subsist and these transactions need not have any significant social component, Melanesians produce for themselves enough to subsist, and exchange is something engaged in pre-eminently for sociopolitical reasons. Melanesian society in some important senses reverses the assumptions of a money-centred market economy. Whereas with us the majority of transactions are purchases, commonly from strangers, and we obtain few goods and services as gifts (presents on certain anniversaries, the occasional gift from one's spouse and so on), in Melanesian societies the opposite applies.

Throughout Melanesia material goods are given largely in social rather than in subsistence-related contexts, occasionally the same objects may feature in both. The passage of material goods from hand to hand is prompted far more often by social obligations than by consumer or utilitarian considerations. This shifts the emphasis to an entirely different plane – from impersonal purchase of commodities from strangers for consumer ends to personal transactions between relatives for sociopolitical ends (both being avenues to, and reflecting, success and prestige). The articulation between material economic issues and the society at large is of a different order: the inhabitants of Melanesia display a concern for their own flesh and blood, community, and sociability in their giving of things to one another. The nearest we come to these transactions is in our giving of Christmas and birthday presents.

We shall return ethnographically to the highlands of Papua New Guinea to examine these issues further, moving south-west from the Maring across the central cordillera to the Wola people (Map 6.1). They occupy similar rugged mountainous terrain in the Southern Highlands, north-east of Lake Kutubu and south-west of Mount Giluwe. They too are typical highlanders, living in small houses scattered along the sides of their valleys in areas of extensive cane grass land, the watersheds between them being heavily forested. Dotting the landscape are their neat gardens. They practise a semi-permanent shifting cultivation and subsist on a predominantly vegetable diet in which sweet potato is the staple. They keep pig herds of considerable size. Their supernatural conceptions centre on beliefs in the ability of their ancestors' spirits to cause sickness and death, in various other forest spirit forces, and in sorcery and poison.

They hand their pigs, together with other items of wealth such as sea-shells and a swamp-tree-sap cosmetic oil, around to one another in interminable series of exchanges marking all important social events. These transactions are a significant force for the maintenance of order in their fiercely egalitarian, acephalous society. Although the exchange procedures, the wealth given, and the events which prompt transactions vary from one society to another, certain themes and elements recur at a deeper level throughout Melanesia. Wola society is as good as any other to draw out these themes, looking in detail at some sociopolitical institutions for ethnographic substance. Furthermore, the interpretation that I place upon these transactions, emphasising individual action over corporate group interest (see chapter 9), is somewhat at odds with that of many others and for this reason I feel more comfortable referring to the people I know at first hand.

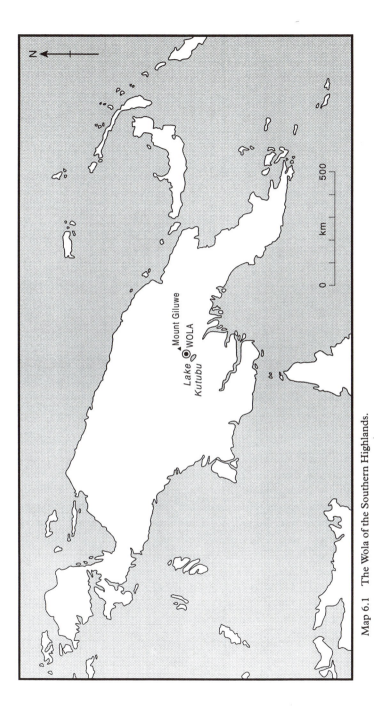

Map 6.1   The Wola of the Southern Highlands.

Pig kills

The Wola exchange pigs both in life-cycle marking exchanges (bride-wealth, mortuary payments and so on) and in recurring grand exchange events which they call *showmay tok lorokmay* (pig kills). These may occur as isolated events or as part of large occasions such as major rituals or stages in complex exchange cycles. They take place when pig herds have built up to considerable sizes and are proving difficult to manage. Thus these events relieve the pressure of the inexorably expanding work that herding the animals demands (see chapter 3). It is important that those taking part arrange their exchange commitments and affairs so as to ensure that they have pigs left over that they can afford to kill. A man who owed others valuables would find himself embroiled in a dispute if he recklessly killed wealth which in effect he owed them.

In the weeks that precede a pig kill there is a flurry of exchange activity not only as men settle their transactional obligations but also as they sort out title to animals. Pig ownership is not simply a matter of those herding animals having rights to kill them, men commonly have pigs in others' households and have to exchange wealth to secure rights to them. An important payment at this time is one that men make to the relatives of women who have herded the pigs they intend to kill, which is usually a payment by a man to his affines through his wife. Also before a kill, usually starting some months previous to it, those taking part prepare an open, grassy, park-like place for the event. They collect firewood and stones with which to cook the pork, along with various leaves for this purpose, and erect substantial horizontal poles on which to display it.

On the agreed day, excited men and women will be up before dawn and, in the chilly half-light, with phosphorescent cloud lying in the valley bottoms below, lead their squealing pigs on tethers to the appointed clearing. Here men quickly kill the animals by clubbing them across the snout (Plate 6.1). They then singe off their bristles over fires and lay out the carcasses on beds of banana leaves, where those who own them, helped by various relatives, proceed to butcher them (Plate 6.2). This is a time-consuming task, involving the removal of the two flanks, complete with fore and rear legs, from each animal. Crowds of people start to arrive as it proceeds. Many of them will feast on titbits of pork given them by relatives and friends, either roasting them over open fires or cooking them with greens in bamboo tubes. Men drape the sides of pork over the horizontal display pole as they remove them. When this is full with red meat it is a pleasing moment for those participating, pregnant with meaning – for it is a display not merely of meat as food

Plate 6.1   While one man holds a pig off the ground so that it presents its snout, another quickly slaughters it by clubbing it across the mandible.

but also of meat as wealth. It shows off the participants' prowess and acumen in exchange – a highly important matter to the Wola, as to other Melanesians, marking some of the men's most outstanding and admired achievements.

Late in the morning, when they have completed most of the butchering, men light the fires to heat the stones for cooking the pork. The day before they will have dug long, shallow pits, arranged wood over them and heaped stones on top. While they wait for the stones to heat up there is a lull, during which people gossip, snack and smoke. When the stones fall into the pit, often with a fireworks-like display of sparks, men quickly remove many of them with split-sapling tongs, together with the charred wood. They line the pits with banana leaves and place the pork in them, together with fresh tree-fern fronds collected a day or so previously. They include hot stones here and there and cover the meat-filled pits with further leaves and a layer of hot stones. After covering these with more leaves, they heap soil over them to create a steaming mound.

Some two hours later, during which there will have been a great deal

Plate 6.2   The son of a big man helps him to butcher a pig, breaking off its head before the pork goes into the oven to cook.

of socialising, often with infrequently seen relatives from elsewhere, men reverse the above process and open the oven (Plate 6.3). They lift the hot pork from the pits and place it on banana leaves for those who own it to cut up for distribution. This is a tense and trying time for the butchers, for they have to remember all those who stand to receive a share and give them a cut commensurate with their expectations. It is no easy task, with scores of people eligible. Finally comes the climax of the event, the exchange, with men holding up pieces of meat above their heads and shouting out the names of the persons to whom they are giving them.

Men give pork to all kin and friends with whom they currently interact. Looked at another way, they give pork to all those who have given them pork previously. At a pig kill we see the outcome of the institutionalisation of wealth exchange in Wola society acted out and, by extension, its effect in other societies throughout Melanesia. Numerous individual transactions take place simultaneously between many, many persons, the kind of transactions which are constantly taking place in countless smaller-scale contexts everyday involving considerably fewer people.

Plate 6.3   While women crowd in anticipation along the edge of a newly opened steaming oven pit, a man pulls out a side of pork from the bed of tree-fern fronds to be cut up for distribution.

Whereas a pig kill is a fairly straightforward event to describe, the flow of pork wealth (from butchers to relatives and from these recipients to others) is extremely difficult to track, involving a staggeringly complicated series of interrelated transactions.

The pigs herded by Melanesians are wealth to them, valued objects exchanged as tokens of sociability and political manipulation, rather than creatures reared for sale and consumption. Although they slaughter and eat them eventually, pigs are not raised merely to supply meat. The effort that highlanders such as the Maring put into pig raising is no longer so surprising. The inhabitants of Melanesia value and exchange not only pigs but also a number of other products that vary from one region to another: from sea shells to boars' tusks and from yams to pottery. Other valuables that the Wola give and receive include: shell-made objects, particularly crescents of pearl-shell and cowries mounted on necklaces; animals other than pigs, among them certain large and infrequently caught marsupials (including the echidna) and the flightless cassowary; colourfully plumed headdresses, notably those featuring magnificent bird of paradise feathers; and, imported from neighbouring regions, fine ornamental stone axes, an impure carbonaceous salt and a thick cosmetic oil.

Stateless social order

The Wola and other Melanesians spend a considerable part of their lives negotiating, arranging and participating in exchanges of these wealth objects in prescribed social contexts. Indeed, it is not overly dramatic to say that they exhibit an obsessive interest in these activities. What is the consequence of this for Melanesian society? It is pertinent here to review briefly the distinction made by anthropologists between societies organised as states, and those which are stateless or acephalous. States have central governments, policemen, courts (or their equivalents) which operate in concert to maintain order. Stateless societies have no such institutions. All traditional Melanesian societies are stateless, and the question is how they maintain order without the elements of state apparatus which in our experience are necessary to orderly social life.

A significant point is population density – the number of people who are regularly interacting socially with one another. It is easy to visualise how social life is regulated within small groups largely made up of closely related kin. A considerable component almost verges on instinctive (relations between parents and children, siblings and so on), and fairly informal mechanisms are sufficient to settle differences and organise action. This is doubly so when, as is usually the case, the members of these small groups are dependent upon one another for their subsistence needs – their very existence.

Problems arise when social groups become considerably larger, for primary kinship bonds then become insufficient to regulate behaviour within them. These close bonds may continue to order relations satisfactorily within the small kin-founded groupings which aggregated compose the wider community. It is in interaction between members of these different kin groups that socially disruptive behaviour is likely to occur. In this event, when the density of social populations increases, we expect to find other culturally sanctioned mechanisms to promote orderly social life. These arrangements are commonly formulated on a kinship paradigm in small-scale face-to-face societies, as extensions of the kin grid that universally structures relations within extended family-like social groups (almost naturally, although with many cultural variations). The norms governing sociopolitical exchange in Melanesian society, for instance, are invariably structured on kinship lines.

The complex exchange institutions which characterise the stateless societies of Melanesia promote orderly political and social relations. Exchange is a very powerful social principle on which to structure an acephalous political order, for it is an aspect of all human interaction. On one level we might surmise that the ancestors of today's Melanesians (perhaps the Non-Austronesians or Papuans in antiquity) discovered long ago that elaborating on the exchanges that took place between individuals was one potent way of dealing with the problem of encouraging naturally wayward human beings to behave with consideration towards one another. Exchange consequently became institutionalised in the structure and order of social life.

The way in which exchange effects such control over behaviour is straightforward. If a society has norms, which members observe and value very highly, that require them to engage in a continuous round of exchanges of valuables with others, then they must remain on amicable terms. They cannot wrong others wantonly (e.g. steal from them) or fight with them and still expect to exchange with them (other than exchanging blows, which is the antithesis of orderly social behaviour), and their personal reputation and esteem depend upon their participating to the best of their ability. It is small wonder that the Wola, like other Melanesians, are obsessed with sociopolitical exchanges.

Marriage exchanges

A look at the series of exchanges that mark a Wola marriage will serve to illustrate what these theoretical considerations imply in real life. The extended series of transactions marking a marriage among them serves to establish a new set of socially meaningful and enduring relations between the parties involved. Some of the participants are even likely to be related to some persons on the other side already by other transactional and social bonds, and this multistranded meshing to-and-fro imparts considerable strength to Wola social networks.

The exchange of wealth regulates marriage and orders relations between the sexes, for to indulge in sexual intercourse without legitimating a relationship beforehand with an exchange of valuables is a serious offence. The Wola are amazed that Europeans marry without exchanging wealth or, as they put it, 'steal girls for nothing'. We might surmise that these transactions help to prevent men and women from fighting over partners, for they have no free access to members of the other sex. A man cannot just take up with a woman, even with her consent, without arranging with her and his relatives for a protracted series of transactions. It is also plausible that they contribute to the virtual absence of forced abductions and even rapes by preventing situations from arising in the normal course of life where these might occur (the threat of revenge and the fear men have that women may poison them with menstrual blood are further important considerations here [see chapters 4 and 12]).

These nuptial transactions also give the resulting marriage relationship considerable durability. They prevent men from taking up casually with women and then abandoning them with children after a brief interval. They promote orderly and stable marital relations because it is very difficult to undo them. They also afford the relatives of young men and women a considerable influence, even control of sorts, over their behaviour, because their cooperation is essential in mustering and distributing the wealth exchanged. This does not imply that men and women are forced together and tied irrevocably in miserable unions: Wola marriage arrangements and relationships render such ideas inapposite.

Two people who are attracted to one another and intend to marry may exchange relatively small gifts with one another, besides courting in other customary, rather constrained ways, such as attending small informal singing parties together, for a year or more before the large bridewealth transaction that will mark their marriage proper. She may give him delicacies such as pork or pandan nuts and he reciprocate in kind. Or she may net and present him with a bag or apron, and he may give her a valuable in return, a pearl shell or maybe even a small pig – which she, setting a pattern that will recur again and again when she receives wealth from her future husband, will pass on to a close male

Plate 6.4   The father of a bride, wearing the crescent wig characteristic of the neighbouring Huli, holds up a pearl-shell crescent, the agreed-upon share of her bridewealth for one of her relatives, for him to come forward and formally accept it, thus legitimating the marriage.

relative. On one or more occasions the young man's gift may be marsupials caught possibly with the assistance of relatives. Some three or four months before the bridewealth transaction is to take place, he makes a large betrothal payment, consisting of six or so valuables, which she again passes on to her male relatives. When they receive this payment they know that the marriage will take place.

The bridewealth transaction is made up of two, three, or more dozen valuables, notably pigs and pearl shells (in recent years considerable inflation has occurred in the size of transactions and changes in the wealth offered). The groom looks to his relatives to contribute wealth to the transaction, and if he is a young man marrying for the first time their contributions will make up the greater part. A similar range of relatives on the bride's side will share it (Plate 6.4). The bridewealth transaction usually takes days to complete because all those on the bride's side who stand to receive something must be satisfied with the wealth offered to them. This can lead to tense, even heated negotiations as they bargain for more valuables from the relatives of the groom. This cannot be interpreted as bargaining to buy a bride; any economic analogy is totally out of place in this social exchange. Once the often protracted negotiations are completed, the bride concludes the marriage by passing each valuable from one side to the other, symbolising her connective position between the two kin networks linked by her marriage. The groom plays no part in the proceedings.

The bride's side makes a return prestation the day following the bridewealth distribution, giving the groom's side three or four valuables, one of them customarily being a large pig. A month or so later the groom's side will hand over any late contributions to the bridewealth, some of which may have been promised and have entered into the earlier payment negotiations. A while after this, helped again perhaps by relatives, the husband may hunt marsupials and give his catch to his new wife's relatives. They in turn will reciprocate with a small payment of one or two valuables. After this, throughout the life of the marriage, items pass back and forth between the husband and his relatives and the woman's kin. The payment mentioned earlier, made by a man to the male kin of a woman herding pigs he intends to slaughter, through her hands, is one such occasion. It is scarcely necessary to belabour the sociological import of such a sequence of exchanges, which is only one of a number that characterise Wola social life; their integrative effect in establishing a new set of affinal relations is clear.

This chapter has been applying what anthropologists call **social exchange** or **transactional theory** to Melanesian society. The constitution of the social order obliges us to do so; Melanesians were early exponents of exchange theory, sensing its sociological potency long ago. Transactional theorists study social life as a complex system of exchanges. One line of enquiry, elaborating on the ideas of the social philosopher Mauss, asks what it is that prompts people to reciprocate the things they receive in exchange transactions and centres on the distinction between commodity and gift. The proposition is that when people exchange commodities, buyers assume outright ownership of the things, whereas when they present gifts to one another, they remain identified in some intangible way with them. The connectivity resides in their social relationship, symbolised in the thing exchanged. We are familiar with this; some part of the giver adheres to any present that we receive and gives it what we call sentimental value. It morally obligates a return, sustaining the relationship. And some of the enduring valuables that Melanesians exchange come to symbolise chains of relationships as they accrete identities through multiple transactions, morally encapsulating entire social networks. In other words, commodities are alienated when exchanged whereas gifts are inalienable. This alluringly straight-forward distinction is intriguingly conditioned by production arrangements in Melanesia, where many of the things circulating in sociopolitical exchanges are not produced but exchanged into existence (see chapters 5 and 8).

Whereas this chapter applies the transactional approach on a macro-level as structuring the sociopolitical relations of entire societies, it can also, of course, be applied to the content of the interactions between individuals. When anyone gives something to someone else, the item offered will signal all manner of things about the state of their relationship, especially as perceived by the giver. What is given and how it is given can convey pleasure or displeasure, even anger – physically containing this disruptive emotion. Where people invest exchange with tremendously high value, as in Melanesia, these kinds of messages can be transmitted with a force we find difficult to comprehend.

The size of a piece of pork given at a pig kill can come as a pat on the back or a slap in the face, and offering a large cut to someone who deserves only a small one is in effect earning social esteem at the expense of another's embarrassment and loss of face. This competitive side of exchange stands opposed to its sociable side and is another issue central to understanding Melanesian society.

FURTHER READING

The ethnographic monographs on which this review is based are:
D. K. Feil, 1984 *Ways of exchange*. St. Lucia: Queensland University Press.
D. K. Feil, 1987 *The evolution of Papua New Guinea Highlands societies*. Cambridge: Cambridge University Press.
R. M. Glasse and M. Meggitt (eds.), 1969 *Pigs, pearl shells, and women*. Englewood Cliffs: Prentice-Hall.
R. Lederman, 1986 *What gifts engender*. Cambridge: Cambridge University Press.
P. Sillitoe, 1979 *Give and take*. Canberra: Australian National University Press.

On social exchange see:
J. Davies, 1992 *Exchange*. (Concepts in the Social Sciences) Buckingham: Open University Press.
P. Ekeh, 1974 *Social exchange theory*. London: Heinemann.
C. Gregory, 1982 *Gifts and commodities*. London: Academic Press.
M. Mauss, 1990 *The gift*. (trans. W. D. Halls) London: Routledge.
M. Sahlins, 1974 *Stone Age economics*. London: Tavistock.
A. Weiner, 1992 *Inalienable possessions: The paradox of keeping-while-giving*. Berkeley: University of California Press.

FILMS

Bird of the Thunderwoman. Australian Broadcasting Commission.
Courtship and music in Papua New Guinea. River Films with La Sept.
The Mendi. Canadian Broadcasting Commission.

7   Big men on Bougainville Island

We have been examining the sociable side of exchange – giving as an amicable act which fosters and requires relative social harmony or order. But exchange can at the same time, as intimated at the close of the last chapter, contain an element of competitiveness: people can compete in what they give and receive, those giving more achieving a higher social standing. In Melanesia those who excel at sociopolitical exchange – who are outstanding competitors – commonly achieve admiration and respect: they are Melanesia's big men.

Big men

A big man is a person of repute and influence in Melanesian society. The term 'big man' derives from a literal translation of the appellation given to such persons in some Melanesian societies, which has passed into the region's Pidgin lingua franca as *bikpela man* and is applied to adult males in general and respected persons of talent in particular. A critical feature of big-manship is that the status is achieved rather than ascribed; that is, it is not inherited (although in some places the son of a big man may be in a better position than others to become one) and consequently has only informal standing. It carries no political authority or power.

The big man differs from a chief in some fundamental regards. The position of chief vests authority in the holder, legitimated by public consensus, to make decisions, issue directions and apply sanctions to other members of society. The chief may have recourse to force to back up his political authority. He governs through formal institutions, frequently delegating authority to lower officeholders for administrative purposes in designated parts of the chiefdom. Those subjected to chiefly authority accept it because it guarantees order and security, but they may also contest it because it justifies and maintains relations of inequality. Although the authority vested in the officeholder presents the possibility of domination, the consent of those subject to the authority that legitimises it serves as a constraint. All of this is quite different from the situation that obtains in big man societies.

Any man endowed with the required qualities can aspire to big man status. These qualities, or the emphasis put on them, vary from one society to another. They range from an above-average ability to contribute to feasts and festivals and manipulate wealth, fearlessness in warfare and an aggressive temperament, skill in oratory and persuasion, specialised ritual knowledge, a reputation for sorcery. The prestige of a big man declines as these qualities wane with age: distinction depends on current ability, not former glory. The influence that accrues to individuals who achieve big-man status varies. In some places big men reportedly exert considerable political control over the activities of small, varyingly constituted local groups by force of character, proven ability and the creation of obligations. Some big men have been described as despotic, others, although first among equals, cannot be said to achieve or create for themselves positions of political leadership.

Although it varies considerably in ethnographic detail from place to place, the big man complex has an underlying consistency, although among Austronesians it has some hierarchical features which have prompted some writers to speak of 'chiefs' (see chapter 11). The prominence of big men in Melanesian societies does not preclude the recognition of women who excel at female-ascribed activities, achieving respect that translates largely into public influence emanating from the domestic domain (see chapter 9).

Bougainville, one of the larger islands to the east of New Guinea (Map 7.1), will serve as our ethnographic illustration of the nature of big-manship. This island comprises two mountain ranges topped by volcanoes and clothed in rain forest, dissected by steep-sided gorges and impassable swamps. In the south-west a wide alluvial plain slopes down from the mountain backbone to swamps along the coast. Here, around the fast-flowing streams that fan out from the mountains, the Siuai live in hamlets of stilted houses. Their staple crop is taro, and they keep sizeable pig herds. They are Non-Austronesians who live in a stateless, egalitarian polity. Their big men, called *mumi*, combine many of the characteristics reported from other places in Melanesia for big men and illustrate a number of issues pertaining to leadership in Melanesian society.

Achieving big man status

Those aspiring to big man status in Siuai society have to demonstrate:
(1) outstanding skill in manipulating wealth in sociopolitical exchange;

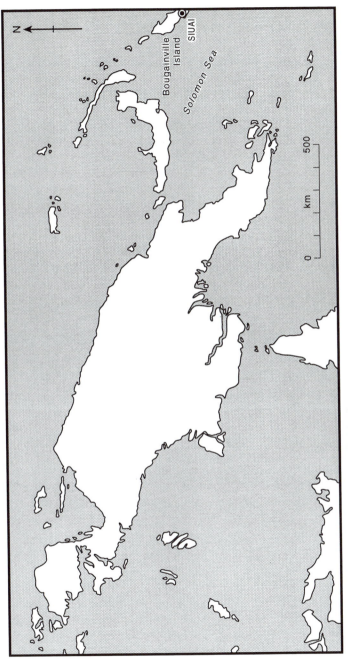

Map 7.1   The Siuai of Bougainville Island.

(2) a reputation for fearless and successful leadership in war;
(3) ritual knowledge and an ability to control and appease powerful spirit forces; and
(4) skill as an orator.

The most significant of these qualifications is the first.

The two principal items of wealth which the Siuai exchange with one another are pigs and sea-shell valuables. The shell wealth comprises lengths of button-like shell discs threaded onto lengths of string. These discs, called *pesi*, are distinguished in terms of shell type, colour, diameter and thickness and have different values, delicate red ones being valued the highest. The Siuai, like other Melanesians, regularly exchange these valuables with one another, often together with meals featuring valued foods and delicacies. Exchanges again frequently mark events in the life cycle, such as marriage and death. Big men play a prominent role in these exchanges; disburse and receive more wealth than other men. The Siuai also exchange wealth at culturally defined as opposed to life-cycle-prompted events which, while unique to them, parallel others throughout Melanesia. These events centre on the men's clubhouse.

A man aspiring to the status of big man has to organise and finance the building of a men's house. The more people are involved in the enterprise the better. An ambitious man strives to include not only relatives living in the same locality but also people from elsewhere. He contracts out the building work to different groups of people, commissioning some to erect the house's frame and do the required ornamental lashings, others to supply the sago-sheet thatch, and so on (Plates 7.1 and 7.2). He arranges large feasts to pay these people for their services. The test of his transactional skills is in providing an adequate or better still, more than adequate supply of choice foods – pork, taro, coconut and sago and almond puddings – for the feasts. A big man tries to see that his local relatives, who will use the house when completed, organise their subsistence activities to ensure a surplus of the needed food items at the required time. Assembling a sufficient number of fattened pigs for these occasions calls for considerable skill. In addition to using the animals raised by female relatives, he may arrange with certain kin and friends to supply him with pigs, perhaps giving them small animals to raise from one of his own litters for the purpose. These suppliers will be compensated with *pesi*. As the event approaches he may seek out men with large beasts which they are willing to sell, and buy these with lengths of *pesi*. He must therefore arrange his exchange affairs in such a way as to have sufficient valuables to make these sizeable payments to others, and the negotiations and transactions do not stop there. The Siuai do not kill their own pigs; instead, they exchange them with others

Plate 7.1   The construction of a house on Bougainville, men lift the ridge-pole into position.

Plate 7.2   A man preparing a sheet of sago-leaf thatch for a house, tucking and securing the frondlets into position.

for animals of equivalent size. It is no surprise that, having picked their way through this maze of negotiations, the Siuai regard the delivery of a large pig for slaughter as a particularly exciting occasion and sometimes arrange a small feast to reward the efforts of those who have transported the animal on a streamer-decked stretcher to the pen built especially to accommodate it before the feast.

When the house is built, it demands furnishing with slit-gongs – robust sections of tree trunk hollowed out with a slit cut down one side (Plate 7.3). These are arranged on log sleepers in the clubhouse, slit uppermost, and men beat on them with the butt-end of pieces of wood to accompany feasts and to signal other important social events. The making of slit-gongs follows the same procedure as the construction of men's houses. The big man of a house requiring a slit-gong arranges with his relatives who frequent the house and, if a particularly able man, with others elsewhere, to supply vegetables, nuts, and pigs for a feast and organises his *pesi* transactions and those of his closest supporters to pay for them. He then enters into a contract with another group of men centred on a men's house elsewhere, to supply a gong, negotiating with its big man, who arranges with someone skilled at making slit-gongs to manufacture one.

The arrival of a new gong and the feast to reward its suppliers is again a grand and exciting occasion. The more people are involved, the grander the occasion and the greater the prestige accruing to the sponsoring big man and his men's house. The Siuai commission enormous gongs to ensure that large numbers of men will be required to move them. Gongs are transported from the forest where they are made to the men's house for which they are commissioned on stout carrying frames made with enormous struts. Those commissioning gongs even engage in magical practices to make the whole load heavier so that it requires more men to carry it (the carriers resort to magic in return to counter this supernatural increasing of their load). The more men are needed, of course, the bigger the feast required to reward them. Not offering a generous feast would diminish the organiser's social standing; indeed, anyone rumoured to be unable to do so will be unable to muster much of a workforce, and therefore end up sponsoring a small, mediocre event which earns him little renown.

Besides filling a men's house with a dozen or so gongs, the Siuai traditionally consecrated it with the heads of enemies. Over time a house acquired a number of slain enemies' heads, all arranged looking towards their homelands to discourage their relatives from seeking revenge. This relates to the second qualification of big-manship: an ability to organise and finance armed hostilities. Big men among the Siuai need not

Plate 7.3   Bougainvillean men hollowing out a slit-gong; two saplings lashed along the top edge act as guides to the slit's width.

personally be fearless warriors found in the thick of every battle with several slayings to their credit as they reportedly must be in some parts of Melanesia. Armed aggression is expensive for the Siuai not just in destruction and death but also in the payments which it requires of those who initiate hostilities to compensate the kin of slain allies. Reparations are common throughout Melanesia; it is in arranging feasts to meet these obligations, in supplying pigs, *pesi* and so on, as necessary, that men validate their status as big men in wartime. The reputations of successful men as reliable and renowned wealth brokers and feast organisers inspire the confidence of others that allows them to muster and press for warriors to fight on behalf of their men's house group when the need arises.

In addition to thinking that enemy heads confer supernatural power on the men's house, the Siuai believe that men's houses and their environs are the home of demons called *horomorun*, which they associate closely with the resident big man. This relates to the third qualification of big men: ritual knowledge and power, which like warriorhood is not as significant or developed among the Siuai as in some other societies of Melanesia. The Siuai believe in a big-man *horomorun* familiar, assisted by lesser demons, which are the same in number as the men who regularly frequent the men's house. These spirits protect the members of the men's house, especially the big man, against being killed out of jealousy, probably through sorcery. They also guard their property; for instance, in anticipation of a feast a big man may supernaturally instruct the demons to protect coconut groves from pilfering. But men, especially big men, have to keep these demons happy or they will attack them and make them sick. To do this they arrange feasts at which the demons can feed on the essence of the blood of the pigs they slaughter. A big man will also hang pieces of pork from a peg on one of the supports of the men's house for his demon to share with the others. When a man aspires to become big, he takes on awesome supernatural responsibilities, and failing to meet them may mean death. It takes little imagination to appreciate what an incentive beliefs in disgruntled and 'hungry' demons must be for men to participate industriously in socio-political exchange activities to ensure sufficient pig slaughters to keep them content.

The fourth quality required of big men is a skill at oratory, both formal and informal. Speeches are made at feasts at which speakers face each other across the dance ground to denigrate their own achievements and praise those of their counterparts (host or guests). (Big men also commission the composition of special tunes played on pan-pipes to commemorate the grand events they organise.) Informally leaders need to persuade others to comply with their plans – to talk others around to their point of view.

The big man legacy

What does a man get out of being big? In the first place, he wins the admiration and respect of others. The achievement of high standing is a significant motive force in human behaviour, perhaps more for some individuals than for others, and some Siuai pursue big man status largely for this reward. Other men try to convert their renown into political capital – to gain some tenuous control over the actions of those living around them. The local groups which they aspire in some sense to lead are variously constituted, including closely and distantly related kin. The Siuai subscribe to a matrilineal ideology – which is significant in certain ritual matters and when someone dies, it also has a sentimental value – and some neighbourhoods are landowning matrilineages with accretions of various other relatives. Other localities are more patrilineal in composition, a cumulative result of men's decisions over several generations to remain at their father's place and with his kin, and these similarly include accretions of other kin. This mixed and random kin constitution of local groups is common throughout Melanesia (see chapter 9). The wide choice afforded to people with regard to residence is an important, indeed, almost inevitable, aspect of Melanesian social organisation. As a result, definition of these groups is difficult, their fluidity compounds problems of drawing boundaries around them.

What a politically ambitious Siuai big man aspires to do is lead those who live in his neighbourhood, and he may use the allegiance of those who frequently visit his men's house as a political base from which to influence the actions of others elsewhere. He goes about this by struggling to win for himself and consequently the men's-house group with which he is associated a reputation that members will take pride in and work to maintain. The struggles between clubhouses can become intense as rival big men battle to demonstrate their supremacy.

When they have built and furnished first-class men's houses, rivals may embark on a round of competitive feasts. These feasts are similar to those staged during house building and gong making and involve the same wealth manipulations and resource organisation, but here the sponsoring big man picks a rival big man over whom he wishes to demonstrate his transactional superiority and gives the feast in his honour. The man so 'honoured' or challenged is obliged to arrange a feast in return of at least equal splendour. If he fails to do so within a year or two, he concedes the challenger's superiority. If he exceeds the feast he received, the original challenger must in turn match this inflated return or lose face. If their feasts more or less match in size then they have established parity of status – until, perhaps, the next challenge.

We have already seen that a big man requires the cooperation of relatives and friends, in particular those comprising his men's-house group. In coordinating their actions to build up to a projected feast, he relies on fostering a strong *esprit de corps*. All those associated with a men's house want to champion it over others because this brings them all renown; the big man benefits more than anyone else, but he is needed to concentrate and coordinate their activities to this end. It is from this thin thread that his leadership hangs, although he may have a stronger hold over one or two men by having them in his personal debt. We have already established that Melanesian societies have no formal government as we understand it, and this conditions the nature and extent of the political leadership we should expect to find in them.

Equal leadership

Leadership in stateless polities is constrained by the notion of **equality**. Melanesian societies put great value on the political equality of all persons, as do stateless societies around the world. The Siuai, like other Melanesians, lead their lives according to an ethos of relative individual political freedom; every person is free to govern his/her own actions so long as he/she does not infringe on the rights of others to do likewise. And through the generations human societies in Melanesia and throughout the world have evolved sets of norms and values, constantly in process of revision, which promote orderly social relations between individuals. In Melanesia, much of this expected behaviour revolves around institutionalised exchange, which places individuals under various socially determined obligations to one another on specified occasions – a powerful force, as we have seen, in fostering social order (see chapter 6).

Leadership in an egalitarian environment may seem a contradiction in terms. It is axiomatic in stateless societies that no person can occupy a position that gives him authority over others. He cannot force others to comply with his intentions; he has no physical or supernatural sanctions at his disposal with which he might coerce their compliance. This places our big men in a precarious position demanding considerable skill and tact. In short, a big man finds himself in a situation that continually tests his ability to lead and circumscribes the limited and tenuous control he extends over others' behaviour. Indeed 'control' is the wrong word, for the 'controlled' go along with his plans only so long as they are in their joint interests. Perhaps 'manipulation' is a better word, for although a big man has no political power he does have influence above the average, influence which accrues to him by virtue of the respect and renown he earns by excelling in activities highly esteemed by all.

If this is the position then we can speak of Siuai big men as leaders only in a limited sense. They exercise a degree of leadership by manipulating their relations with their men's house associates – by persuading them that the course of action they have in mind will bring prestige and standing to all concerned and by inspiring confidence that they have the ability and energy, reflected in previous achievements, to accomplish the task that is being contemplated. One of the qualities we listed at the beginning as a necessary qualification for big man status was the ability to sway others with talk. Here we see the importance of that skill.

When some event is mooted that will require several men to cooperate and coordinate their actions, they discuss it at length in and around the men's houses (Plate 7.4). A majority opinion gradually crystallises, and it is as this emerges that a big man relies on his persuasive and manipulative skills to swing it in the direction he favours. To try to force the issue against the wishes of a significant number of those who frequent his clubhouse would undermine his tenuous political influence, for men would simply cease to turn up there. A Siuai is free to frequent any men's house he pleases, or at least any one where he has kin connections and friends who will admit him to their circle. He may even move from one locality to another, from one territorially defined group of relatives to another. Consequently, men can withdraw their support from any big man who irks them and even shift their allegiance to a rival of his. If a big man demands more from his associates than they see themselves as receiving in return, they will desert him.

Big men in the Eastern Highlands of Papua New Guinea have been characterised as persons who successfully mediate between two conflicting values of their society: 'equivalence' and 'strength'. We can see this juggling act clearly with Siuai big men as in trying to direct others they must allow for their individual rights or risk antagonising them and losing their cooperation altogether. Perhaps, given the precarious and fluid nature of their position we should call big men not leaders but coordinators and energisers of social action.

Another social value that comes to prominence through the strivings of big men is sociability, the creation and maintenance of cooperative and harmonious social relations. Among the Siuai, 'the circulation of goods is materially increased by the quest for high rank', and 'the activities of leaders result in the formation and intensification of social relationships inside their own neighbourhoods'. They also have 'the effect of increasing interaction among residents even outside the context of men's society activities' and furthermore 'bring about the creation and intensification of social relations between neighbourhoods' such that 'neighbourhoods having active high-ranking leaders possess more *esprit de corps* and better morale than most others. As evidence we might

Plate 7.4　Men meeting for a discussion on the sitting platforms outside two houses.

cite their greater number of communal undertakings and the fewer number of factional quarrels and litigations' (Oliver 1967: 441–47).

These comments help us to appreciate why the Siuai, like other Melanesians, place such a high premium on exchange and accord renown and even a measure of influence to those who excel at it. The continual strivings of big men stimulate the exchange-founded interaction found throughout Melanesia, interaction which fosters a stable and integrated stateless political environment. They help to ensure cooperation and social order without any centralised authority. It is small wonder that those who excel at exchange are considered 'big'. The social accolades that they win encourage their wholehearted commitment, even obsession, with sociopolitical exchange, and their strivings for personal glory stimulate them further.

An intriguing issue is what prevents ambitious big men from trying to consolidate their tenuous influence – to establish more secure positions of leadership over others. It seems reasonable to assume that like politically ambitious human beings elsewhere they would like to have more control over the actions of their peers. Melanesian society has many features which conspire to prevent the breakdown of the stateless order and the loss of individual liberty to authoritative officeholders. Sociopolitical exchange and the values that surround it serve as a significant bulwark. Others concern the production of things; for example, arrangements for the manufacture of artifacts, which prevent control from falling into the hands of particular interest groups and their exploiting others.

FURTHER READING

The ethnographic accounts drawn upon in this chapter are:

D. L. Oliver, 1955 *A Solomon Island society.* Cambridge: Harvard University Press (republished in 1967 by Beacon Press).

D. L. Oliver, 1973 'Southern Bougainville'. In R. M. Berndt and P. Lawrence (eds.), *Politics in New Guinea.* Seattle: University of Washington Press.

On leadership elsewhere see:

R. M. Berndt and P. Lawrence (eds.), 1973 *Politics in New Guinea.* Seattle: University of Washington Press.

M. Godelier, 1986 *The making of great men.* (trans. R. Sawyer) Cambridge: Cambridge University Press.

M. Godelier and M. Strathern (eds.), 1991 *Big men and great men.* Cambridge: Cambridge University Press.

K. E. Read, 1959 'Leadership and consensus in a New Guinea society'. *American Anthropologist* 61: 425–36.

8   Technology in the highlands fringe

The traditional cultures of Melanesia were Stone Age ones and some of them remained so well into the twentieth century. Such cultures are generally portrayed as primitive and their technologies as relatively inefficient, but this is a false impression. Although the technologies may be modest, they are highly effective in the environments in which they are used.

Primitive technology

It is *only* in a technological sense that anthropologists will countenance talk of one culture as 'primitive' compared with another. It is undeniable that a horse-drawn wheeled cart can carry more things quickly over a given distance than a human being, that a motorised vehicle will do so even more effectively, that an aircraft will do so better still, and so on, but it is quite another matter to assume that people without wheeled or mechanised transport lead impoverished and deficient lives. We now acknowledge that we have no grounds for making such a judgement. How can we say that any religion, form of family organisation, or political system is preferable to another? These are relative, not absolute questions, and the answers will depend on the society into which one has been socialised, one's place in it and your consequent experience of life. Nonetheless, the question remains why in Melanesia and many other parts of the world people remained content with primitive technologies, coming nowhere near setting off industrial revolutions and in some places not even going beyond hunting-and-gathering to horticulture. One possible explanation for their contentment with their lot is that a primitive tool kit may testify to a particularly sound relationship both among human beings and between them and the natural world. At the outset I should stress once again that whatever the technology it would be erroneous to suppose any intellectual inferiority of those who produce and employ it.

Technology is subject to both cultural and ecological constraints.

First, there are those relating to the political-economic ordering of Melanesian societies. An industrial revolution demands in the first instance the political environment of the nation-state, where a few have the opportunity to co-ordinate and facilitate experimentation and technical development and the power to direct it as necessary – and even, consequently, to make the lives of others abjectly miserable. This is unthinkable in acephalous political contexts like those of tribal Melanesia. The question becomes not why these people never experienced a technological revolution but why they have maintained truly democratic and liberal political orders to the equal benefit of all individuals while other societies allowed power to fall into the hands of a few.

Secondly, there are constraints relating to cultural values. An industrial revolution depends in some measure on feelings of material dissatisfaction – perhaps induced somewhat by population increases and growing pressure on and consequent scarcity of resources. Melanesian people, besides blocking the concentration of power, capital, resources and so on, in a few hands and thwarting the centralisation of political power necessary for industrial developments, have apparently never experienced these feelings of commodity inadequacy. They seem, on current evidence, to have remained content with their lot for millennia, considering their standard of living quite adequate and existing in a state of 'original affluence' until now, when, affected by contact with the Western world they recognise its inadequacy in comparison with what is industrially achievable.

Thirdly, there are ecological constraints. The populations of Melanesia had sound relations with their natural environments; their technologies ensured that they stayed within well-regulated ecological niches. The question again becomes how our ancestors managed to override the environmental constraints placed on them to the point that with our awesome technology we now threaten to destabilise the entire planet as a habitat fit for human beings and other creatures.

These points, to my mind, more than adequately account for the continuance of Stone Age technologies in Melanesia. Indeed they put them in a favourable light. Although it is undeniable that industrial technology is more advanced in terms of the capacity to modify and control (and also destroy and dislocate) the environment, this is only one of its aspects. In other regards it may be seen as giving rise to a lifestyle that is less advanced than that of technologically simple people. If one values relative liberty and equal opportunity for all, conservation and living in balance with the natural environment, and relative contentment and fair sharing, then the 'primitive' culture may be preferable. The important question is whether the costs of acquiring the benefits of

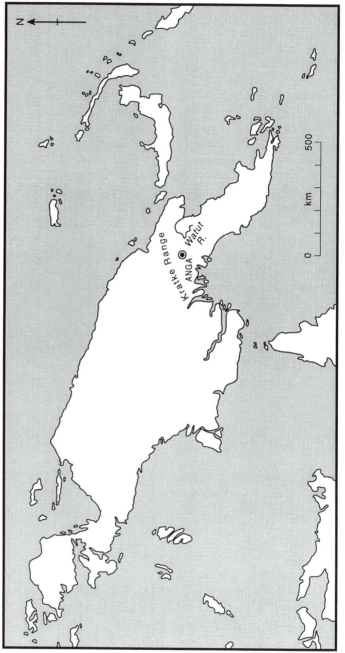

Map 8.1   The Anga and the Kratke Range.

modern technology are inevitable. In our review of technology in Melanesia we shall turn to the Anga speakers of the highland fringe of Papua New Guinea. They are a widely dispersed people occupying the region from the Kratke Ranges to the Watut River (Map 8.1). They wear characteristic bark-cloth capes from their heads and the men wear voluminous sporran-shaped codpieces of dried reeds. They live in scattered hamlets, practise shifting cultivation with sweet potato as their staple crop, and keep domesticated pigs. They hunt wild pigs and various marsupials and birds in the extensive forests of their region. They traditionally had a fearsome, warlike reputation and are well-known for their elaborate male initiation rites.

Stone technology

The principal Anga man's tool is the stone adze, and the principal woman's one is the digging stick. The adze, haft held vertically, resembles a figure 7 in shape. The Anga manufacture the stone blades from a range of rocks, largely metamorphic ones including phyllite, greywacke and schist which they find in the beds of streams. Men knap them roughly to begin with, using pebble hammerstones. When they have chipped them to the required size and elongated oval shape, they proceed to grind the blades down. They employ coarse-grained abrasive rocks such as volcanic tuff (sometimes large stream-bed boulders) for grindstones, rubbing adze blades against them, with water as a lubricant. The extent of grinding varies, but men commonly leave the surface of the adze part-ground after they have produced a cutting edge honed to their satisfaction. Over time, with repeated resharpening, they may eliminate all the chipped irregularities remaining from the initial knapping of the blade. The manufacture of a stone adze blade, in particular the grinding of it, is hard and monotonous work, and men do it working in bursts over several days. The finished stone blades, especially those resharpened several times, vary considerably in size and shape, the retouching of accidentally chipped cutting edges producing eccentrically shaped implements, but whatever their shape and size, all adze blades serve as all-round tools.

The Anga mount their adze blades on one-piece hafts (Figure 8.1). They manufacture these from 40-centimetre or so lengths of branch wood with 15–20-centimetre lengths of parent trunk wood attached to them. They select hard, straight-grained timber with a certain elasticity, often from *Garcinia* sp. and *Claoxylon* sp. trees. They pare the branch to a readily graspable haft, tapering it to a point and rubbing it smooth with a handful of abrasive leaves. The trunk piece attached crosswise to

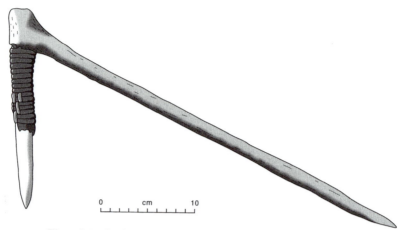

Figure 8.1   An Anga adze.

the top of the haft is shaped into a socket to accommodate the stone blade. The knot of the natural fork gives the haft great strength where it takes most of the stress of the blows delivered with the adze. Men hollow out a socket cavity on the top side of the trunk section to the dimensions of the butt-end of the blade, trying the stone head for fit at intervals, and shape the remainder of the socket piece to suitable rounded dimensions. When they have completed the haft and the socket to their satisfaction, men place the adze blade in the socket recess and bind it tightly in place with pared rattan strands, winding them around and around socket and blade and finally tucking the ends into the binding to secure them (Plate 8.1). It takes between four and six hours of work to prepare a haft and mount an adze blade.

The adze or *tsila mouné* is a man's everyday tool, used to fell trees and clear other vegetation in establishing gardens, collect and cut up fire-wood, shape timbers for house building, and fashion a range of wooden artifacts such as bows, arrows, shields, clubs, adze hafts and digging sticks. The Anga had come into possession of steel equivalents, both adze-like mounted carpenter's plane-blades and conventional steel axes, by the middle of the twentieth century, these implements diffusing along traditional trade routes from points of European penetration into their region and the highlands beyond (e.g. the gold fields at Bulolo). According to Godelier's (1973) statistics, it took 3.4 times longer to complete work felling trees with stone adzes than with steel axes (although, as he notes, comparison was difficult because of differences in the work undertaken with the different tools).

Plate 8.1 A man binding a stone adze blade in place on a socketed haft,
using a bone awl to prise up the tight rattan binding to insert the strand.

Other Anga implements are typical of a Melanesian tool-kit and
include, besides digging sticks, chert-flake knives and scrapers, broad-
bladed machete-like wooden knives, awls and needles made of cassowary, wallaby and bat bone and razor-edged internodal bamboo knives.
Other manufactures include cooking implements, such as bamboo
tongs, bamboo tubes, gourds, a range of bamboo tobacco pipes and fire-
lighters of split sticks and bamboo strips. Their weapons, used by men
in fighting and hunting, include finely shaped and polished palm-wood
bows strung with strips of pared bamboo culm and a range of arrows,
from plain palm-wood points to leaf-shaped bamboo blades and from
prong-headed arrows to blunt-ended club ones for shooting birds
without damaging their plumes, all mounted on cane grass shafts and
sometimes engraved with designs. They produced war clubs too, some

Plate 8.2   A woman plaiting a mourning 'bib' from bark-fibre string, worn around the neck; relatives sometimes decorate it with small objects that belonged to the deceased, such as cowrie shells.

of hardwood, sword-like or knob-ended, and others with laboriously fashioned stone heads, ranging in shape from balls to disks, from stars to pineapples. Warriors carried for defence roughly hewn, oval wooden shields.

The netted string bag is perhaps the artifact more than any other that characterises Melanesian culture. Women are responsible for netting these, and make other things, from bark-fibre string which they prepare by rolling strips of bast together between palm and thigh (Plate 8.2). Among the Anga, as elsewhere, women carry large bags knotted from the head and for men they produce smaller ones to be slung over the shoulder. Anga men and women wear bark-cloth capes and skirts of similar manufacture, and for decoration they produce among other things woven armbands, cowrie-shell necklaces and baldrics, pig-tusk and bone nasal-septum ornaments, and various bird-plume arrangements for the head, such as fringes of wispy cassowary feathers. The division of labour along gender lines which characterises both artifact manufacture and swidden cultivation is significant for the definition of womanhood and manhood in this and other Melanesian societies.

Artifacts and value

It may seem nonsensical to associate the relatively meagre material assemblage of Melanesians with an absence of material dissatisfaction in the light of the value they place on the things they employ in their sociopolitical exchanges. But they are not acquisitive materialists; they do not strive to own things. Rather, they are transactive materialists, eager to have things passing through their hands in social transactions. The things that they covet to give away, as we have seen, include pigs, various sea shells (such as cowries and pearl shells), colourful bird plumes (notably bird of paradise feathers), game animals (such as cassowaries and various marsupials), fine everyday items (such as shapely clay pots and elegantly netted bags) and various consumable goods (such as decorating oil, salt and prized foodstuffs). The valuables exchanged by the Anga include pigs, hunted game, cowrie-shell finery, ornamental stone axes and consumables, notably bars of salt.

The Anga produce their salt from a cane grass related to Job's tears (*Coix gigantea*) that takes up and stores significant amounts of potassium from the soil. The grass is cultivated on irrigated plots and harvested by women annually during dry periods. Men collect the wood needed to incinerate it and after leaving the cane to dry for a week or so they burn it on specially prepared fires and then leave the ash under thatched shelters for several months. Next they fill open-ended lengths of bamboo or gourds, one end blocked with burrs which act as a filter, with the saline ashes. They pour water into these containers and catch the salty filtrate that flows through in a bamboo trough which in turn discharges into a long bamboo container. They continue topping up the ash with water until the water trickling from the filter no longer tastes salty. Next the saline solution is evaporated. This is done by a specialist who knows the appropriate magic and possesses the equipment needed. Rectangular moulds in the top surface of a stove made of stones, earth and cement-like ash deposits are lined with large impervious leaves (e.g., banana fronds) and filled with salt solution. A carefully tended fire inside the stove (the solution should not boil) evaporates the water from the salt, yielding blocks of salt 60 to 70 centimetres long by 10 centimetres or so wide in three to six days. Finally, the Anga stitch the bars of salt removed from the moulds into bark wrappers.

The salt producers and their neighbours esteem the salt highly. It clearly has use-value as a commodity, a consumable good, but all those living in salt-producing regions have the opportunity to produce all the salt they need. Consequently, we may conclude that it is not its use-value among themselves that determines its high exchange-value. This

Plate 8.3   A man with a bark-cloth cape draped across his shoulders and a range of finery from cowrie-shell chest band to pig-tusk nose ornament; propped against the house behind him are a war shield and a bow and arrows.

value seems in part acquired in commodity transactions with neigh-bouring tribes. Salt producers exploit their saline resources to produce a commodity which they can transact with others for goods that they wish to acquire from them such as stone for axes and bark-cloth for capes (Plate 8.3). The demand for salt consequently exceeds the supply – a situation which does not obtain among the salt producers alone. The Anga who make salt (e.g. the Baruya people) produce amounts beyond their dietary needs to barter for other things that they desire from elsewhere. The assumption is that people strike a rough parity between things in terms of their comparative use-value to them, with the relative supplies of and demands for these items determining exchange rates. There are three issues to consider here: labour time, skill and resource supply.

The time that people invest in making something is likely to influence the value that they put on it. In this regard, we can compare the time it takes to produce salt against that required to make articles for which it is bartered and contrast their rates of exchange. One of these goods is bark-cloth capes. The Anga produce bark cloth from the inner bast layer of the bark of *Ficus* trees. They strip bark sheets of the required size off trees (taking care not to tear them around knots), pare off the outer bark, and hang the bast up to dry overnight. Before beating the fibrous sheets, they moisten them with water, and they continue to do this periodically during beating (sometimes squashing pieces of banana stem on them). They use beaters made from stream-bed stones of appropriate size and oval-elongated shape (schist being a popular rock) in the same way as adze blades, knapping them to shape initially and then grinding them smooth. On the hammer face they scratch a hatched design with chert blades, sometimes tying on a bamboo template with grooves cut in it to act as a guide. It is tedious work, but a beater lasts for years. Bast sheets are beaten on a log anvil, and as the sheet increases in size it is periodically folded in half, first in two and then in four, and so on, to keep it thick enough to beat without making holes in it (Plate 8.4). The finished bark-cloth is coarse compared with the fine work produced on some Pacific islands. Women make more bark-cloth than men. The Anga use most of what they produce for capes, trimming sheets to an appropriate size and then turning them over and stitching a hem along one shorter edge through which they thread string and pull it tight to create a loop by which to hang the cape from the head. The tuft of hair which the Anga characteristically cultivate on the crown of the head serves as a knob for holding a cape in place. Stiff at first, the capes become soft and comfortable with use.

A comparison of bark-cloth cape manufacture against salt-bar

Plate 8.4   A woman seated under the eaves of a house beating a folded sheet of bark-cloth using a stone hammer against a tree trunk; both children are wearing bark-cloth capes.

production indicates an unequal rate of exchange according to time put in: one salt bar, which takes one-and-a-half to two days to produce, is exchanged for six bark-cloth capes, which take four days to produce. The bark-cloth cape makers are clearly investing at least twice as much labour time in manufacturing their product as the salt makers are in the production of theirs. But labour is not a scarce resource for the Anga, as one man commented, 'If we receive enough, then work belongs to the past, it is forgotten.' The important point is that they obtain enough goods to satisfy them in return, for what they consider to be a reasonable amount of work, not that parity is struck over labour time. It has been pointed out that if we view the production time comparison in terms of the sexual division of labour, then the time that men work is nearer equal. Men do 61 per cent of the work of salt making, putting in 1.2 days, but only 40 per cent of the work of producing capes, amounting to 1.6 days. The suggestion is that because men dominate the distribution of these goods, they think only in terms of the labour they invest in them, discounting that of women (see chapter 9). Nevertheless, labour rates remain unequal regarding salt and cape manufacture even after allowing for this supposed gender discrimination. Furthermore, when we consider time rates in relation to the exchange of salt for other things, such as stone axes and ritual *niaka* nuts, they are considerably more skewed (the former being cheap in terms of the labour put into producing them and the latter very expensive), and they are not amenable to more favourable recalculation for men along gender lines.

If the time people spend working does not systematically determine the value they put on things, this leaves us with the second issue – that if something demands skill to produce and only a few people have the skill, this can influence its value. The scarcity of competent producers may restrict supply relative to demand for the thing and consequently increase what people are willing to give in exchange for this limited good. Although specialists evaporate salt into bars, they do not apparently use this as a craft monopoly among themselves; all those living in salt-producing areas receive all the salt they require for personal use and trade. But there may willy-nilly be some restriction here, because the specialists can physically produce only so much salt. Therefore their neighbours have to take what they can produce with their limited technology and few skilled salt makers (minus the salt they keep back for their own needs), and exchange-rates of salt to other things accommodate to this supply.

The point is that Anga salt producers are unlikely to be manufacturing all the salt they could; the specialists doubtless could work harder if supplied with more of the salty filtrate. Melanesian people rarely strive to utilise their resources as fully as they might; they do not calculate economically at the margins but are invariably content with a certain modest level of production which adequately supplies their needs. Which brings us to the third issue that could conceivably influence the determination of value – the supply of raw materials needed to produce the things bartered. The Anga salt producers can only grow so much salt-yielding cane, having limited areas suitable for its cultivation. If they were processing all the cane they could grow, then natural scarcity would be determining exchange rates. However salt-yielding cane is not so scarce as to limit producers; they can manufacture all the salt they wish without cutting all the cane that grows in their region.

We have here a far more complex balancing of forces, uniquely conditioned by Melanesian social and political expectations. Anga salt producers have no monopoly of salt production; their neighbours manufacture it for themselves too, but they apparently do not rely on it to the same extent to obtain other goods. If they started to calculate economically to make a profit, restricting supply to force up exchange rates, their neighbours would consider this unfair and withdraw. They could increase their own salt production, having access to the same technology and cane grass growing on their territories. But as it is they are content to have others supply some of their needs in return for things that do not 'cost' them too much to produce for this purpose.

Also, very important, this arrangement facilitates exchange and consequently regular social interaction. Exchange, as we have seen, is central to the constitution of Melanesian society. Customary social exchange obligations ensure that some of the salt produced reaches relatives living elsewhere; it is not all distributed by trade. The Anga have archaic soot-encrusted salt bars which no one ever intends to consume. They have become, through exchange, 'useless' valuables like the shell wealth exchanged elsewhere in Melanesia (e.g. Trobriand armbands and necklaces [chapter 5]). They are symbols of sociability and tokens of sociopolitical competition, not consumable commodities at all. An important factor contributing to the value of salt, like the other things listed previously as wealth, is their use as valuables in socially validated exchange transactions. Regarding valuables such as sea shells, which have no consumable or utilitarian worth, it is easier to accept their socially founded evaluation, for without it they would be valueless. (We can largely discount both the very rare use of these objects for personal decoration and their use as tokens with which people can occasionally purchase consumables.) Regarding salt, we have economic factors conditioned by sociopolitical exchange expectations. The assumptions of supply, demand, scarcity, and so on, apply here more as limiting factors than as controlling ones. Furthermore, the neighbours of the Anga, and people beyond are obtaining an item of wealth without producing it, and this is an important arrangement for Melanesians. Exchanging things with one another which they have not produced obliges them to keep on exchanging indefinitely. The only way to obtain things to give away is to receive them from someone else to whom in turn one becomes indebted.

Production power

Every Anga family has *equal* access to the natural resources, capital and labour it requires to sustain its material existence, and none of these appears scarce given current wants. They do not even conceive of time, while inevitably limited, as a scarce resource. In short, there appears to be no scope for individuals or groups to gain power over others through controlling access to resources essential to their subsistence. But the valuables that the Anga, like other Melanesians, hand round in social exchange contexts are scarce. To qualify as wealth they must be in relatively short supply; if everyone had unlimited access to them, they would presumably no longer value them in the same way. Although, sociologically speaking, it is irrelevant what they give to each other, because it is the act of giving that is socially significant, in real life they will not accept just anything. The exchange of objects makes sense to people only if they value the things, and their evaluation is a tantalising amalgamation of material and social issues.

Several of the objects exchanged by the Anga and by Melanesians generally originate elsewhere and reach them ready-made. The inability of people to produce these, lacking the necessary raw materials in their region, and, indeed, their frequent ignorance of how they are made and where they come from reflect the situation with wealth production in general: those who exchange valuables should not produce them. Once in circulation these objects may change hands many times in socio-political exchanges (almost indefinitely in the case of durables such as sea shells) with no productive input required; they exist and are exchanged. But valuables do not come into existence spontaneously, although this is almost the illusion created. Although Melanesians may not directly manufacture these items, they must do so indirectly – that is, make things to exchange and trade for them as the Anga make salt.

We should expect men to be busily engaged in producing such locally manufactured wealth, both to give in trade for imported valuables and to exchange directly. But this is strangely not so: the Anga, for example, do not spend large amounts of time manufacturing salt or regularly travel long distances to other regions to secure imported wealth. Their production of valuables is only desultory. No one can manufacture archaic pieces loaded with the symbolism and emotive value that come from having been presented in countless transactions, and this probably acts to dampen production. The situation is reminiscent of shell armband manufacture in the Trobriand Islands (see chapter 5). Nonetheless, if they have the resources and skill, we should expect to find people more busy making the things they value, whereas what people produce barely keeps pace with the destruction of wealth in use.

People transfer locally made valuables to the social exchange sphere by paying wealth to producers. It becomes similar to imported wealth from elsewhere. The crucial point is that no one should directly produce wealth to use in sociopolitical exchange. People must hand over wealth to others to redeem what they are responsible for producing from the productive realm; the cost of bringing something into the social exchange realm is the wealth forgone, which they could otherwise have used in another social exchange context. Consequently, men do not produce wealth; they exchange it into existence. The danger is that, valuing these objects highly, Melanesians may be tempted to acquire them by producing them in quantity, thus placing their social order in jeopardy (see chapter 6). Where the objects handed around come from is of little significance, so long as they are continually handed around. It is not the production of valuables which should engage transactors but the time-consuming social activities of arranging, negotiating, viewing, giving and receiving them in exchange. The conventions regarding production and exchange, isolating one from the other, safeguard these stateless political arrangements. Men are socially conditioned to regard exchanging valuables as giving them worth – as being the proper thing to do.

But there is more at stake here than the stimulation of social transactions alone. If men should turn to producing wealth to achieve prestige, this would threaten the egalitarian political order. Some men would inevitably work hard, cheat others and by a series of unpredictable steps secure control over some aspect of the production process. The ethos of production to earn status and achieve influence over others would be established. The disjunction between subsistence and social exchange systems would eventually be eliminated. Those who excelled would as a result extend some control over the subsistence requirements of others (making essential raw materials scarce by restricting access or supplying finished goods), which would amount to a power base in the marxist sense from which to extend some rule over others' lives and exploit them.

The thesis of Marx, put simply, is that when certain social groups or classes control access to natural resources and capital, they will use this power to exploit other groups, forcing them to sell their labour on unfair terms to secure their livelihoods. They impose the tyranny of production on others. This is a theory that many anthropologists have attempted to apply to other societies. Marxian political economy (predicated on a society's division into social classes) has two elements, inextricably linked: productive resources or the means of production (land, capital

MODE OF PRODUCTION

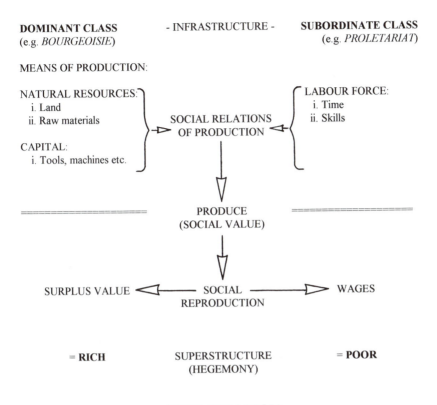

DOMINANT CLASS   - INFRASTRUCTURE -   **SUBORDINATE CLASS**
(e.g. *BOURGEOISIE*)   (e.g. *PROLETARIAT*)

MEANS OF PRODUCTION:

NATURAL RESOURCES: LABOUR FORCE:
  i. Land   i. Time
  ii. Raw materials   SOCIAL RELATIONS   ii. Skills
                             OF PRODUCTION

CAPITAL:
  i. Tools, machines etc.

                             PRODUCE
                             (SOCIAL VALUE)

SURPLUS VALUE ◁—— SOCIAL ——▷ WAGES
                    REPRODUCTION

  = **RICH**   SUPERSTRUCTURE   = **POOR**
                         (HEGEMONY)

EXPLOITATION

Figure 8.2   The marxist model of political economy.

and raw materials) and the disposal of the output. The social relations of production link these two and, together with the forces of production (technological processes), constitute the infrastructure. This and the superstructure (social institutions and cultural values that regulate the system) make up the mode of production (Figure 8.2).

The significant point is the existence of inequalities between groups in their control of productive resources and hence the distribution of wealth and power between them, with some owning a disproportionate share of the means of production and others having only their labour to apply to production. These dominant relations of production are reflected in a society's class structure. The upshot is that one segment of society exploits another, appropriating an unfair proportion of what it produces by virtue of its control of capital, land and so on, and this is legitimated by hegemonic ideologies that justify the privileged social positions of the wealthy, often fostering false consciousness among the dominated.

The marxist perspective is holistic, considering all aspects of a society as inseparable; it is dialectical, focusing on contradictions; and it is dynamic, locating the potential for conflict in these tensions, notably in relations between social classes which influence the direction of social change. In any society in any period there are dominant ways in which groups relate unequally to one another to effect production, and tensions between them influence the course of history. Marxists have distinguished several different modes of production: the capitalist, wherein the working class sells its labour to the productive-resource-owning capitalist class on unfair terms; the feudal, wherein serfs labour directly for local overlords; the Asiatic, wherein control of production is centralised under an all-powerful ruling elite; and the kinship, wherein the equivalent of classes is identified in unequal relationships based on age and gender differences (though here marxism appears to be a theory looking for a home).

By definition a stateless egalitarian polity should not involve exploitation in the marxist sense. This has reduced marxist commentators on tribal society either to a misguided search for petty exploitation in the domestic sphere or to a virtual materialist determinism – the idea that economic, social and other institutions, even history, are predicated on different modes of production. Both are a far cry from Marx's thesis. The deterministic isolation of his dated historical materialist assumptions not only emasculates his ideas but is also dubious for its evolutionary implications (running from technologically primitive to advanced postindustrial societies). Without exploitation his theory evaporates, and we are left with the general organisation and supposed evolution of productive arrangements. Nonetheless, the proposition that the absence of social classes structuring unequal access to means of production will reduce the social tensions that promote change is intriguingly correlated with the comparatively static appearance of tribal societies over long periods of time.

In Melanesia we find the subsistence economy (essential to animal survival) walled off from the exchange system (essential to social survival) in such a way that a man who excels at exchange has no control over other people's livelihoods. Many valuables are of no practical use, and those which are consumable are luxuries. And transactors cannot plunder these things at will from the productive sphere but must possess other valuables to substitute for them, validating their right to recently produced wealth as opposed to that originating in exchange. Whereas capitalist economies oblige people to labour productively to earn scarce material rewards, which bring prestige and reflect their power if they extend to some control over the livelihood of others, the acephalous structure of Melanesian society precludes this. In some senses Melanesian society approximates to Marx's crude fantasy of a primitive communistic order without exploitation. It places Marx's ideas in a significantly different context: the arena in which men compete for political status and influence is divorced from production, and because subsistence is disassociated from the achievement of social position or power, exploitation is averted. Making things in Melanesia is more than the mere manufacture of goods; here technology takes us to the very heart of the political order.

FURTHER READING

The ethnographic accounts drawn upon for this chapter include:
B. Blackwood, 1950 *The technology of a modern stone age people in New Guinea*. Pitt Rivers Museum Occasional Paper on Technology 3.
B. Blackwood, 1982 *The Kukukuku of the Upper Watut*. (ed. C. R. Hallpike) Pitt Rivers Museum Monograph 2.
H. Fischer, 1968 *Negwa: Eine Papua Gruppe in Wandel*. Munchen: Klaus Renner Verlag.
M. Godelier, 1969 'La "monnaie de sel" des Baruya de Nouvelle Guinée'. *L'Homme*. 9: 5–37. (In English: 'Salt money and the circulation of commodities among the Baruya of New Guinea,' in M. Godelier, 1977 *Perspectives in marxist anthropology*. Cambridge: Cambridge University Press: 127–51.)
M. Godelier and J. Garanger, 1973 'Outils de pierre, outils d'acier chez les Baruya de Nouvelle Guinée'. *L'Homme*. 13: 187–220. (In English: 'Stone tools and steel tools among the Baruya of New Guinea' *Social Science Information*. 18: 663–78.)
P. Lemonnier, 1984 'La production de "sel" végétal chez les Anga (Papouasie Nouvelle-Guinée)'. *Journal d'Agriculture traditionelle et de Botanique appliquée*. 31: 71–126.

See also:
S. M. Mead, 1973 *Material culture and art in the Star Harbour region, Eastern Solomon Islands*. Royal Ontario Museum Monograph 1.
L. Pospisil, 1963 *Kapauku Papuan economy*. Yale University Publications in Anthropology 67.
P. Sillitoe, 1988 *Made in Niugini*. London: British Museum Publications.

On material culture and technology studies see:
B. Cotterell and J. Kamminga, 1990 *Mechanics of pre-industrial technology*. Harmondsworth: Penguin.

P. Lemmonier, 1992 *Elements for an anthropology of technology.* University of Michigan Anthropology Museum Paper 88.

B. Reynolds and M. A. Stott (eds.), 1987 *Material anthropology: Contemporary approaches to material culture.*

FILMS

The arts and crafts of Papua New Guinea: Kundu drum and bark belt. Institute of Papua New Guinea Studies Pacific Video-Cassette Series 21.

Towards Baruya manhood. Australian Commonwealth Film Unit.

9 Gender relations in the Western Highlands

Women and men are different; this is an indisputable biological fact. But are natural differences inevitably elaborated culturally into discriminations which esteem and rank one sex (usually men) above the other? It is widely thought that women throughout Melanesia are socially inferior to men and ethnographic reports (such as those on Manus [chapter 4]) read in the context of contemporary Western values and expectations confirm this impression. But this contradicts the egalitarianism described earlier as a key value throughout Melanesia, and the contradiction calls for closer examination of the facts.

Gender issues

In the past two decades or so some anthropologists have given more attention than previously to the position of women in other societies. They have looked at the definition of the person according to gender-specific categories, the cultural construction of women's roles, and the nature of relations between the sexes. Many of these feminist studies draw heavily on marxism, arguing that men take advantage of women, as capitalists exploit the working classes. The increased interest in women's issues has paralleled recent women's emancipation campaigns in the West, and there is some danger that ethnocentric carryover from these experiences will encourage the inference that gender differences everywhere must evidence inequalities. Indeed, where women apparently do not perceive inequalities this is sometimes explained as evidence of 'false consciousness', their male-dominated society having duped them with the values that it has inculcated during socialisation. These interpretations illustrate how the values and beliefs of anthropologists and the readers of their ethnographies may inform their understanding of others' social lives.

Critics of Melanesian ethnography have argued with some justification that until recently fieldworkers have overlooked or underplayed the place of women in the societies that they have studied. They have

131

pointed out that male anthropologists cannot gain meaningful access to the social world of women in these cultures, which maintain a marked distinction between the domains of the sexes. This is just comment, although the corollary that female outsiders cannot expect to gain significant access to the men's world has not yet been addressed. Again ethnographers' backgrounds, here gender, inform their work. This overlooking of women cannot be attributed solely to men's having dominated anthropology in Melanesia, because a number of prominent researchers in the region have been women. The problem is one of the representation of womanhood. Its recent recognition reflects our tendency not to address issues until they become prominent intellectual concerns in our society, at which point we impose them on others.

Feminism is an issue whose time has come, and feminist anthropology's agenda is to overcome the discipline's male bias and the analytical invisibility of women by reformulating social theory. According to contemporary feminist critiques, male dominance of the structures of society inhibits expression of alternative female views. These critiques seek to discredit the pernicious assumptions that women are always and everywhere subordinate to men. Hence the subject of feminist anthropology is not women but gender relations and gender as a social construct, albeit largely from the women's perspective. Anthropologists agree, regardless of gender, however, that there exists in traditional Melanesian society a major cultural divide between women's and men's domains, although they may dispute the nature of the division and the extent to which it implies subordination and domination. In our inquiry into the position of women in Melanesian society we shall return to the highlands of Papua New Guinea, this time to the Melpa. They occupy the broad Wahgi Valley in the Mount Hagen region (Map 9.1), a large grassy plain flanked by forested mountain slopes where archaeologists have uncovered evidence of very early agriculture (see chapter 1). They are archetypical central highlanders living in scattered homesteads, made up of squat houses with separate dwellings for women and men. Their staple food is, again, sweet potato. They value pigs and pearl shells highly and exchange them on many social occasions, one of which is the *moka*, in which men compete for status. Men dominate this public exchange-centred domain in Melpa society, but women are not totally eclipsed and reduced to subordinate status. They have their place too in the cultural order.

Women in Melpa society

The lives of Melpa women centre on the household domain (Plates 9.1 and 9.2). Women assume the responsibilities of adulthood at marriage.

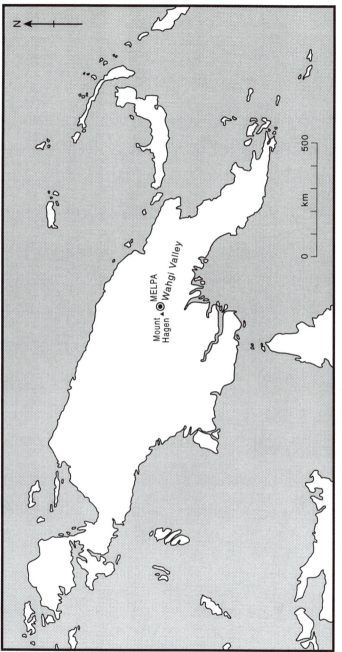

Map 9.1   The Melpa of the Western Highlands.

Plate 9.1   A woman of the Western Highlands, characteristically carrying a young child – sweet potato in each hand to keep him quiet.

Plate 9.2   A Melpa woman stripping bark fibre off a sapling – the raw
material for making the string used to produce netted artifacts like her bag
– which is quintessentially women's work, an aspect of the marked sexual
division of labour that characterises this society.

Until then girls usually reside with their mothers or other close female
kin and assist them, albeit sometimes desultorily. It is after marriage that
the full weight of a homestead's horticultural, pig-keeping and everyday
household duties fall on her shoulders. One of the intimations of a girl's
relatively free-and-easy life is the scope allowed her in choosing her
marriage partner, which will establish a relationship that will change her
life markedly and circumscribe her freedom of action (Plate 9.3). While
the affinal kin connections established at marriage are important in
structuring Melpa social life and subsequent wealth exchange activity,
parents rationalise that there is little point in trying to force daughters to
marry certain boys because they particularly wish to establish an alliance
with their kin, for an unhappily married girl is likely to cause trouble for
all. The option of taking refuge from her husband and affines with her
natal kin affords a Melpa woman one of her most significant safeguards
in ensuring her relative autonomy within an apparently male-dominated
society.

The freedom extended to spouses-to-be to choose their partners is
not absolute. Their relatives may express preferences and exert some
pressure, and in addition there are rules prohibiting certain unions as

Plate 9.3   A nubile girl decorated to take part in a dance, her colourful appearance having an element of courting behaviour. Once married, women are prohibited from wearing finery and participating in such events.

incestuous, for example, marriage with close clan kin or relatives of persons already married to close kin with whom exchange relations currently exist (such a marriage duplicating an established alliance would waste an opportunity to establish a new all-important exchange connection). Nonetheless, girls are free to court and even flirt within culturally defined limits, and some 'strong headed' ones force on their kin unions upon which they frown. On occasion chaperoned girls may attend courting sessions at which there is singing with couples kneeling facing one another, rubbing their foreheads together, in amorous play called 'turning heads' (Pidgin *turnim het*). Couples attracted to one another may also exchange betrothal gifts of beads, shells, marsupials and so on. These are a prelude to the exchanges of bridewealth which will establish the marriage (see chapter 6).

Once married, a woman usually moves out of her parents' household and into that of her husband's relatives, although this is not mandatory. Her daily routine revolves around her new homestead and the gardens in which her husband and perhaps some of his relatives have allocated her areas to cultivate (Plate 9.4). Although it is men who claim rights to garden land through their kin connections to its custodian descent groups and who are responsible for the initial heavy work of site clearance, it is women who are responsible for the bulk of the day-to-day cultivation, tilling the soil and planting and tending the majority of crops, notably the staple sweet potato (see chapter 3). The principal tools associated with either sex – the axe of men and the digging stick of women – characterise this division of labour. The digging stick is a simple yet versatile implement breaking up the soil, heaping it into mounds and dibbling crops. Women generally visit their gardens every day, sometimes accompanied by their younger children, engaging in horticultural work (tilling, weeding, planting etc.) and harvesting suffi- cient food for their households' daily needs; little food is stored – fresh produce is gathered daily from their living-pantry-like gardens. When they return home, usually in the afternoon, women are responsible for preparing most of their families' meals, including their husbands' (one way in which disgruntled wives can express their displeasure and make life uncomfortable for their husbands is by refusing to cook for them).

A large proportion of the tubers that women bring home of an afternoon are fed to the pigs in their charge. It is as pig keepers that they achieve positions of esteem and can acquire (albeit covert) influence. An able woman who can competently manage the logistics of herding large numbers of pigs earns an appellative which is the female equivalent of 'big man'. Pigs are an important item of wealth in sociopolitical exchanges such as the *moka*, the arena in which men vie publicly for

Plate 9.4 A couple prepare an earth oven; while stones heat on a fire he lines the pit with banana leaves and she scrapes and prepares the vegetables.

status and influence. A woman's standing is a direct reflection of her husband's; he translates her labours in rearing pigs into social status through sociopolitical exchanges. A man relies on a woman to manage the pigs with which he will finance the distributions on which his reputation depends. As the Melpa might say, a man 'needs a woman at his back'.

In order to value women as persons in their own right we need to interpret their domestic associations sympathetically and not impose Western preoccupations on them. The Melpa make a symbolic and a social connection between domesticity and femaleness. It is in this domain that they define womanhood, and here women manage activities that determine their social standing and value. It is as important as the public sphere – indeed, from a woman's perspective, more important. The nature of the partnership between women and men is caught in the characterisation of women as Melpa society's *producers* and men as its *transactors*. Without an able woman or women backing him up at home, the ablest man cannot hope to achieve much on the ceremonial dance ground. Women occupy a pivotal place, as a consequence, and it gives them some say. They also fill a crucial structural position in their acephalous polity. Controlling significant aspects of production, they serve as guardians of political power. A disgruntled wife with a sizeable herd under her control has only to threaten to leave her husband to call attention to his dependency on her; only a severe breakdown in their relationship would be likely to induce a woman to embarrass and incommode her husband by abandoning her marital homestead and herd.

When exchanges such as the *moka* occur, women are particularly concerned to see fair treatment of their own relatives, often lobbying their husbands to present certain pigs that are in their care to their kin. Their behaviour reflects another key structural position that women occupy in Melpa society. A marriage among the Melpa connects two sets of previously unrelated kin by establishing an affinal link between them which, with the subsequent birth of children, will become a consanguineal one (the woman's kinsfolk then standing as matrilateral kin to the man's relatives). These kin links are significant in structuring subsequent exchanges of wealth; they are connections along which valuables move to-and-fro. The Melpa capture this when they speak of marriages creating 'roads' along which wealth travels. They perceive married women as embodying these connections in that they are related to and move between the two groups of kin. They speak of women as standing 'in between' two groups of in-laws, and from the point of view of men, the married women between them link them together for transactions. The notion of in-betweenness is not merely a metaphor for social relations between groups, but in fact has substance, for women act as go-betweens, helping to arrange and negotiate transactions in which they take pride and sometimes bearing valuables from one side to the other. They derive prestige from this role. Although they are not ultimately responsible for determining whom to bestow any gifts upon, as the vehicles for the movement of things between groups they none-theless play some behind-the-scenes part in determining their destina-tion. They have influence with which men must reckon.

Descent group controversy

The in-between position of women in Melpa society relates not only to narrow social issues pertaining to wealth transactions between small groups of kin but also to wider political processes in the society at large. Marriages link the large, patrilineally defined corporate descent groups which structure political relations in the Mount Hagen area. A marriage forges a potential alliance of broader political significance from which support may be forthcoming not only for the large sociopolitical exchanges in which descent corporations vie for status with one another but also in times of war. The nature of descent groups in highland New Guinea societies has been the subject of debate for some decades, and the controversy is a classic illustration of how the uncritical transfer of a social theory from one ethnographic context to another can confuse our interpretations.

The nub of the controversy is the extent to which New Guinea societies display unilineal segmentary descent. Derived from the theory called structural-functionalism, which presupposes that the social insti-tutions of a society are arranged in an orderly structure and function to maintain social cohesion and order within it, the idea of segmentary descent was used to good effect from the 1940s onwards in under-standing African stateless polities. In these African societies political order appears to be maintained through the balanced opposition of unilineally conceptualised descent groups (i.e., comprising people related by descent through one line, either the male [patrilineal] or the female [matrilineal]). The argument, greatly simplified, is that highland New Guinea societies are also ordered in this way – that descent-conceived groups (tribes, clans, etc.), are locked in relationships of balanced political opposition, which they express peacefully in exchange competition and violently in periodic bouts of warfare (see Figure 9.1).

The celebrated fluidity of Melanesian social groups, however, rules out any straightforward imposition of the African model. Whereas in

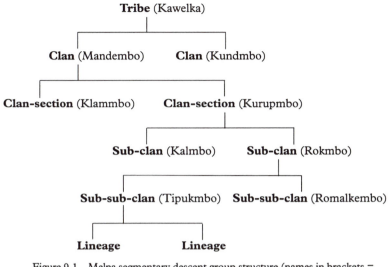

Figure 9.1 Melpa segmentary descent group structure (names in brackets = examples of actual segments). (After M. Strathern, 1972; A. J. Strathern, 1972).

African descent systems persons are ascribed to one group only for life, here they can detach themselves from one descent group and affiliate themselves to another with ease. Again, when someone moves his place of residence in Africa, he does not change his descent group affiliation (and therefore in any location several agnatic lines are likely to be represented), and in some situations (ritual, revenge etc.) the recruitment of groups is ideologically determined according to descent affiliation alone. In New Guinea, in contrast, people identify descent groups geographically with particular locales, and when someone moves his place of residence he transfers his group association while living there to that connected to the new locale. Consequently, people affiliate with these localised descent groups by a range of kin connections, not ones defined by descent exclusively – a radical idiomatic departure from the African situation.

Land tenure rules ensure that local groups in New Guinea remain kin constituted, complete strangers are unable to claim rights to land. The inclination of men to reside in the same place as their fathers, obliging their wives to comply with their virilocal residence preference, results in local groups' appearing like agnatically constituted descent lines. But people apparently do not unambiguously conceive of them as unilineal descent entities and show little interest in tracing descent connections; the groups have very shallow genealogies. The tendency for local groups to develop a unilineal character because of the pragmatic decisions of individual men to reside at their fathers' places rather than to any intention to ensure continuity of descent line identity has been termed 'patrifiliation'. A deal of impressive intellectual wrestling has occurred to accommodate this behaviour to descent theory. A significant distinction has been made between descent as an *ideology* by which people conceive of the structure, continuity and solidarity of local groups and descent as a *recruitment principle* by which they regulate group composition, applying descent connections rulewise to define membership. We may interpret descent notions in Melanesia idiomatically, but ties of filiation better account for group recruitment.

The problems we have defining the form and make-up of local groups reflect again the difficulties we encounter in delineating categories in the Melanesian region (see chapter 1). Where we have an urge to define and pigeon-hole, Melanesians tend to obfuscate and blend. No one is denying that kin-constituted social groups exist in Melanesia or that people may make statements suggestive of descent conceptions; what we are disputing is the segmentary nature of these groups and the part they play in people's lives. Any kin-related group may be conceived in descent terms given the facts of biology, but this may receive little cultural elaboration.

My experience in the New Guinea highlands has led me to question the interpretation of territorially focused kin-composed corporations as segmentary descent groups which structure political interaction. It is not my understanding that those residing in the same territory act in concert out of concern for the group's interests (their clan's prestige, land-holdings, regional standing, etc.) or that certain successful persons, the big men, lead the group (as opposed to influencing it) and represent its corporate interests to others (see chapter 7). The extent to which this understanding derives from the idiosyncrasies of the Wola highlanders I know I leave to posterity to assess.

According to my view, local territorial groups are neighbourhood-like entities, loosely knit communities of some hundreds of persons. They are named, stay in existence for generations, and consist of several interrelated families the blood ties between which render them ideally exogamous. It is their occupation of geographical territories that gives them permanence; the rules that control their membership are those that govern land tenure, which have wide bilateral scope (although it may appear restricted because men commonly claim land where their fathers lived). On every neighbourhood there centres a social universe which extends geographically to all those locales in which its resident members maintain social relations. Each neighbourhood has a somewhat different social universe, and these interlock with one another across large regions. Neither of these two social categories is an organised group. Both focus on geographical areas, one a small territory on which residents and potentially their kin elsewhere claim rights of land use and the other a larger area marking spatially the extent of their social interaction. They have fuzzy boundaries and shift over time as people come and go.

Pursuing any collective action (exchanging wealth, fighting battles, etc.) assumes organisation into groups. It is significant that individuals are not expected or obliged to support particular permanent groups, however constituted. Although action-sets may sometimes correspond closely with neighbourhood groups, this does not imply that these are political corporations. It is the result of residential propinquity; individuals are more likely to join in activities with those they live among and interact with every day than with those residing elsewhere. Men are free to decide for themselves on the basis of their own interests whether to participate with relatives and friends in any proposed collective activity, and if they deem it not to be to their advantage to join in they are at liberty to abstain. The groups that form are thus transient collections of people who think that it is in their individual interests temporarily to coordinate their actions to achieve some goal. A group with exactly the same membership is not likely to come together again.

Considerations that prompt men to participate in an action-set include a concern for their reputations, a wish to share in the glory of some large occasion, or the desire to avail themselves of the benefits of a joint effort. When a few men instigate an activity they can expect support from several relatives in their neighbourhood with whom they interact constantly, and these become the focal group for the event. In turn, some of these men's relatives from elsewhere may join in and possibly even recruit others from their own networks. The group makes decisions and coordinates its actions by discussing matters until the majority opinion becomes clear. All have an equal right to voice their opinions in these discussions, in which they try to persuade each other to act in ways which they think best suit them as a group; their success depends largely upon the advantages their plans offer to those they are trying to influence. Some individuals, the big men, as we have seen have more influence than others, but they cannot by virtue of their prestige lead or coerce others (see chapter 7).

Some of the contradictions evident in the Melpa ethnography suggest that some downplaying of descent groups as political corporations may be in order. For example, '*Moka* can be conducted quite privately between individual partners; or a clan, divisions or combinations of clans, may come together in public display, each man giving to his own partner, but jointly celebrating the whole wealth of the group ... Success for men comes from the manipulation of partnership networks, not from attainment of some office within the clan community or from an assumption of rank. While clan and personal prestige are to some extent bound up with one another, it is chiefly from their individual standing that men are accorded renown' (M. Strathern 1972: 10, 309). Whatever conclusion you draw from this diversion into the byways of the applicability or otherwise of unilineal descent theory to highland New Guinea society, it will not invalidate the representation of women as those who stand in between, joining hitherto separate kin networks, and that this interstitial position gives them considerable scope in defining their womanhood and relative independence.

Between women and men

It is clear that women's position, perceived as joining together in their marriages two previously unlinked kin networks, gives them some degree of influence and autonomy. They have it in their power seriously to disrupt relationships if badly treated. The wife of a domineering husband can return to her natal kin for refuge, and if she is in the right they will defend her interests. It costs a man not only socially but materially to wrong his wife, for if she is justified in her flight he is obliged to present her kin with wealth to indicate good faith and repair the damaged relations. However, as with many sociopolitical interactions the difference between justified and unjustified action is not unambiguous. The divided loyalty of a woman, for example, particularly early in her marriage, between her husband's interests and her blood relatives' interests results in a hazy line between justified flight and running off to force a man to give more than he had intended to his wife's relatives. The latter is a high risk strategy, however, and an abused husband may push his wife into a divorce.

The option of divorce is also available to abused women. Often the threat of divorce, coupled with his wife's running away to consanguineal kin, is sufficient to induce a man to improve his behaviour. The temporary disturbance to his domestic organisation, particularly pig herding arrangements, and to affinal exchange agreements intimates the serious disruption that will ensue if a divorce occurs (see chapter 6). Nonetheless, divorce is possible, and indeed, even quite common in Melpa society, particularly in the early days of a marriage (a survey confirmed something like 68 per cent of first marriages extant). The position of Melpa women varies significantly according to their age. A young wife without children experiences more sharply divided loyalty and her husband and his kin perceive her as a possible threat to their security and interests. A matriarch with adult sons, in contrast, will have settled fully into her husband's community, to which her natal kin are now connected by indissoluble matrilateral blood relations, and she is unlikely to be suspected of harbouring any malign intentions towards her offspring and their relatives.

Gender symbols are central to the position of women in Melanesian society, relating to stereotypes that have considerable rhetorical resonance (albeit these metaphoric qualities of femaleness and maleness may not suit actual individuals). The idea that women may have evil intentions, for example, and the capacity to put them into effect and damage men's interests, even threaten their lives, is one that Melpa males take seriously. They believe that women not only have the option of leaving them and thus disrupting their social and exchange arrangements but also have the capacity to pollute and poison them. These fears are an important bulwark to women's autonomy. Although the threat may be more imagined than real, it nonetheless influences men's attitudes towards women. Men believe that menstrual blood and anything associated with birth can pollute and kill them. Women are obliged to protect them from such matter; for example, during menstruation they avoid contact with men and offer them no food.

While women may not use their menstrual polluting powers to menace men openly, for to do so would be tantamount to threatening to kill them, they can intimate by all manner of subtle devices how accidents might occur. In addition to their fears of menstrual pollution, the Melpa believe that women may carry poison between enemies, as emissaries of their relatives, and administer it furtively to their husband's kin. Again, no woman would openly suggest such things; to do so would invite her husband's kin to kill her in revenge for any deaths subsequently attributed to her nefarious dealings. But men's fears of such clandestine attack must prompt them to watch their behaviour; a contented wife is unlikely to agree to administer poison at the behest of her relatives, but a disgruntled one may very well be tempted to do so. Men's fears of menstrual pollution and enemy poison are potent threats colouring their attitudes towards women and restraining any domineering behaviour. Men symbolise women as dangerous and potentially powerful, while they talk of them as harmless and weak. Although some men may act high-handedly in public, women demand consideration and respect.

Women's position

It is evident that we should not take the dominant public position of Melpa men or their dismissive remarks about women's 'soft heads' too literally, for women have considerable influence and latitude of action. The sexes occupy quite different and distinct sociocultural domains, but one does not necessarily subjugate the other. Even the circumstances of polygynous marriage, with which several Melpa women have to contend, are not entirely negative and demeaning. Although jealousy between co-wives sometimes occurs as they compete for their husband's favours, these differences centre more on practical than on sentimental issues. And there are many polygynous marriages where co-wives come to some agreement over their relationship – sharing resources, work-loads, child-rearing responsibilities, and so on – to their joint advantage, even presenting a united front to their husband to pursue their interests at his expense.

It would be erroneous apparently to suppose that Melpa women resent their status. They subscribe to the same values, revolving around their culture's political, exchange and religious institutions, as men, and in their actions, most notably as intermediaries, they support these shared values, thus ensuring their integral place in the sociocultural system. They have different perspectives and interests, of course, but women rarely undertake joint action on the basis of their gender, have no subculture of their own, and do not form exclusive associations. Instead of thinking in terms of antagonism between the sexes it is perhaps fruitful to conceive of their relation as a partnership. Neither women nor men can exist economically, politically, or socially without the other or lead complete adult lives. There is no sex war apparent among Melpa and any intimations of it have more to do with men's fears and suspicions than they do with women's resentment and subjugation (M. Strathern 1972: 314). Nonetheless, male perceptions of its declaration afford women a degree of genuine independence.

The last few chapters have conjured up the image of social forces conspiring to ensure order and harmony, but how harmonious is social life on the Black Islands? Divorce is quite common among the Melpa and fear of violence, both physical and supernatural, frequently encountered. Reference has been made at several junctures to disputes, hostilities and warfare, to head-hunting and sorcery. These decidedly unsociable activities suggest that life in Melanesia is fractious and violent on occasion. It is time to look at how they cope with these frequent outbursts of antisocial and disruptive behaviour.

FURTHER READING

The ethnographic accounts on which this review draws include:
M. Strathern, 1972 *Women in between*. London: Seminar Press.
M. Strathern, 1988 *The gender of the gift*. Berkeley: University of California Press.
A. J. Strathern, 1971 *Rope of moka*. Cambridge: Cambridge University Press.
A. J. Strathern, 1972 *One father, one blood*. Canberra: Australian National University Press.
E. Brandewie, 1990 *Contrast and context in New Guinea culture*. Anthropos Institute Monograph 39.
F. Merlan and A. Rumsey, 1991 *Ku Waru*. Cambridge: Cambridge University Press.

On the study of descent see:
J. A. Barnes, 1962 'African models in the New Guinea Highlands.' *Man*. 62: 5–9.
M. Fortes, 1953 'The structure of unilineal descent groups.' *American Anthropologist*. 55: 17–41.
M. Fortes and E. E. Evans-Pritchard (eds.), 1940 *African political systems*. Oxford: Oxford University Press.
M. Meggitt, 1965 *The lineage system of the Mae-Enga of New Guinea*. Edinburgh: Oliver and Boyd.

Other studies of gender issues in Melanesia include:
P. Brown and G. Buchbinder (eds.), 1976 *Men and women in the New Guinea Highlands*. American Anthropological Association Special Publication 8.
F. Errington and D. Gewertz, 1987 *Cultural alternatives and a feminist anthropology*. Cambridge: Cambridge University Press.
M. Jolly, 1994 *Women of the place*. Amsterdam: Harwood Academic Press.
L. Josephides, 1985 *The production of inequality*. London: Tavistock.
M. Kahn, 1986 *Always hungry, never greedy: Food and the expression of gender in a Melanesian society*. Cambridge: Cambridge University Press.
A. Kyakas and P. Wiessner, 1992 *From inside the women's house: Enga women's lives and traditions*. Buranda (Queensland): Robert Brown and Associates.
D. O'Brien and S. W. Tiffany (eds.), 1984 *Rethinking women's roles: Perspectives from the Pacific*. Berkeley: University of California Press.
M. Strathern (ed.), 1987 *Dealing with inequality*. Cambridge: Cambridge University Press.

On gender and anthropology see:
H. Whitehead (ed.), 1981 *Sexual meanings: The cultural construction of gender and sexuality*. Cambridge: Cambridge University Press.
H. Moore, 1988 *Feminism and anthropology*. Cambridge: Polity Press.

FILMS

The Kawelka: Ongka's big moka. Granada Television Disappearing World Series.

10   Dispute settlement around the Paniai Lakes

Melanesians, being only human, have their differences. Previous chapters have looked at the centripetal forces consolidating Melanesian society, contributing to a bonded social entity, and it is now time to look at those centrifugal ones militating against social order, threatening to tear the social mass apart. We have seen that Melanesians lack legal institutions as we know them. The intriguing issue is how they manage to contain and resolve disputes.

The anthropology of law

There are two sides to power relations and political organisation as seen by anthropologists: how people organise themselves into collectivities, notably to pursue coordinated and cooperative actions, and how they cope with and settle disputes which threaten to disrupt collective organisation, even social life, beyond a small circle of close relatives. The anthropology of law concerns itself with the comparative study of the institutions and processes found around the world for resolving differences between human beings and forcing into line those individuals whose behaviour threatens the orderly continuance of social life.

Throughout Melanesia we find that people have some clear, and some not so clear, conceptions of right and wrong behaviour and expectations of one another founded on the rights and duties which they conceive persons to have towards one another. Anthropologists refer to these variously as customs, norms and mores, even rules and laws (although these latter two terms sit uncomfortably with stateless legal assumptions and practices). When a man and his wife clear and plant a garden, for instance, it is wrong for anyone else to harvest its produce without their permission; to do so is to steal from them. Similarly, in many parts of Melanesia it is wrong for a couple to engage in sexual intercourse before the bridewealth exchanges are completed and they are formally married; to do so is referred to in many languages as 'stealing a woman' and provokes claims for recompense from the woman's relatives. Rape is a heinous offence which provokes strident social condemnation and firm, often violent, retaliation.

In any society there will be a range of such injunctions which people are brought up to respect and observe. The people who feature ethnographically in this chapter, for example, are reported to have 121 such legal 'rules'. But the status of such 'rules' in a stateless context should be approached with some caution and open-mindedness. Few people asked were apparently able to cite many of the 'rules', and probably no single individual knew them all. When this ideal code of expected behaviour, rights and appropriate settlements was compared with actual disputes over infringements and their resolution, only 50 per cent of cases complied with it. The lack of agreement is expectable in an acephalous and nonliterate society which lacks a formally codified set of laws. The informality of judicial concepts in stateless societies imparts a degree of flexibility to the legal system which we find it difficult to conceive; as we shall see, situational factors can determine the outcome of disputes as much as people's ideas about what ought or ought not to be done about any dereliction.

The people who feature in this chapter are the Kapauku, who live around the Paniai (or Wissel) Lakes in the mountains at the western end of the island of New Guinea (Map 10.1). This rugged country of steep-sided valleys and high peaks is similar to that found along New Guinea's central highland backbone. The people are likewise sweet potato staple swidden cultivators who keep sizeable pig herds and engage in sociopolitical exchange. The stocky men, like all those who live in the central cordillera west of the Strickland River are phallocrypt wearers. They occupy villages, otherwise these people are similar in appearance and lifestyle to the other highlanders featured so far in this book.

The Kapauku ethnography was the first major study of the *corpus juris* of a Melanesian people, giving 'legal rules' as enunciated by informants and examining them against actual cases. It requires careful reading, however, because the ethnographer, trained as a lawyer, uses the terms and concepts of Western jurisprudence in this stateless judicial context. He refers, for instance, to codified 'rules' or prohibitions (*daa*) making up the Kapauku body of law and to big men as authoritative persons, almost judges, both of which assertions sit uneasily with the ethnographic evidence and are difficult to reconcile with the stress put on the people's marked individualism and stateless egalitarianism. It is, however, instructive; the ethnographic record is coloured not only by anthropologists' genders and personal histories but also by their disciplinary background and attendant intellectual assumptions.

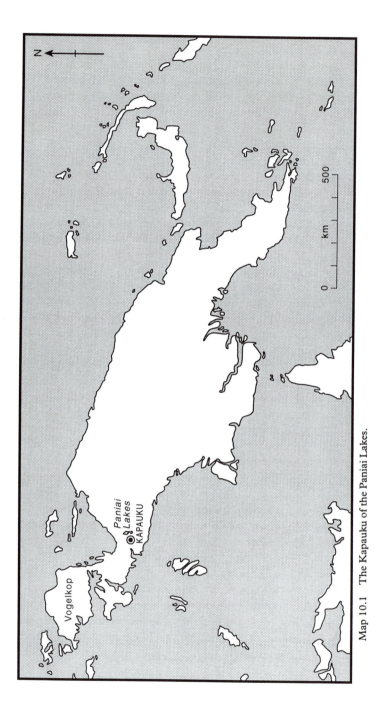

Map 10.1   The Kapauku of the Paniai Lakes.

Handling disputes

The Kapauku handle disputes by arguing, keeping their tempers in check to varying extents, until they settle the matter to both parties' satisfaction, one admits having been wrong and makes amends, or the plaintiff either lets the matter drop or resorts to some action to redress the grievance (Plates 10.1–10.4). This last course of action may cause the dispute to spiral, the other party interpreting the action as unjust and demanding damages, and so on. Two factors which have a significant influence on the course of a dispute are the relationships between the disputants and the seriousness of the offence. These determine the number of people likely to become involved or at least to show an interest in the dispute and the strength of their feelings about the matter. A minor dispute between close relatives will probably pass with few, if any, other persons interfering; a quarrel between two brothers over ownership of a tree planted by their father, for instance, or a domestic row between husband and wife over the harvest of food from their garden are unlikely to attract much interest or give rise to long-lasting argument. A serious offence between persons distantly related or unrelated will, in contrast, involve considerable numbers of people siding with their kinsmen, may drag on for some considerable time, and is likely to give rise to a serious violent encounter; a man accused of raping an unrelated woman living elsewhere, for example, will find himself embroiled in an acrimonious dispute in which the tempers of many indignant people will run high, with demands from the woman's relatives for considerable compensation and probable rebuttals from his kin that the accusation is unwarranted.

Anthropologists customarily illustrate general issues regarding social control with case histories, and a couple of cases will substantiate these points. Both of these case histories and several of those that follow concern a man called Awitigaaj, a big man of Botukebo settlement (see Figure 10.1, page 152). The first illustrates a minor dispute involving few persons and soon settled:

Case 1

Awitigaaj's sixth wife Oumau was jealous of his fifth wife Enaago because she was his favourite. She constantly picked quarrels with her favoured co-wife (a common situation in polygynous marriages) and one day started a fight with her, hitting her with a stick. This provoked Awitigaaj to intervene and threaten Oumau with a beating; bickering he would have to tolerate, as a polygynously married man, but not physical

Plate 10.1   During a dispute, the big man Awitigaaj squats among arguing relatives, his hand raised to his head in a gesture of exasperation.

Plate 10.2   Gesturing in the heat of a dispute, Taajwiijokaipouga, one of Awitigaaj's enraged relatives, makes a point.

Plate 10.3 One of Jokagaibo's wives, Goo Amaadii, accused of adultery, stands with her hands tied behind her back during a dispute over her infidelity.

Plate 10.4   After a dispute, a Pueta man settles a debt that he owes, taking
wealth from a string bag to display on the ground in a public demonstration to
validate settlement.

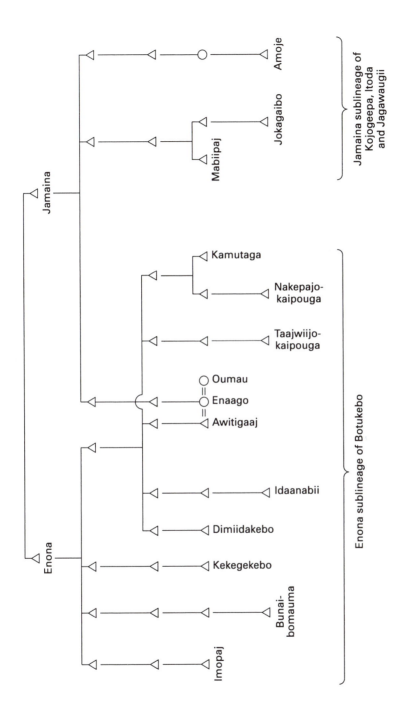

Figure 10.1   Genealogy of Kapauku involved in dispute cases.

fighting among his wives. No one else was involved, and his wives settled back into their uneasy rivalrous relationship.

The second case documents a dispute involving many people over a serious offence against distantly related persons. It also illustrates the point that the history of people's relations is an important consideration in understanding their behaviour in disputes. The dispute concerns how Awitigaaj married Enaago, and it helps us appreciate better Oumau's jealous outbreak by putting it in its wider context.

Case 2

Awitigaaj ought never to have married his fifth wife, Enaago. According to the norms that govern Kapauku marriage, she was too closely related to him; for them to marry was, in a sense, incestuous. But when Enaago was a young woman they eloped together into the forest and hid. Both his and her relatives were furious at their indecorous act and searched for them in the forest for days without success. Tiring of this and realising that they faced a *fait accompli*, Enaago's father and her relatives from neighbouring Kojogeepa demanded that Awitigaaj's kin start making arrangements to pay them bridewealth. They were enraged by this demand. It was a questionable union forced on them by deplorable tactics, and they were being obliged by Awitigaaj's cunning behaviour to sponsor another bridewealth transaction for him when he already had several wives. They refused to cooperate; the bridewealth was Awitigaaj's business, not theirs. By this time entire sublineages (Jamaina and Enona) had mobilised on either side. A flashpoint was reached, and many angry men started fighting with sticks. The result was some bruises and a stand-off. Later, when things had calmed down, Awitigaaj and Enaago returned, and he arranged a bridewealth exchange to legitimate their questionable union.

No justice

Another significant issue regarding dispute reconciliation in Kapauku society and throughout Melanesia generally is that people place no premium on justice. All those who live in a locality will have some vested interest in any dispute and its outcome, being related in one way or another to one or both parties. The way in which the relatives of disputants customarily unite and give them their support, as described, reflects their partisan attitudes. The idea of an impartial judge who can mete out justice fairly according to the law is clearly inappropriate in such a society, as we should have predicted from our discussion of the egalitarian acephalous political ordering of Melanesian society. The following case, again involving the big man Awitigaaj, illustrates clearly how the interests of others bias their attitudes.

Case 3

Awitigaaj received a large pig from a relative of his wife Enaago living at Kojogeepa, for which he contracted to exchange sixty cowrie shells. Later, after handing over 180 beads (worth some six cowries only), he maintained that things were square between them. The other man, not surprisingly, was annoyed by this, and a dispute erupted. While these wranglings were going on, Awitigaaj craftily promised to give a quarter of the pig to a neighbouring big man and relatives in Botukebo if they supported his assertions that he had adequately met his obligations over the pig. His distant affinal relative was apparently overcome by the aggressively voiced opinions of these two influential men and their kin at Botukebo and returned home to Kojogeepa, letting the matter drop.

Any notion of administering justice is clearly inapposite in this society. We have established that it is the big men of Melanesia who can be spoken of as exerting some measure of influence, if not control, over the actions of their fellows (see chapter 7). Although these individuals, given their renown and influence, can play an instrumental part in settling disputes, this is not as impartial arbitrator but as one who can prevail on others to come to some settlement, even though perhaps somewhat disadvantageous to them. Their influence in this regard often centres on their wealth-manipulating skills, which enable them to contribute significantly to any compensation required to effect a settlement. Everyone expects them to use their influence to their own and their relatives' ends.

The contribution of relatives, whatever their social status, to the resolution of disputes is probably more significant than the interventions of big men in promoting settlements. The efficacy of the counsel of kin increases when they are related to both parties because they can then give advice and exert pressure on both sides to bring about a settlement and may act if necessary as trusted intermediaries. A serious dispute between distantly related or unrelated individuals concerns many people, and they may need to exploit points of kin connection between them to communicate and effect a peaceful settlement. A dispute will disrupt the social flow of all their lives to some extent, with those related to both sides experiencing this disruption most acutely. It is probable that all of these people will wish to see life return to normal as soon as possible and will attempt to manoeuvre the disputant to whom they are related to settle the issue or if caught in the middle, will negotiate between the two sides. This possibly explains why Awitigaaj's pig-giving affine somewhat timidly gave up his demands for payment (uncharacteristically for the volatile Kapauku, who regularly resort to violence when thwarted in such situations). Perhaps other kin of Enaago's persuaded him to let the matter drop, being consanguineally related to him and affinally related to Awitigaaj and not wishing to find themselves in the middle of an embarrassing and violent dispute between them. The following case, involving Awitigaaj again and the bribed big man of the previous case and another of their relatives illustrates how those related to both sides negotiate the settlement of disputes.

Case 4

The big man of Case 3 borrowed 240 cowries, 20 bead necklaces, 420 beads, 20 bush knives, and 30 axes from a relative living in Botukebo, who himself had received them in an exchange associated with warfare. When, after some two years, the creditor demanded repayment, the big man maintained that he was unable to repay him. This angered the creditor, who knew that the big man regularly handled many valuables, and the ensuing argument erupted into a fight in which the creditor's forearm was broken. After the mêlée, when tempers had cooled, the relatives on both sides started pushing for a settlement. The big man Awitigaaj, one of their kinsmen, played a prominent role in these sometimes heated negotiations, which ended for the interim in the debtor's handing over 60 cowries, 5 bead necklaces, and 120 beads and promising to meet the remainder of the debt in the future. The recalcitrant big man sickened and died within a few months of the brawl, others put it down to supernatural punishment for his spoiling ways (his creditor would have received some recompense for the outstanding debt from the mortuary payments attending his death).

There is another side to the issue of the opposing parties being related in some way to one another. It concerns a paradoxical aspect of this relatedness that may militate against an enduring settlement. We have blandly accepted that, in the absence of an impartial judge to settle any issue, the objective among the Kapauku is to reach, if possible, an amicable settlement by argument – a settlement that is acceptable and, given the facts of the case, satisfactory to both parties. The problem is that as they are related we have to take into consideration the history of the interaction that has taken place between them in the course of their relationship because this predictably influences their behaviour and expectations and thus the probable outcome of any dispute between them. If those related to one another already have strained and difficult relations, a dispute between them will exacerbate these and make it likely that they will reach only a precarious settlement.

The extended case method

What all this means is that in a society like that of the Kapauku we cannot treat a dispute as an isolated event that demands arbitration and settlement. Among the Kapauku, where disputants and would-be arbiters are related or at least certainly not strangers, we must see a dispute as one event in a chain of probably lifelong encounters. Apparent wrongdoers may consider their actions justified from this perspective because, as hinted earlier, they even the score for some wrong suffered previously and that wrong itself may have been intended to balance an even earlier misdeed.

It is not clear who is right or wrong in these situations or who has suffered the greater damage. The judicial context in Melanesian society is fairer than ours in some senses, for it automatically allows for the particular circumstances surrounding any dispute. The specific social context conditions people's interpretation of their normative expectations, transgressions of which are not infringements of laws that carry codified punishments but trespasses against flexibly interpreted customary responsibilities. It would be inappropriate in some regards to think in terms of the final and absolute settlement of disputes. It is more apt to consider disputes and their resolution as episodes in a lifelong tit-for-tat.

Many wrongs, perhaps the majority, are committed not directly as retribution for a previous wrong but during the course of everyday interaction when people's interests come into conflict. Nonetheless, even when one dispute is not directly related to another, the personal relations between those involved will condition how they behave towards one another if they become embroiled in a dispute. Anthropologists use what is called the extended case method (or situational analysis) to accommodate this obvious and important point in the study of small-scale societies. It derives from the case method, which features prominently in the anthropology of law, as it does in Western law. The differences in the use of cases between the two illustrate the gulf between state and stateless legal systems. In the state system the case method serves to establish precedent in the legal code; in the stateless one it demonstrates not merely the principles involved in dispute resolution but the role of social relations. It amounts in anthropology to the use of events – cases – from real life, reported in varying detail, to illustrate and substantiate these points. The extended case method traces the connections between one case and another and considers how they impinge on events. In short, it investigates how the history of the relations among a small number of people influences and conditions their behaviour when they quarrel.

The big man Awitigaaj of Botukebo has purposefully been featured in the cases related so far to illustrate in a limited way the extended case method and to show how knowing what has happened in the past helps us understand people's behaviour in disputes. The presentation of cases as isolated events to illustrate the 'rules' of Kapauku law, as in the Kapauku ethnography, makes some of them difficult to understand and illustrates the importance of the extended case method in studying people's actions in disputes. Why, for instance, did Enaago's relative apparently let Awitigaaj cheat him over the pig transaction in Case 3 when he could have called on his relatives to press his claim? They may have dissuaded him from this course because of their touchy relations with Awitigaaj; other events suggest that relations between them were tense, perhaps because of Awitigaaj's incestuous union with Enaago (Case 2). They may have considered Awitigaaj's action over the pig justifiable retribution for something they had done and have been disinclined to push the situation and provoke further wrongdoings. We can trace the saga of their strained relations in several other cases, as follows.

Case 5

Awitigaaj and two Botukebo relatives, Kamutaga and Kekegebo, went hunting and wounded but failed to kill a wild pig. Another man killed it later that day. In this situation the Kapauku expect the killer to share the game with those who initially wounded it, but he did not. He took the sow to Kojogeepa and shared it with Enaago's relatives of the Jamaina sublineage. When Awitigaaj and his relatives turned up in full cry, a stick fight broke out.

Case 6

Imopaj, one of Awitigaaj's relatives, who collected some wood on Jamaina territory, was apprehended by a big man who lived there and ordered to return the wood. When the Jamaina man knocked the wood off Imopaj's shoulder they almost came to blows – an unusually violent response, even for Kapauku, over such a petty issue.

Other cases relating to Botukebo also make more sense knowing something about the state of relations within the neighbourhood and Awitigaaj's life history.

Case 7

When Awitigaaj let it be known that he was thinking of marrying for the eleventh time, this brought to a head the way his relatives felt about his socially disruptive and overly self-centred behaviour. Three men – Bunaibomauma, Nakepajokaipouga and Taajwiijokaipouga – led the opposition. They pointed out that he had been tardy in contributing to the bridewealth payments of other relatives and that he had tricked them into accepting his marriage to Enaago (and had subsequently incestuously married two other close female relatives). They urged no one to contribute to the bridewealth that he would have to amass, and as it turned out no one joined in the pig kill he staged or helped him to build a new dance house.

It appears that these were only a few of many wrongdoings; besides the pig debt episode related in Case 3, the ethnographer records four other cases in which men claimed that Awitigaaj had cheated them in exchanges. It was small wonder that his relatives were refusing to co-operate with him and help him, perhaps in the hope of checking his somewhat unruly and socially disruptive behaviour.

Equivalence equals settlement

Big men are regularly involved in disputes more often than milder and less ambitious men: 4.8 disputes each compared with 1.6 for others (and the four big men in the locality in which the ethnographer collected a considerable number of the cases reported were involved in a staggering 15.8 disputes each). We are presented with an interesting paradox: those whose activities do most to promote social integration through sociopolitical exchange are also those who most often threaten social order by becoming embroiled in disputes. This suggests that, as the ambitious members of their society, they would be the ones most likely to upset things in a self-interested rush for gain if such drives were not channelled in socially benign directions.

The paradox detected in the behaviour of big men reflects the antinomy inherent in exchange itself. We have seen how, from a somewhat abstract sociological perspective, exchange encourages social integration and order, whereas from the perspective of the individual pursuit of personal aggrandisement it can on occasion apparently give rise to the reverse. However, so long as people seek to negotiate a compromise settlement, the higher sociological purpose continues to be worked out. Many of the disputes among the Kapauku focus on pigs and other wealth. It is predictable that big men will be embroiled in disputes more often than others, because they regularly overreach themselves and find their creditors clamouring for recompense.

We are, of course, considering exchange yet again here; we cannot go far in discussing Melanesian ethnography without this central issue entering onto the stage, and it continues to occupy the limelight in the drama of dispute settlement in the role of compensation payments. A very important way of settling disputes throughout Melanesia is for the wrongdoer to make a payment to the wronged party. Knowing what we have established about Melanesian society, it will be clear that such compensation payments are not mere indemnity for a loss. Although the moral and symbolic meaning of the passage of valued items between people in this part of the world is beyond our experience, we can glimpse how a payment is not just to make good a wrong but symbolises the continuance of amicable social relations.

A cardinal principle regulating dispute settlement among the Kapauku and Melanesians generally is equivalence, a principle with which we are already familiar (see chapter 7). The aim of those embroiled in disputes is to balance the score between them; handing over valuables in compensation makes good the loss suffered by the plaintiff and simultaneously, given the centrality of the exchange principle in Melanesian life, signals and re-establishes amicable relations between them. If the wrongdoer obdurately refuses compensation, the plaintiff may redress the balance by taking retributive action, that is, by wronging him back in revenge. It is incorrect to think of this as meting out just punishment; it is the reverse of compensation and socially negative. It is an act aimed at securing an equivalence of losses on the two sides. The following case, in which some pigs damaged a garden, illustrates these principles at work.

Case 8

When a garden owner found some pigs rooting over his sweet potato crop, he fired bird arrows at them to scare them off. He demanded at least sixty beads from their owners in compensation for the damage they had done but they offered him only a mere two. Enraged, he knocked down their garden fences and chopped down sugarcane in their gardens. One of the pig owners went in turn to retaliate by further damaging the man's sweet potato garden but was stopped. An acrimonious argument ensued and they almost came to blows. The garden owner stormed off again, this time to burn down the pig owners' houses, but his relatives intervened and stopped him, persuading him and the others that the damage done on either side more or less balanced.

Sometimes men go beyond using harmless bird arrows on pigs that break into their gardens, as in the following case.

Case 9

A garden owner shot and killed a pig that had entered his garden and was rooting over his crops. His fence was not in good repair, however, and the sow had done little damage. His action had therefore over-redressed the balance in the heat of the moment, and he gave twenty-one cowries to the pig owner in compensation. The pig owner, in return, gave the garden owner a quarter of the pig. Both parties gave and received. Compensation balanced the wrongs and went further, in typical Melanesian fashion, to reaffirm relations.

Reading the Kapauku or almost any other Melanesian ethnography, one gains the impression of surprisingly fractious and violent societies. This is common among acephalous peoples the world over; proud of their independence, they are quick to defend physically infringements of it. We see that social life in Melanesia is a question of compromise – an ever-shifting balance between sometimes paradoxically opposed forces that exist in a dynamic relationship. Society is in constant flow as individuals daily accommodate to the interpretations of values and actions of others.

We can appreciate why people without state judicial apparatus do not wrong one another with impunity. The interrelated forces that ulti-mately help keep them in check include the following:
(1) the existence of some fundamental, and highly valued urge among well-adjusted Melanesians to maintain stable and orderly social environments in which to live;
(2) the intervention of relatives not directly involved in disputes, especially those related to both sides, who value orderly behaviour highly; and
(3) the loss of social respect and self-esteem that antisocial individuals

experience if they fail to make proper amends, which may extend to forgoing others' co-operation in everyday life or even the breakdown of social relations and violence.

These amount to powerful coercive sanctions which account for individuals paying compensation and thus settling disputes amicably when there is no authority forcing them to do so or accepting others' redressive action as fair without retaliation. However, there are other forces, some of them effective on an occult plane. The next chapter considers one of them: sorcery.

FURTHER READING

The ethnographic accounts on which this review draws are:
L. Pospisil, 1958 *Kapauku Papuans and their law.* Yale University Publications in Anthropology 54.
L. Pospisil, 1963 *The Kapauku Papuans of West New Guinea.* New York: Holt, Rinehart and Winston.

Other studies of dispute settlement in Melanesia include:
R. M. Berndt, 1962 *Excess and restraint.* Chicago: University of Chicago Press.
K. J. Brison, 1992 *Just talk.* Berkeley: University of California Press.
A. L. Epstein (ed.), 1974 *Contention and dispute.* Canberra: Australian National University Press.
L. Goldman, 1983 *Talk never dies.* London: Tavistock.
L. Goldman, 1993 *The culture of coincidence.* Oxford: Oxford University Press.
A. J. Strathern, 1993 *Voices of conflict.* Pittsburgh: University of Pittsburgh Press.
M. Strathern, 1972 *Official and unofficial courts: Legal assumptions and expectations in a highlands community.* Port Moresby: Australian National University New Guinea Research Bulletin 61.

11 Sorcery on Dobu Island

Throughout Melanesia we find that people live in fear of sorcery. The so-called black arts have great potential in the Black Islands for effecting social control and in some regions they have even played a part in the development of limited political offices vested with a modicum of authority and a degree of inequality. At the same time, they are riddled with paradoxes and apparent contradictions, to the point that as categorical thinkers we have to struggle to comprehend how they exist at all.

Sorcery and witchcraft

In anthropology we customarily make a distinction between two kinds of malicious supernatural activity, sorcery and witchcraft. Although we cannot make the discrimination rigidly for all cultures around the world, it is relevant to many regions throughout Melanesia.

Sorcery is the conscious manipulation of things to bring about illness and death, often things associated personally with the victim which he or she has touched or owned. A person can learn the procedures involved and then set out deliberately to attack victims through the manipulation of the prescribed rites and spells. Witchcraft is the product of some inborn malignant power over which those so afflicted commonly have no conscious control. Indeed, they are often unaware that they possess it. People often believe that, whatever the force is, it leaves witches when they are asleep to perpetrate its evil deeds. A person obviously cannot learn to be a witch; he or she either is or is not one. But one can learn how to detect witchcraft attacks, how to restore their victims to health, and perhaps even how to defend people from such misfortune. We label these activities divination. There are customary divination practices associated with the detection and prevention of sorcery, too, and specific rites believed to cure its victims.

We find sorcery and witchcraft beliefs throughout Melanesia, together with associated divinatory practices. In the Massim area, the locale of

165

this chapter's ethnography, people such as the Trobriand Islanders and Dobuans believe both in sorcery and in flying witches that spread fire and destruction from their pubes.

The unfortunate terrorised population featured in this chapter lives on Dobu, a small island situated off the eastern tip of New Guinea in the D'Entrecasteaux Archipelago (Map 11.1). They are neighbours of the Trobriand Islanders (see chapter 5) and like them are Austronesian-speakers and participate in the *kula*. Their island is a steep-sided volcano rising abruptly from the sea, with clear coral-lined bays and precipitous forest-covered ridges, the trees apparently falling over themselves to reach the water. It offers relatively few sites for settlements and gardens. The Dobuans live in stilted houses, collected into villages on the relatively few sizeable level locations on the island (Plates 11.1 and 11.2). Their staple crop is yam, supplemented by fishing and other plant foods, such as the sago palm. They have a matrilineal ideology, particularly with regard to inheritance, in contrast to the more common patrilineal preference elsewhere (chapter 9).

The Dobuans, crowded together on this ruggedly beautiful but uncompromising island, have a particularly dark and sinister reputation even by Melanesian standards. To be fair to them, it is suggested that the ethnography reflects to some extent the views of the anthropologist who lived with them in its exaggeration of their black reputation compared with their neighbours, but this is not exceptional. We have already noted in a number of instances how anthropologists' personal histories and preoccupations are reflected in their ethnographic accounts.

Dobuan sorcery

Dobuans believe that many diseases result from the recitation of spells specific to each sickness, different people knowing different spells. It is the spell that they think is efficacious; once it has been recited over something, anyone who comes into contact with that thing will contract the associated disease. These spells are rich in symbolism, with metaphoric plays, allusions and antitheses combined in potent chants. In one spell, for instance, which is associated with a disease that eats the nose away, the reciter makes a great play on the hornbill, contrasting this bird's gigantic beak with the antithesis of no nose. On Dobu, to contract this disease is to get the 'hornbill'. All spells are larded with such elliptical references to what will happen to those on whom they are unleashed and use special esoteric language. In another spell the crab is the occult motif, referred to not by the everyday word *lakua* but by the mysterious word *mokakasi*:

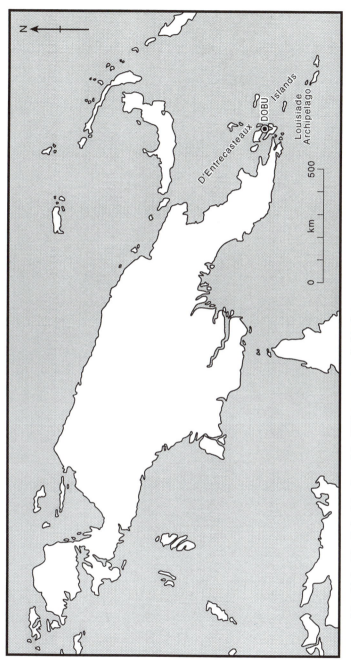

Map 11.1   The Dobu Islanders of the D'Entrecasteaux Archipelago.

Plate 11.1   On the beach in front of a Dobuan village, a group of women, some of them with baskets on their heads, prepares to set off for their gardens.

Plate 11.2   Everyday transport around and between nearby islands in the
Massim Archipelago – a Dobuan paddling a dugout outrigger canoe with a
stem of bananas in the rear.

        crab
    inside your earth cave
        your throat clogs up
        (as the crab clogs up his hole)
        your body fat congeals
        your foot crouches bends
        your seat of the voice rots
        your heel gives under your standing
        your seat of urine secretion clogs up
        your tongue hangs out with spue vomiting
        your intestines flow out of your anus
        your throat (i.e. mind) I roll up
        your heart I crumble up
        I crumble up striking dead
        your throat (seat of mind) I roll up

                                        (Fortune 1932: 169)

The recitation of this spell leads to a physiologically blocked condition
followed by a lethal spewing out.

    A sorcerer who wishes to strike someone down will obtain some of the
victim's personal leavings, called *sumwana*, and recite a spell over them

Plate 11.3   A man identified in the archives as a sorcerer holding a lime
container (from which lime is spooned with a spatula, and is chewed
together with the narcotic-like betel nut).

Plate 11.4   A Dobuan man sorting out personal possessions, favoured for
bespelling by sorcerers, on the day sitting platform outside his stilted house,
with dogs scavenging nearby.

(Plates 11.3 and 11.4). Personal leavings suitable for this purpose
include remains of meals, excreta, body dirt and even footprints. If the
sorcerer cannot readily obtain any of these, he may breathe the spell into
a length of vine and string it across a track that the victim uses and then
hide nearby to retrieve it once the victim has brushed against it. He
takes the vine home and smokes it for a day and then he crumbles it at
night over a fire until it is all burnt, mimicking as he does so the writhing
of the victim in the agonies that his actions induce. This will kill the
victim. Alternatively, the sorcerer may parcel up the vine or any other
sumwana leavings. This sends the victim into a crazed delirium; the
binding induces convulsions, the Dobuans say, just as the winding of a
cuscus's tail around a branch accounts for that animal's sudden jerky
movements.

   Before embarking on any nefarious activities a sorcerer prepares
himself. Hotness is a recurring symbolic theme. The Dobuans believe
that heat makes sorcery effective, and therefore the sorcerer drinks salt
water and chews ginger to heat up his body and his spells. He also
refrains from eating for some twenty-four hours, believing that an empty

0   cm   5

Figure 11.1   An elaborately carved Massim lime spatula.

stomach induces intense body heat. He needs to take care in following his procedures. If a spell is not word-perfect its disease-inflicting potential will rebound on the reciter. The learning of spells and techniques is particularly dangerous for neophytes. Sorcery is a risky business.

Another sorcery technique which is widespread in Melanesia and of which the Dobuans stand in awe, involves a spell which makes the sorcerer invisible (the ethnographer does not give the spell, although he says that someone told it to him so that 'you can go into shops in Sydney, steal what you like, and get away with it unseen' [Fortune 1932: 78]). Once he is invisible, the sorcerer approaches his victim, causing him to scream and faint. He takes a lime spatula (Figure 11.1) over which he has recited a spell and mimes cutting open the victim, removing through the gaping 'wound' his heart, lungs and entrails. A feigned tap with the spatula makes the victim whole again, and a spell whispered over the spatula puts him back on his feet. Before commanding him to go home, the sorcerer asks the victim three times if he can recognise him, rapping him each time on the temples with the spatula. The dazed victim then staggers home, where he collapses into a tormented writhing heap and dies the next day.

At this juncture let us note that the Dobuans also know of genuinely toxic substances such as the seeds of the dog-bane plant and gall from the globe-fish, both of which contain poisonous substances. Someone wishing to kill another person may introduce some of these substances into their food or tobacco, without need of a spell. In parts of Melanesia, particularly the New Guinea highlands, we distinguish between these practices and other nefarious activities such as sorcery and witchcraft, calling them poison, even where the substances used are not scientifically toxic (a commonly cited supposed ingredient being menstrual blood [see chapter 9]).

Effectiveness of sorcery

There is probably no material connection between acts of sorcery and fatalities attributed to them, and therefore it is puzzling to us that people can believe in such practices, which we assume that experience or experiment would soon demonstrate to be ineffective. But this is to adopt the wrong intellectual stance. The Dobuans' magic volcanic crystals demonstrate the point. They believe that when released these can fly into a victim's body. Many people own crystals, and individuals who know the spells to shoot them into other people can also remove them. Commenting on this technique, Fortune (1932: 298) says, 'The presence of the crystal in his hand after he has projected it magically at a victim, or before he has ejected it from a patient is immaterial. The immaterial on the contrary is material in effecting his purpose.' In other words, the Dobuans do not expect a demonstrable material connection – an attitude which, of course, precludes scientific experimentation. These are symbolic acts and expressions and therefore on a different plane altogether.

The attitude of Dobuans to failed attempts at sorcery reflects this. We might assume that many attempts to kill others nefariously fail. Not only would sorcerers keep their failures to themselves out of embarrassment and explain them as resulting from their own mistakes and inadequacies but also they have made their symbolic gesture an end in itself. Furthermore, people do not go around talking openly about trying to kill others with sorcery, which would be tantamount to discussing murder. It is a secretive business, not one widely debated. They would not question the general efficacy of the rites; it would be inappropriate to do so, and the opportunity would be unlikely to present itself in such a society or occur to people socialised into its sorcerous cultural traditions. A few aberrant characters might question them, but others would be unlikely to heed them unless social conditions were changing and the social atmosphere conducive to some acceptance of such heretical thoughts.

The considerable amount of sickness and relatively high death rate occurring in societies like that on Dobu Island would also result in a fair number of apparent sorcery successes, which we might assume would be sufficient to cancel out any doubts arising over failures. There are important psychological issues associated with these beliefs too. People who believe in the potency of such practices can reportedly think themselves into a morbid state if they consider themselves the target of sorcery (see chapter 14). There was a case, described in detail by Fortune (1932: 158–61), in which such suggestion made a man ill when there was nothing organically wrong with him; he had gone to collect poles in the forest to train his yams on and had met someone believed to be a powerful sorcerer with whom he had disputed land rights.

The use of sorcery as sanction no longer seems far-fetched. If people fear these practices to the point where they can think themselves into sickness, perhaps even death, then they have a powerful force for social control of deviant behaviour. When normal dispute procedures fail (chapter 10), then the threat or fear of sorcery can help promote a settlement. The belief that they might be sortilegiously attacked for wrongdoing encourages socially expected behaviour. The Dobuans are aware of this: 'You have your rifles – we have *tabu*, witchcraft, and sorcery, our weapons' (Fortune 1932: 157). The following case illustrates how the Dobuans use the threat of sorcery to force the settlement of disputes:

Case 1

Two men, while collecting poles for house-building, came across another man's pig, which they thought was wild, and killed it. When they realised their mistake, they hid the animal and returned home, hoping to escape detection. The pig's owner started to search for it when it failed to return home. He looked for days and did not find its speared corpse until it was partially decomposed. Others told him that they had seen the pole cutters in the vicinity about the time the pig disappeared, and he let it be known that he had collected their footprints in wet sand. The implication was clear; either they compensated him for his pig or he might very well resort to sorcery in retaliation. They soon made an adequate payment to him and settled the dispute.

The Dobuans do not stop at settling disputes by threatening sorcery; they also prevent them with it. They protect their property by charging it with sorcery; for example, a man may breathe a spell into some leaves and tie them around the trunk of a fruiting tree that belongs to him in such a way that anyone climbing it to steal the fruits would come into contact with the charged foliage and be attacked by the sorcery in it. There is no need of locks and burglar alarms in a society like that on Dobu Island, because no one who lacks a spell to counteract sorcery is going to risk a gruesome death to steal something. Even with such a spell there are dangers; a sorcerer may cancel its protection.

Beyond this, the Dobuans turn illness attributed to the black machinations of others to judicial advantage. Fortune's (1932: 166) observation that 'where there is the fire of sorcery or witchcraft there has been very often the smoke of quarrel' suggests the connection between sorcery-ascribed illness and dispute settlement. The divination procedures employed by the Dobuans to identify the cause of sickness and name the sorcerer exploit the probability of this connection. Persons with the knowledge can detect a sorcery-caused illness from the victim's body odour or by gripping his or her middle finger by the first joint to see whether the fingertip flushes. If they suspect sorcery, diviners identify the individual responsible by gazing either into a wooden bowl of water sprinkled with hibiscus flowers or into a volcanic crystal charged with the appropriate spells, in which they can see reflected the spirit of the sorcerer. The diviner will be keenly aware of any disputes or disagreements in this small island society, and the scene is thus set for his bringing up the matter for discussion and settlement. When he names the individual he 'sees' in the water or the crystal, the victim or his relatives will approach the person named and request him to revoke his spell in return for an adequate settlement of the difference between them. If the diviner knows of no dispute in which the sick person is involved he will turn to some other cause, such as witchcraft.

It is reasonable to assume that recourse to sorcery has a cathartic effect for those frustrated in disputes. It is an alternative to open violence, which can disrupt social life considerably (chapter 10). Wronged by someone and thwarted in their justified claims against them, individuals can turn to sorcery taking pleasure in their opponents' anticipated agonies. Again, it is a symbolic gesture. But can we so paint the 'black art' sociologically and psychologically white? This brings us to another Melanesian paradox. The contradiction contained in sorcery might be called the 'fearful friends syndrome'. Sorcery encourages demonstrations of amicability for fear of the possible consequences of a serious rift with others, but people are guardedly friendly to those outside a small circle of relatives because underneath their sociable show they are terrified of one another. Sorcery fears inhibit secure relationships. The Dobuans believe that sorcerers strive to become friendly with their victims before striking because this is likely to give them access to some juicy *sumwana* to work on. Suspicions like these breed tense social relationships, even disputes. Thus, whereas sorcery promotes social order in some circumstances, in others it can be divisive. If a death occurs from an illness attributed to sorcery, Dobuans attempt to identify the sorcerer by watching the deceased as mourners file past; they believe that when the sorcerer approaches it the corpse will twitch.

The politics of sorcery

The paradoxical nature of sorcery does not stop at simultaneously encouraging social interaction and discouraging it; it also promotes both social inequality and equality. Whereas Melanesia's Non-Austronesian or Papuan groups are characterised, as we have seen, by markedly informal leadership limited by the premium placed on equivalence between persons, Austronesian-speakers such as the Dobuans have chief-like offices that are hereditary (that is, ascribed not achieved), ideally through primogeniture. On Dobu the rule of inheritance of chiefly office is that the eldest son of the senior female line should succeed to the position. Under the matrilineal system of the Dobuans, like that of the nearby Trobrianders, certain rights and property are inherited by men from their mothers' relatives (probably mothers' brothers) and handed on by them to their sisters' children. This gives rise to a complicated alternating residence pattern on Dobu and considerable friction between a man's mother's place (where he will hand on rights to his sister's sons) and his wife's group's place (where his children will receive rights from his wife's brothers). The tension is reflected in a high divorce rate. It is not fanciful to suggest that the strains induced by this convoluted social organisation probably contribute to the treacherous Dobuan social environment and the exaggerated fear of sorcery.

Because of changes induced by colonial authorities in the political regime before ethnographic enquiry, it is not clear how many chiefs there were traditionally on Dobu or how their offices were related. There are reports of leaders of villages and localities (village clusters) and elsewhere there are references to a precontact commander-in-chief of the entire island. Similarly, the jurisdiction and the limits of the weak authority vested in these offices are hazy. Some chiefs could apparently censure those locked in disputes. According to Fortune (1932: 84) one

was to be heard now and again in *guguia*, the public admonishing of a member of his own village. He would commonly talk for half-an-hour or so in loud, angry staccato sentences. The other *tai sinabwadi*, big men of the village took no part, but listened quietly. On these occasions one of the big men commonly whispered to me in a reverential tone, *i guguia*, he is laying down the law, and motioned to me to sit down and be silent. There was complete silence, no reply or repartee, although obviously one or two persons and a small party of sympathisers were seething in revolt at being most severely tongue-lashed.

Chiefs' authority extended beyond such admonitions to organising people for collective activities. The authority of a chief, for instance, 'extended over his whole locality of several villages for fixing the sailing dates for overseas expeditions when the whole locality acted at one time' (Fortune 1932: 85). And the commander-in-chief could apparently mobilise the entire island for military expeditions (Fortune 1978: 675).

The question prompted by these observations is why some persons are willing to stand up and admonish those embroiled in disputes or tell others what to do for some community event. They are very likely to offend people in talking to them this way, and they are apparently sticking their necks out in a society in which all fear that anyone crossed by another may retaliate with sorcery. The chiefs seem to be running a grave risk in carrying out the functions of their office, for 'bringing a man to book in a society where sorcery flourishes is playing with the most dangerous fire' (Fortune 1932: 47). The answer is that the chiefs are believed to possess the most powerful sorcery and so can counter any such attack. They inherit this sorcery knowledge; it is an important aspect of the office they occupy.

If people believe that certain persons in their society are far more powerful sorcerers than others, this gives these persons the opportunity to coerce them. Chiefly sorcery not only protects those who know it when intervening in disputes but also gives them the authority they require to direct the actions of others. It legitimates their position and is the source of what power accrues to it. They can use their knowledge and control of believed powerful sorcery – not necessarily openly but by subtle suggestion – to maintain a degree of political control over others.

In addressing the question of why some titled individuals risk interfering in and even directing others' affairs, another question arises. Why has Dobuan society not passed from stateless to state instead of hovering uncertainly on the divide? The supernatural source of chiefly political coercion and power might have been expected to lead to the development of full-blown chiefly polities, even kingdoms. Instead, the chiefly offices of Austronesians are markedly informal and carry little political authority; it is as if they reflected the influence of the egalitarian ethic of their Non-Austronesian neighbours. This returns us to the paradox that sorcery beliefs simultaneously promote both inequality and equality in social relations.

Although sorcery is a significant sanction in the nascent Dobuan political hierarchy, it also checks its further development and the accumulation of power. The Dobuans believe that if chiefs are too high and mighty and too successful, then others will become resentful and use sorcery to harm and injure them, to pull them down, perhaps even kill them. In another apt fire metaphor playing on the efficacy of heat in Dobuan sorcery symbolism, Fortune observes that in disputes 'they are inhibited considerably by fear of anger flaring up to the heat which kindles sorcery' (1932: 56). The combined sorcery assault of those who are offended and opposed to a chief's overbearing behaviour will exceed his supernatural power to defend himself. The combined onslaught will overwhelm his magical defences and so injure him. And chiefs are as likely, of course, as others to fall sick and die, thus giving credence to people's beliefs that their sorcery can strike down leaders. The upshot is that persons who are believed to inherit more powerful sorcery knowledge than others, legitimating the tenuous political offices they occupy, are very circumspect in their use of the limited authority this gives them; it is very dangerous to overstep the mark.

The Dobuans object not only to anyone's exerting more than a modicum of influence over their individual affairs but also to anyone's flaunting his successes in life. It is dangerous to appear markedly better off than others. Dobuans value equality highly and use sorcery to attack anyone who offends their sense of fair dealing and symmetrical relations. They have 'nothing except anger for any differences in success due to ability. The black art is used against an over successful gardener, since he is believed to have stolen other persons' yams from their gardens by magic. The black art is used against rivals who interfere with one's own success in overseas exchange ... Even a man who has too many domestic pigs is in danger – his greater wealth is regarded as an affront' (Fortune 1932: 176). The use of sorcery to even the score between people is common throughout Melanesia, where revenge is another central principle of life. It is even more evident when armed hostilities occur than it is in sorcery's surreptitious expressions of aggression.

FURTHER READING

The ethnographic accounts on which this review draws are:

W. E. Bromilow, 1909 'Some manners and customs of the Dobuans of S. E. Papua.' *Australian Association for the Advancement of Science.* 12: 470–85.
W. E. Bromilow, 1912 'Dobuan (Papuan) beliefs and folklore.' *Australian Association for the Advancement of Science.* 13: 413–26.
W. E. Bromilow, 1929 *Twenty years among primitive Papuans.* London: Epworth.
R. F. Fortune, 1932 *Sorcerers of Dobu.* London: Routledge and Kegan Paul.
R. F. Fortune, 1960 'Folk medicine in the Dobuan Islands' *Journal of the Polynesian Society.* 69: 31–33.
R. F. Fortune, 1978 'Dobuans.' *Family of Man Encyclopaedia.* Part 25: 673–75.

On sorcery elsewhere in Melanesia see:
B. M. Knauft, 1985 *Good company and violence: Sorcery and social action in a lowland New Guinea society.* Berkeley: University of California Press.

P. Lawrence and M. Meggitt (eds.), 1965 *Gods, ghosts and men in Melanesia*. Oxford: Oxford University Press.

M. Stephen (ed.), 1987 *Sorcerer and witch in Melanesia*. New Brunswick: Rutgers University Press.

M. Zelenietz and S. Lindenbaum. (eds.), 1981 'Sorcery and social change in Melanesia'. *Social Analysis*. special issue no. 8.

On anthropological studies of sorcery and witchcraft see:

A. C. Lehman and J. E. Myers (eds.), 1993 *Magic, witchcraft, and religion*. Palo Alto: Mayfield.

M. Marwick (ed.), 1970 *Witchcraft and sorcery*. Harmondsworth: Penguin.

A. Sanders, 1995 *A deed without a name*. Oxford: Berg.

12   Warfare and cannibalism in the Balim Region

When disputes become deadlocked in societies with no purportedly impartial judicial institutions, the parties are likely to fight. When this happens in Melanesia and a serious injury or fatality occurs, armed hostilities between the two parties and their relatives are probable. Armed encounters in Melanesia appear uncontrolled and disorganised, with relatives fighting against one another, even sometimes changing sides in a conflict, but their singularity follows inevitably from what we have established about the region's acephalous social orders, combined with the peculiar propensity for intraspecific killing of the human animal.

The hostilities that occur in Melanesia are of a different order from war as we know it. While sometimes bloodthirsty they are less relentless and in some regards more merciful, outward barbaric impressions notwithstanding. There is no idea of all-out war, of defeating and conquering the enemy at all costs. The saying that 'there are no winners in a war, only losers' is particularly apt for Melanesia, where people fight with no idea of winning or losing but only of balancing losses. This striving for a balance in blood is another manifestation of the all-important equivalence principle that governs Melanesian life.

Armed hostilities

Melanesians are not exceptional in engaging in hostilities quite different from our idea of war. The notion of unlimited war is alien to many tribal societies, and the restricted hostilities in which they engage take a wide variety of forms. Anthropology has evolved a limited vocabulary to describe these aggressive activities. The two terms that feature most prominently in the ethnographic literature are feud and war, which can be broadly differentiated as follows:

A feud is a never-ending hostile relationship wherein peace between the enemies is inconceivable. The motive force is revenge; when one side kills and avenges a previous wrong, the other incurs a loss and must avenge it, and so on. Feuds are characterised by violent acts separated by quiescent periods. The hostilities frequently take the form of stealthy military encounters such as ambushes, in which there are only one or two fatalities at a time.

A war is just about any other kind of hostility in which the parties involved can usually make peace if they wish. The reasons for wars are varied, but a common motive is gain, whether economic (e.g. resources), political (e.g. authority and suzerainty), or religious (e.g. converts and a place in paradise). Although the time people spend fighting varies and is often quite brief, both sides actively prosecute hostilities during a war. There may however, be lulls in the fighting, even cease-fires to attend to essential tasks such as harvesting crops. Besides stealthy military encounters such as raids and ambushes, battles are also common in wars, and many people may be routed and killed and their property destroyed in one encounter.

The hostilities that occur in Melanesia are commonly referred to as wars, but this does not accord strictly speaking with the above definitions. Fighting throughout the region blends features of both feud and war. This is another example of our vocabulary being inadequate to express what we find in other cultures. The culturally unique hostilities that occur in Melanesia demand their own name (a possible contender might be 'belligerence') but lacking any generally accepted alternative we shall continue to use 'war' with appropriate qualification.

In our look at the quintessentially chaotic and apparently anarchic hostilities of Melanesia we shall turn to the Yali (or Jalé), who live in the mountains to the east of the Balim River in the central cordillera of New Guinea (Map 12.1). Their homeland is rugged and precipitous, like that of other highland dwellers, with steep-sided valleys along which flow turbulent rivers. The men wear masses of cane hoops around their bodies above their penis sheaths, the women brief sedge skirts (Plates 12.1 and 12.2). The Yali live in villages made up of clusters of round huts with their gardens nearby. They subsist by swidden agriculture, with sweet potato again the staple crop. Humans and pigs alike depend on the tubers. Pigs are again a highly valued source of wealth, which they exchange in 'the validation or reaffirmation of social relationships' (Koch 1974: 42).

Yali warfare

In our discussion of dispute settlement (chapter 10) we saw how wronged parties may retaliate if the issue under dispute is not settled to

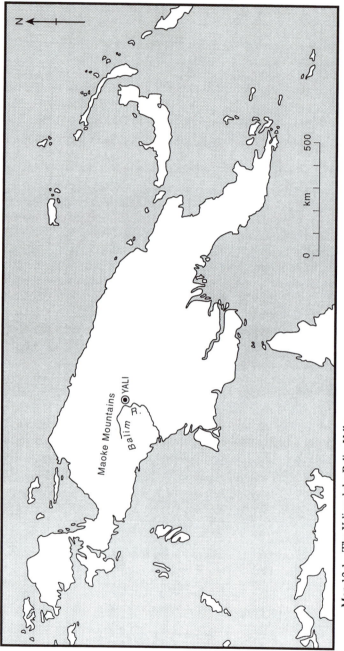

Map 12.1   The Yali and the Balim Valley.

Plate 12.1   Yali men singeing the bristles off joints of butchered pork over a
fire heating stones for an earth oven.

Plate 12.2   A group of Yali women and children look on
expectantly at an event.

their satisfaction. This resort to aggressive self-help is understandable where we find no policemen to intervene in grievances, but it is a risky strategy. The attitude of the 'defendant' to such action determines what is likely to happen next. He may, as we have seen, consider himself in the right and view the act as a wrong against him, or he may think that the act goes too far in redressing their differences. In this event, he is likely in turn to seek to redress the balance in some self-help action, giving rise to a potential chain of linked wrongs and disputes. We can readily appreciate how such an unstable situation can end in a violent confrontation.

It does not require a chain of redressive acts to provoke an eruption of violence; one dispute can spark fighting. It is understandable in a society in which there is no authority to impose a settlement or punishment that people locked in disputes may become exasperated and resort to violence in an attempt to secure what they consider their due. Hostilities may also start on occasion over deaths attributed to sorcery or revenge killings. These may look like new wars, and people may talk of them as such, but they are invariably part of a chain of violence going back to some previous, perhaps even ancient, forgotten dispute that resulted in an unrequited fatality.

The Yali recognise that wars are caused by the wrongdoing of individuals and the violent responses that follow and clearly identify the responsible parties. They call them the 'men of the arrow's stem', and it is around these individuals that relatives come together for warfare. It is an enormous responsibility to be an 'arrow-stem man'. The Yali emphasise the moral responsibility assumed in causing hostilities, in which relatives and friends may die fighting on one's behalf, by making the 'arrow-stem men' liable for the extensive sociopolitical exchanges required to compensate the kin of those killed fighting on their side. We can apprehend the social and political implications of these payments from our earlier discussion of exchange (see chapter 6). They reaffirm social relations between those who have lost one of their number, and they can take years or even generations to complete. Failure to do so can destroy social relationships and even inspire new hostilities. We can understand how these enormous responsibilities act in some circumstances to curb violent behaviour in disputes; no one becomes an 'arrow-stem man' without good reason.

The Yali's principal offensive weapon is the bow, with a range of varyingly pointed bamboo and palm-wood unfletched arrows. For defence, warriors arrange net bags around their necks and heads; the hoops they wear around their waists and buttocks also afford them some protection. The military encounters that characterise their fighting are informal, even somewhat confused, lacking any command to order their tactics. The Yali fight both by stealthy raids and in battles.

In raids a few armed men lay ambushes for unsuspecting enemies in regions they are likely to frequent – perhaps adjacent to a spring, a path to a remote garden, or a trap in the forest – and slay anyone, man, woman, or child, who comes along to collect water or harvest crops or check for game. During hostilities people are careful when visiting possible ambush locations and men commonly lie in wait in vain. The raid often results in a fatality and it is often dangerous for the raiders as well, who may have penetrated deep into enemy territory and have to retreat with their opponents in hot pursuit.

The battle, for all its aggressive clamour, is less dangerous. It is a fluid encounter, usually between two fairly evenly matched sides, in which individuals fight as they think best, taking orders from no one. The numbers of men involved on either side are relatively small, and according to Koch (1974: 77) they fight in:

a loosely co-ordinated pattern of individual engagements. The techniques of arrow warfare, terrain conditions, and the greater peril of getting hit if the warriors form attack units make dispersed fighting positions a tactical expediency but they also impede any ready co-ordination of movements. Fighting on open land, a warrior looks for vantage ground from where he can attack with a shoot-and-run technique. He advances as far as the topography affords him cover, quickly discharges one or more arrows, and then hurries back to escape the reach of enemy shots.

In lulls between skirmishes men light fires, smoke and chat. If the two sides are evenly balanced the battle front remains more or less static as they exchange arrows until one of the lulls becomes the end of the day's fighting. But if the numbers on one side exceed the other they may drive them back to their village, where the engagement becomes one of sniping around houses. Sometimes the invaders rout the defenders, who may retreat to their men's house, in which a ritual convention protects them from further attack; the victors then pillage and burn the other houses.

Conflict theory

As in the management of disputes (chapter 10), the course of violent events depends critically on the relationship of the opponents. Close relatives and those living as neighbours in the same locality are unlikely to resort to serious violence. Other kin will intervene and restrain them if they seem on the point of going too far in the heat of the moment. If a close relative did maim or kill another, it would probably be by accident in a rage, and revenge would be unlikely. The culpable party would probably pay compensation to his kin and reaffirm the relations that his calamitous act had disrupted. It is disputes between more distantly related people and strangers that are likely to lead to warfare.

The Yali acknowledge that the relationship between the parties influences the seriousness of any fighting that occurs between them by distinguishing between two kinds of hostility, which they call *wim* and *soli*. *Wim* wars are those they fight against people who live nearby, in localities where they have several relatives and regularly interact socially. These wars are fairly easily settled and usually of short duration with few deaths. The latter, *soli* wars, are those they fight against people living some way off (e.g. in the next valley), where they have few relatives and visit irregularly. These wars are almost feudlike in that the establishment of stable peace between those involved is extremely difficult and precarious. It is on *soli* enemies that the Yali practise cannibalism.

It is understandable that *wim* wars are more easily settled, given the importance of kin relations in small-scale societies. The anthropological approach called conflict theory, which might perhaps be more aptly called conflict-of-loyalties theory, builds on this insight to investigate the forces that tend towards social order in these otherwise apparently anarchic contexts. It argues that when persons are related to both sides in a dispute, they experience conflicting feelings that prompt them to push for a peaceful settlement, acting as go-betweens trusted by both sides. Although the ethnographer who studied the Yali holds that conflict theory is inapplicable to them (Koch 1974: 166–68), his ethnography and case material suggest otherwise.

The Yali observe marriage rules which result in men marrying women from groups against which they may find themselves ranged as enemies. The geographical dispersal of marriages means that those living in any neighbourhood will have relatives spread over a wide area – affinal relatives in the first generation and consanguinal kin in subsequent ones. Among the Yali and other Melanesians these cross-cutting ties within and between settlements are commonly insufficient to prevent the outbreak of hostilities. When indirectly related people find themselves locked in acrimonious disputes, the fact that they have third-party relatives in common is not likely to prevent them from fighting.

When hostilities do break out, those with divided loyalties, while actively fighting on one side or the other, or even both on different occasions in the same war, will find their lives seriously disrupted and press for a settlement. The effectiveness of their lobbying will depend on how many individuals find themselves in this unenviable position. If the cross-cutting ties are numerous and many people are affected, then they will be a significant force, and hostilities are unlikely to go on for long. The number of deaths on either side is an important consideration too. If they are no more than one or two and they balance, then a quick peace settlement is more probable.

The role of those who experience a conflict of loyalties becomes apparent when opponents agree to abandon their hostilities. They cannot meet one another, fearing treacherous violence, but those related to both sides can go between them without fear and convey the feelings of one to the other. In this way peace negotiations open and proceed. Indeed, it is probable that those related to both sides will have been in contact throughout the fighting, continually communicating the other's intentions. When both sides are in a mood to stop the hostilities, one or the other approaches within shouting distance of the enemy's village and dances to songs expressing a wish for peace such as the following (Koch 1974: 83):

> Fighting is a bad thing, so is war,
> Like the trees we will stand together,
> Like the trees at Fungfung.
> Like the trees at Jelen.

A formal peace ceremony follows in which the two parties meet and slaughter a pig. The arrow-stem men responsible for the hostilities take half the pig each and share it with those who have been fighting on their behalf, and a series of dances and pig exchanges follows.

Reasons for war

The hostilities that we are considering here are not of a kind that we would readily recognise as war. The fact that close relatives may fight on opposite sides brings this home. Although they will not directly engage one another in any action, they are nonetheless nominal enemies, the most they are likely to exchange being a few verbal shafts (possibly of encouragement). Furthermore, some men who live in the same village may decide to help relatives fighting on different sides. They may even decide to fight for both sides at different times. These are peculiar ways to conduct a war, and we clearly have to try and make sense of such apparently subversive behaviour to understand Melanesian warfare.

The cause of hostilities in societies structured like that of the Yali is readily understandable. Violence is inevitable, as we have established, in any fairly dense population where the numbers of people are such that informal kin coercion loses its force and where there is no third-party arbitrator to step in and prevent fighting when naturally aggressive human beings differ strongly over an issue. But why does the violence spread to include so many others?

On one level it is perhaps understandable that kin become embroiled in any fight; after all, it is difficult to envisage a man's relatives standing by while he is beaten up or killed. This would not only offend against the supportive sentiment that relatives the world over feel for one another but also offend against a cardinal value of Melanesian society – the equivalence principle which we have previously established as central to acephalous orders. If one man physically assaults another, he is trying to force him to comply with his wishes. He is treating him as less than equal, attempting to subject him to his will. Here we come across another paradox: while such behaviour may be inevitable given the acephalous structure of Melanesian society, it is also an attack on the fiercely egalitarian ethic central to the society's identity. In order to understand warfare in Melanesia we need to answer the question of how societies resolve this paradox. The key to this understanding is the principle of revenge, which dictates the behaviour of the Yali and other Melanesians when conflicts erupt.

The Yali, like all inhabitants of Melanesia, are taught from birth to place a high value on revenge – to believe that they have a moral obligation to wreak vengeance on anyone who seriously injures or maliciously wounds and kills one of their kin. When a killing occurs, for example, the Yali perform a special ritual that underlines their resolve to seek revenge. They tear some flesh from the corpse of their slain relative while it lies on its cremation pyre and attach this to an arrow. They then stalk as near as they dare to the killer's or enemy arrow-stem man's village and fire the arrow towards it or, better, into it. This, the Yali believe, ensures a revenge killing when they retaliate. Men on the killer's side prepare an arrow too, attaching pig fat to it and shooting it into the forest to protect themselves from illness inflicted by the slain person's ghost.

The desire to retaliate violently is not felt as a hot emotion by all those who take up arms, or even by the majority of those who join in the hostilities. They may experience moral outrage and indignation but not a strong urge for revenge. They mobilise because of the value which they have been taught to invest in vengeance. We have to account, then, for this emphasis on revenge and we have already foreshadowed the answer. Revenge is an integral aspect of the acephalous political order. It is a bastion against any person's physically dominating others and subjecting them to his will. It keeps political power beyond the reach of human beings, so that it cannot evolve into institutionalised authoritative offices. The institutionalisation of retaliation is one of the forces that keeps this society stateless and democratic. Any person who tries to force another to comply with his wishes when they confront each other over some issue – who attempts to force a settlement in his favour and seriously wounds or kills the other party – instantly faces a number of people mobilised to wreak vengeance. The killer's relatives in turn unite to fight not only because in all probability they think their side in the right in the homicidal confrontation but also to defend themselves, for they are all fair game for settling the blood account.

We can speculate on how such physically coercive behaviour, if unchecked by the revenge sanction, could undermine the egalitarian political order. Initially some strong and wily individuals might manipulate and then dominate others by force, coercing them to do as they said. If this happened the stateless order, with its emphasis on the equal rights of all persons to determine their own actions, would collapse, and those exercising power over others would consolidate their positions into governmental offices giving them legitimate authority to rule. We cannot know what form such a state would take, but some centralised hierarchical order would replace the current acephalous one. Revenge is an inevitable extension of the equivalence ethic that pervades everyday life, expressed blackly as a balance of deaths. It is noteworthy that this striving for blood-debt equivalence sustains the political equivalence of individuals in the context of a balance between conflicting social processes.

Cannibalism

The Yali expand further on the all-important principle of revenge. They do not stop at killing enemies in vengeance; they eat them, too. They have lifted the art of revenge to a high level in cannibalism, and, replete with vengeful symbolism, it is their nemesis. Warriors try in *soli* warfare to snatch the bodies of enemies to eat or, failing that, if they think they are in danger of a counterattack and need to retreat quickly, they hack off their limbs to carry back home. The killers present the human flesh to kin who have lost a relative in the fighting, whose death the corpse avenges. The avenged's kin reciprocate with a salt-seasoned cooked pig, and they present further pigs later, which the killer-recipients repay in turn.

There is dancing and singing in celebration of the revenge and the cannibalistic feast (Plates 12.3 and 12.4). The recipients butcher the corpse, lopping off the arms and legs and splitting the torso in two along the sternum and spine, and they carefully remove the flesh from the head. They put the flesh in an earth oven to cook, except for some titbits

Plate 12.3   Grasping bows and arrows, chanting men parade around a mound
heaped over an earth oven of the kind used to cook human victims of
cannibalistic feasts.

Plate 12.4　Women perform a dance in which they rush to-and-fro around the earth mound heaped over an oven while its contents cook.

which they roast over an open fire. When it is cooked, the 'owners of the body' distribute cuts of flesh to relatives and friends of the person avenged by the corpse in a socially salient exchange of meat similar to that at a pig kill (see chapter 6). An exchange at this time reaffirms the social network weakened by the death of one of its members. The large bones of the victim they collect after the feast and put in a nearby tree to remind everyone of the event.

When asked, the Yali maintain that they eat enemies because it is their custom adding that human flesh makes a tasty meal. Some writers, attempting to go beyond these indigenous explanations of cannibalism, have argued that it has a nutritional compulsion, supplying people with needed protein, rather like pigs. This is a difficult line to defend. It has been pointed out, for instance, that the number of corpses eaten by cannibals is not nutritionally significant and that to make it so a cannibal population would have to eat its own number in a year, which would amount to an unsustainable force of depopulation. Furthermore, cannibals I have spoken to around Lake Kutubu maintain, in contrast to the Yali, that they found human flesh rich, describing it as relatively pale and fatty and adding that it made many of them sick. Beyond this, people living in ecologically similar regions in Melanesia and on the same diets (for example Western Highlanders) are not cannibals. If the practice of cannibalism related directly to dietary needs, we would expect those with similar diet deficiencies to resort, if not to the same remedy at least to comparable ones to supplement their protein intake. Instead we find cannibals living in thinly populated regions with fairly good supplies of animal protein (e.g. the Kiwai [chapter 2]) and noncannibals in densely populated areas where they subsist largely on vegetable foods (e.g. the Maring [chapter 3]).

The eating of enemies relates to the cultural importance of the revenge obligation. The behaviour of the Yali indicates clearly that for them cannibalism is an aspect of revenge. What little ritual attends one of their cannibalistic feasts relates to it. After decapitating the corpse, for instance, they pin its mouth and eyes closed with skewers made from the bones of opaque bats' wings to blind the deceased's ghost and prevent it from guiding relatives back to exact revenge. Similarly, people wrap the head in fig leaves, and then drag it around on a length of vine while others shoot reeds into it; this ensures them future revenge killings. The songs they sing during the feast (Koch 1970b: 51) also express their vengeful intentions:

> Your brothers, may they come! We shall cook them!
> Your sons, may they come! We shall cook them!
> Your mother's kinsmen, may they come! We shall cook them!
> Those with bad eyes, may they come! We shall cook them!
> Those with bad noses, may they come! We shall cook them!
> Those with bad legs, may they come! We shall cook them!

The day after the cannibalistic feast, those who have shared in the meal exorcise the victim's ghost so that it can do them no harm, coaxing it to return to its own territory, vigorously exhaling in that direction, forcing the victim's breath out of their bodies, finally ritually blocking the path in the direction of the victim's village to prevent his ghost from returning with a revenge party.

Revenge is foremost in the Yali's mind. Their cannibalism is replete with vengeful symbolism and meaning; 'the eating of a slain enemy . . . [is] a symbolic expression of spite incorporated in an act of supreme vengeance' (Koch 1970b: 55). It is hard to imagine a more devastating and effective manner in which to exact revenge. A pertinent question is why we have not found cannibalism everywhere in Melanesia, given the value people put on revenge throughout the region. Another intriguing question, given the bellicose and war-like environment in which Melanesians live, is how, besides inculcating an unwavering respect for revengeful action, they instil in men the high regard for warriorhood that is essential to any community's continued social existence.

FURTHER READING

The ethnographic material on which this account draws is:

K. F. Koch, 1974 *War and peace in Jalémó*. Cambridge: Harvard University Press.

K. F. Koch, 1970a 'Cannibalistic revenge in Jalé warfare.' *Natural History.* 79: 41–50.

K. F. Koch, 1970b 'Warfare and anthropophagy in Jalé society.' *Bijdragen Taal-Volkenkunde.* 126:37–58.

See also:

K. G. Heider, 1970 *The Dugum Dani*. Chicago: Aldine.

K. G. Heider, 1979 *Grand Valley Dani: Peaceful warriors*. New York: Holt, Rinehart and Winston.

R. Gardner and K. G. Heider, 1969 *Gardens of war*. London: Andre Deutsch.

On warfare elsewhere in Melanesia see:

C. R. Hallpike, 1977 *Bloodshed and vengeance in the Papuan mountains*. Oxford: Oxford University Press.

S. Harrison, 1993 *The mask of war*. Manchester: Manchester University Press.

M. Meggitt, 1977 *Blood is their argument*. Palo Alto: Mayfield.

FILMS

Dead birds. Harvard University, Peabody Museum Film Study Center.
The Yali of Moon Mountain. The Discovery Channel (US).

13   Initiation rites on the Sepik River

The ceremonies found around the world that anthropologists commonly call initiation rites are often prolonged and dramatic compared with the brief, effervescent celebrations that we arrange to mark coming of age. One reason put forward for these rituals in Melanesia is that they promote a ferocious male ethos and encourage harshness and disdain of physical pain, important traits in the context of the violent acephalous Melanesian political environment. Throughout Melanesia we find initiates thoroughly frightened and subjected to terrifying ordeals as adults introduce them to some of the secrets of their ritual world. Coming of age in Melanesia is no mean feat. Initiates have flexible canes thrust down their gullets to induce vomiting and bleeding; are beaten with sticks, thorny branches or stinging nettles, have holes savagely pierced in their nasal septa or ear lobes to accommodate pig-tusk, sea-shell or other ornaments, have rolls of abrasive leaves thrust violently up and down in their nostrils to induce copious bleeding; and find their penes slashed, frequently circumcised, and even shot through the foreskin with arrows.

Rites of passage

Initiation rituals fall into a broad category of rites which mark changes of status – from single to married, for instance, or from childless to parent. We customarily call these rituals of transition rites of passage after van Gennep (1909). As he observed, 'life itself means to separate and to be reunited, to change form and condition, to die and to be reborn. It is to act and to cease, to wait and rest, and then to begin acting again, but in a different way. And there are always new thresholds to cross' (van Gennep 1960: 189). He pointed out, in a comparative study, that when human beings around the world pass from one status to another they mark their passage with rites which are strikingly familiar. These rites have three phases, elaborated to varying extents in different contexts and different cultures, labelled (1) rites of separation, (2) transition rites, and (3) rites of incorporation (Figure 13.1). Anthro-

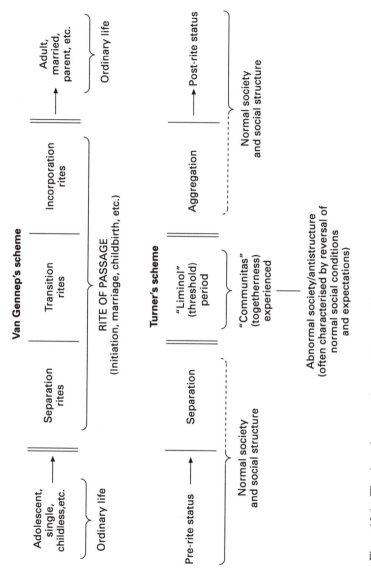

Figure 13.1 The rites of passage after van Gennep and Turner.

pologists have subsequently elaborated on this scheme, with some terminological changes. They have tended to emphasise the middle rite of transition, which Turner (1969), for example, calls the 'liminal' period (from *liminaire* for 'threshold', after van Gennep). This is where the emphasis of rites of passage occurs, Turner argues; participants in them frequently experience 'communitas', a feeling of togetherness, often heightened by abnormal social conditions (or what he calls anti-structure) and reversal of expected behaviour (during initiations, for instance, the terrorising of initiates by relatives and the imposition of ordeals).

An illustration may help to put this abstract scheme in cultural context. University students undergo a rite of passage that we might call an 'initiation to degree' (Figure 13.2). First, they experience separation; isolating themselves from normal life to study and revise. Second comes the transition, during which they must endure periods of extreme separation cloistered in halls taking final examinations. A camaraderie develops between them and their peers at this stressful time as they are drawn together by their ordeal and their abnormal social circumstances – a manifestation of 'communitas'. Finally comes the incorporation, when the initiates return to society as graduates. Graduation is a phase that we unhesitatingly recognise as a ritual, when high-ranking officials of the university, wearing full ceremonial academic regalia, with due pomp and circumstance publicly admit those who have passed their initiation ordeals to a degree at their institution.

In our investigation of rituals of this genre in Melanesia, we shall take as our ethnographic example the initiation rites of the Iatmul, who live on the wide, meandering Sepik River, which rises in the central cordillera of New Guinea and, after flowing across very extensive low-lying fen-like flood plains, enters the Pacific on the north coast (Map 13.1). The people living here have adapted to a riverine existence: their houses are on stilts to protect them from the river's seasonal flooding, and they travel nearly everywhere in dugout canoes. They subsist by fishing, processing sago from the palms that thrive in their region's swamps, and growing crops, notably yams, in gardens established on riverine mud flats. The climate is hot and sticky. And the insect population, which includes malarial mosquitoes, makes what is a difficult environment even worse; people spend the sultry nights cooped up in large tightly woven sago-bast bags to avoid them.

The society is organised into totemic patrilineal clans divided into two moieties. The people live in villages adjacent to the waterways. They are renowned for their men's cult houses, large and magnificent constructions furnished with carved masks and other sculptures now highly

Rite of passage: Initiation to degree

Separation	*Transition*	*Incorporation*
Seclusion and revision	Examination ordeals	Graduation ceremony

Undergraduate → ... → Graduate

Figure 13.2   Initiation to an academic degree as a rite of passage.

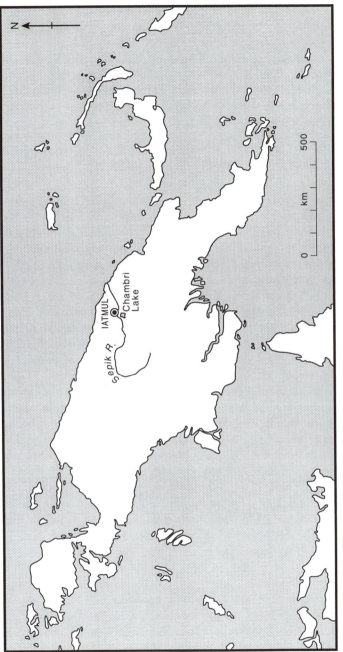

Map 13.1   The Iatmul of the Sepik River.

valued in the Western art world. Hostilities were traditionally common, and ornamented head trophies featured as ritual objects in the men's houses, along with slit-gongs. Their initiation rites centre on these cult houses and the revelation to initiates of the ritual objects they contain. The crocodile, an animal which inhabits the Sepik River, features as a symbol throughout the ritual, which focuses on gender identity and relationships. Here again, the interpretation may bear the particular ethnographer's impress, this time in giving unusual emphasis to emotional issues.

Iatmul initiation

An initiation is set in train by the novices' fathers 'calling for the crocodile', as the Iatmul refer to their challenge to those responsible for initiating their sons. By accepting a payment of food and betel nut (a narcotic-like palm fruit chewed throughout Melanesia), they signal their readiness to arrange the ceremonies. They erect a fence of palm and other fronds around the men's cult house, and they construct a model of a crocodile's head around the entrance through the screen (the novices having to pass through the teeth-lined jaws to enter the initiating enclosure behind). They decorate water drums for the coming ritual. During the preparations they observe a taboo on sexual intercourse and reside in the men's house; if they did not the wounds they inflicted on the novices during the ritual would suppurate. One evening when all is ready, some men sound the crocodile rhythm on the slit-gongs in the men's house, and throughout the following night the initiators dance the crocodile procession around the ceremonial ground, forming two lines with one man leading as the crocodile's head. They pass back and forth through the crocodile-jaw entrance in their leafy barrier. The novices dance in procession with their parents: all the participants intone songs featuring the names of clan crocodile totems.

In the morning, the initiators form two rows inside the enclosure and hit the naked novices as they enter through the crocodile's jaws with their fathers, who protect their sons and lead them on to break down another fence behind which are the decorated water drums. This marks the shift from separation to transition (Figure 13.3). The initiators take the novices and, after washing them, scarify their bodies. The novice, stretched out on an upturned canoe and supported and comforted by a male relative on his mother's side, lies first supine while an operator cuts rows of short nicks on his chest with a bamboo sliver and then prone while the operation is repeated on his back and buttocks (Plates 13.1 and 13.2). When healed the scars will resemble the horny protuberances

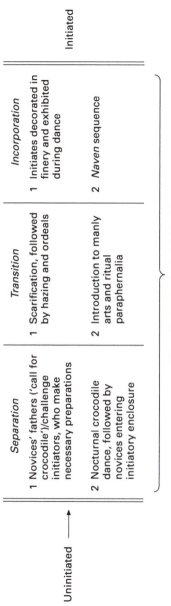

Separation	*Transition*	*Incorporation*
1 Novices' fathers ('call for crocodile')/challenge initiators, who make necessary preparations	1 Scarification, followed by hazing and ordeals	1 Initiates decorated in finery and exhibited during dance
2 Nocturnal crocodile dance, followed by novices entering initiatory enclosure	2 Introduction to manly arts and ritual paraphernalia	2 *Naven* sequence

Uninitiated ⟶   Initiated ⟶

Rite of passage: Iatmul initiation

Figure 13.3   Iatmul initiation as a rite of passage.

Plate 13.1   Stretched out on an upturned canoe and supported by a maternal
relative, a young man endures scarification to give his body a knobbly,
crocodile-skin-like appearance like that of the men initiating him.

of a crocodile's skin. The people say that the community's ancestral
crocodile is responsible for 'eating the backs' of novices and that after
the ceremony it returns to a peaceful sleep.

After this painful ordeal, the initiators may lead the smarting novices
to water and suddenly and violently push them in. The relatives who
have been sustaining them throughout lead them back to the men's
house, where they apply a soothing sap to their wounds that promotes
their healing into raised cicatrices. The novices' trials are not over
however. There follows a week or so of torment for them as their
initiators subject them to a range of cruel tricks and painful harassment.
These include being tricked into drinking quantities of filthy water and
having their faces severely slapped until they are spitting blood. A
masked figure is responsible for the face slapping, pretending to divine

Plate 13.2   A blood-stained novice, seated on a canoe keel used previously as an operating table, eats a meal that includes the baked sago in the basket.

that the novices have stolen things and hitting them in punishment. On some days the novices are forbidden to eat or drink. The initiators inspect their mouths to see that they observe these food prohibitions: they force open their mouths with a piece of crocodile bone, invariably to discover that the boys' mouths are unclean and viciously jab the bone into their gums until they bleed (Plate 13.3). When the initiates are

Plate 13.3   An elaborately masked man torments young initiates in the men's house, inspecting their mouths for evidence of forbidden food consumption and jabbing a sharpened object into their gums.

allowed to eat, they must not touch their food with their fingers but have to pick it up with small bamboo tongs or a folded leaf. The bullying concludes with a ritual washing of the novices' tender healing backs, which the initiators scrub and douse with cold water until the boys are sobbing in agony. The transition stage then enters a second phase, during which the initiators hunt for game and collect considerable quantities of food to 'fatten up' and strengthen the novices and also instruct them in various manly and esoteric matters. They 'show' them how to make bat-fur penis sheaths and cassowary-feather headdresses, how to carve and dance, how to sweep out and cut the grass around the men's house, and so on, but they carry out this instruction in a facetious way. When instructing them in sweeping, for instance, one of the initiators makes an enormous broom and pretends to sweep away the novitiate rubbish. Besides the water drums, the initiators introduce the boys to the sacred flutes and the bullroarers that contain the spirits of the novice-eating crocodiles. They also tell them stories introducing totemic and sacred knowledge.

The revelation of ritual secrets to the initiates suggests the existence of a hierarchy, of those in the know and those ignorant, which sits uneasily with the Melanesian emphasis on egalitarianism. The sacred knowledge associated with men's house cults and known only to initiated men suggests inequalities between elder males and younger ones and women. It certainly marks a difference between them, although whether this amounts to inequality in the marxist–feminist sense is questionable (see chapters 8 and 9). Among the Iatmul it would be a distortion to imply the existence of classes, for every male eventually comes into the knowledge. And everywhere we accept that children, as minors, are different and have yet to learn about life. We have established that while women and men occupy different culturally defined domains – their worldview and social life being predicated upon this – it is quite another thing to interpret this as one party being unequal to the other.

Six to eight weeks after their 'crocodile-eating' scarification, the boys are prepared for the incorporation stage of the rites. Until this time they have lived secluded from everyday life, spending much time in the men's house and going about hidden under cowl-like capes with men warning women and uninitiated children to hide by swirling bullroarers when they go abroad. On the day they emerge from seclusion, after receiving various gifts from their initiators which mark their manly status (such as lime spatula and box, and drum), the novices are decorated and led out to stand in the ceremonial ground, where admiring women dance around them. About this time a *naven* sequence is staged. While strictly speaking not a rite of passage, the *naven* is a ceremony that celebrates some achievement and consequent informal change in status. The principal actors in it are usually male relatives on the maternal side (mother's brothers and others classified as such) of the person who has accomplished the act to be marked, together perhaps with other relatives (predominantly female, including mother, sister, father's sister, elder brother's wife, mother's brother's wife, and wife's brother). They wear the dress of the other sex, men aping decrepit widows and women swaggering warriors, and they assault the achiever in a variety of ways – ducking him, beating him and various others of his kin, rubbing their buttocks up and down his legs, tossing lime powder into his face – depending on the nature of the act celebrated and the wealth exchanged by those taking part. A central feature of the *naven* is wealth exchange; mother's brothers and wife's brothers present the achiever and his father with food and pigs, which they reciprocate with shell wealth and ornaments.

Psychological issues

We can approach this rite-of-passage behaviour from three interconnected viewpoints (after Bateson 1936): psychological, sociological and symbolic. The psychological approach considers attitudes of mind and gender issues. We can appreciate how attending and participating in many initiations throughout their lives and similar vicious events such as those associated with warfare and head-hunting might condition and reinforce harsh, warrior-like attitudes, producing what the Iatmul call 'hot' men. We have to imagine what it must be like to be cruelly terrorised when young with the compliance of one's close relatives, including parents, and then some years later to find oneself in the bully role, with peers expecting, even urging, one to haze likewise a cohort of youngsters. It understandably promotes a ruthless and reckless disposition.

The interpretive approach current in anthropology views initiation rites as expressing gender as a cosmological principle, reflecting a worldview in which male and female elements are structurally opposed. They suggest that whereas those aspects of life associated with women are natural and innate, robustly coming into being, those associated with men are cultural and tenuous, demanding ritual interventions to create and maintain them. We can even interpret some aspects of initiation rites as necessary to make men, to define and strengthen their masculine identity; this idea is made explicit in some societies where initiates ingest semen during ritualised homosexual acts to build up their manhood.

We see in initiation the detachment of young males from the female mother-centred world in which they have grown up and their assimilation into the male, father-centred one in which they will live out their adult lives. The two worlds have different emotional emphases. The women's one is predictable, private, quiet, unostentatious and even jolly on occasion, whereas the men's is unpredictable, public, histrionic, proud and sometimes frightening. They are virtual opposites. During the first phase of the transition stage, when the initiators scarify and haze the novices, they refer to themselves as 'husbands' and to the boys as their 'wives'. Here they are expressing their contempt for the boys, using kin terminology not only to associate them with the male-enfeebling women's world to which they are still emotionally attached but also to classify them with their wives, towards whom, of all women, men feel wary and even sometimes hostile. Although they rarely if ever treat their wives as violently as they do novices, their bullying of novitiate 'wives' during initiation suggests that some men may occasionally desire to do so. In any case, their terrifyingly malicious behaviour demonstrates their vicious disregard of women's values and violently knocks any association with them out of young men. When they have aggressively expunged this female connection, in the second phase of the transition stage the initiators adopt a parental role feeding and instructing the novices. During this time they call the boys their 'children', marking their induction into the men's house world, where no one countenances any female timidity.

The marked distinction between male and female domains is, as we have seen, common throughout Melanesia. It is not invariably associated with initiation ceremonies of the kind described here. In many parts of the highlands men express it as fear of the supposedly toxic properties of menstrual blood, which gives rise to elaborate systems of taboos and rites to protect them and reflects the separation of their social sphere from women's (see chapter 9). This pronounced cultural differentiation between the sexes, which manifests itself in a variety of ways in different places, may be interpreted as another expression of a distinction cited previously as central to Melanesian society – between men as transactors and women as producers – and all that this implies for political power in acephalous contexts.

This marked gender differentiation is often seen, in the Freudian psychoanalytic tradition, as essential, in hostile, warlike environments like that of Melanesia, to ensure the survival of social groups. Initiation incorporates young men into the aggressive male domain. Some writers argue that at a deep level it breaks the mother bond which would otherwise persist for life and contaminate the ruthless male ideal. Others interpret the emphasis on different cultural domains for the sexes, of which initiation is an exaggerated expression, not as an aspect of personality and emotional management but more as a manifestation of the deep-rooted unconscious inferiority men feel with regard to the natural reproductive capacity of women. Men invented and participate in initiations it is suggested, to promote the belief that they are essential to the reproduction and continuance of their society. They prohibit women as natural rather than cultural reproducers of life, from taking part and even accuse them of dangerous, subversive intents.

Sociological issues

The sociological approach to initiation rites centres on their significance for forging social identity and promoting social integration. The initiation experience operates on an individual level, contributing to the moulding of the social identity of persons. Before initiation males are juveniles; after it they are adult persons, with all that that change of status implies for rights and obligations. Their masculine identity is impressed upon them. The implication is not that they all have the same perception of or assume the same roles. Personhood is a more individual quality. Different life experiences (see chapter 4) contribute to the making of markedly different persons. It would be incorrect to suppose that during initiation all novices have similar experiences or perceptions of events. It is probable, for example, that the initiators treat younger boys and timid and popular ones more gently than older and particularly obstreperous and unruly ones. The extent to which their relative-guardians defend novices also probably depends on similar issues. The actors are not picking up standard norms that will guide their behaviour, they differ in their perceptions of the social world and their place in it.

It is possible to argue on another level that initiation not only develops a warlike personality in individuals but also bonds the warriors into a strong group. The shared experience of having endured the trauma of initiation in one another's company, the sense of 'communitas' felt, breeds an enduring ethic of togetherness which living together and cooperating in the men's house cements throughout life. Being 'eaten' at the same time by the crocodile ancestor spirit creates a substantial emotional bond among those involved and gives them a sense of solidarity important to the survival of their community in a war-like world. They can rely on each other's support in any violent encounter.

It can be suggested on yet another level that initiation rites socially integrate entire Iatmul villages, which are large by Melanesian standards, numbering up to 1,000 people. Preventing such large populations from violently splitting apart is a considerable problem in an acephalous polity (see chapter 6). The Iatmul achieve this in some measure through a social system in which communities are split into two for certain purposes. They double the integrating effect achieved through this dual organisation by having two independent cross-cutting moiety systems; one controlling marriage and the other initiation.

The moieties governing marriage are made up of patrilineally defined totemic clans. The general rule in Iatmul society is that a man should marry a woman from the opposite moiety. The prescription of actual marriage partners occurs at the clan level, where an elaborate system of preferential rules specifies the ideal kinswoman for a man to marry. Iatmul say that men should exchange clan sisters and that preferred spouses should fall into the kin categories of father's sister's daughter, father's mother's brother's son's daughter, or father's mother's brother's daughter. These rules structure ties of alliance between clans (chapter 9). Alliance theory distinguishes between preferential and prescribed marriage rules, which commonly centre on marriages between cross cousins (a man and his mother's brother's daughter or father's sister's daughter) and less often between parallel cousins (a man and his mother's sister's daughter or father's brother's daughter). We can appreciate how dividing up a society like this, making each segment dependent on the other for marriage, and the consequent elaborate structuring of uterine and agnatic relationships has an overall integrating effect, even when many marriages, as among the Iatmul, do not actually follow the ideal rules.

The moieties governing initiation are called *Kishit* and *Miwot*. Each is divided into two sections, giving four groups of three or four cohorts each, depending on the stage in the initiatory cycle (Figure 13.4). These cohorts are made up of men of about the same age. They alternate from one moiety to the other – when Cohort 1 is in Kishit, Cohort 2 will be in Miwot, Cohort 3 in Kishit, and so on. Over time they replace one another in the hierarchy, and therefore when all Kishit Cohort 1 members are dead Miwot Cohort 2 becomes Cohort 1, by which time a new Cohort 7 of youngsters will have formed on the Kishit side to replace Miwot Cohort 6 when it moves up to become Cohort 5. The members of any cohort refer to those in the one immediately senior to them in the other moiety as 'elder brothers'. It is these men who will have initiated them. And as there are two matched sections in either moiety, at any initiation there may be two sets of initiators and novices. According to this system of alternating seniority, men from either moiety take it in turns to initiate boys from the other one. This arrangement interdigitates the men in any community into a series of

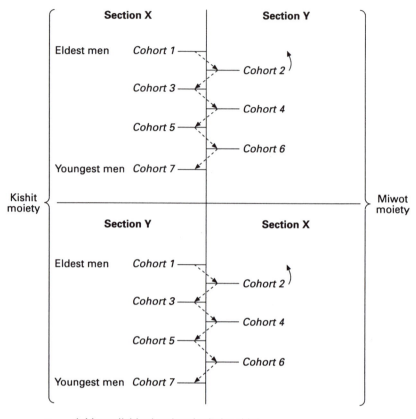

--- ► --- Initiates ('elder brothers' relationship)

As *Cohorts 1* die off *Cohorts 7* are formed. When *Cohorts 1* are
extinct, *Cohorts 8* become new senior cohorts (new
Cohorts 1 = alternating seniority).

Figure 13.4   Iatmul moiety and section system.

structured groups, each dependent on the others for its place. Further-more, these groups cut across the other social groupings by which Iatmul society is organised (for example, members of the same family or clan are in different initiatory groups, depending on their age). Again, we can surmise the significant socially integrative effect.

In addition to the moiety system there is the *naven* ceremony, which structures participants according to other rules. It is relations between affines that the *naven* particularly strengthens, these being the weakest relationships in Iatmul society. It is along affinal lines that communities break apart, the patrilineal clans that comprise them proving more solidary. (Ideally this should result in a split between the marriage moieties, but this does not occur because many marriages are contracted contrary to the rules.) That wealth exchange is a central feature of the *naven* is not surprising, given its socially integrative significance (see chapter 6). Among the Iatmul exchanges not only attend the *naven* sequence but also occur when the fathers of novices challenge the initiators in the opposite moiety to stage an initiation and again after these men have scarified their sons. Again we find sociopolitical ex-change featuring centrally in the organisation of a Melanesian polity.

Symbolic issues

The symbolic approach looks at initiation for the cultural intelligence that it communicates. A symbol is anything that represents by cultural association (i.e. not by its intrinsic features) something other than itself (for instance, as for Christians a cross represents Jesus Christ). It can express things about the thing that it symbolises (for instance, as a cross demands reverence of believers), and cryptically convey condensed messages, especially when arranged with others in some culturally sanctioned sequence. The study of symbols in other cultures is informed by the anthropological theory of structuralism, and it is important because many people do not depict their emotions or represent their social world in words. Instead they communicate about and intellectua-lise on these matters using symbols, arranging and juxtaposing them to convey ideas, often on the subconscious plane.

Symbols are commonly polysemous, that is have import on several levels simultaneously, whereas we have separately traced the psycho-logical and sociological aspects of Iatmul initiation behaviour and comments on it, Iatmul symbolism embraces all of these at once. For example, there is considerable crocodile imagery throughout Iatmul initiation, and we might surmise that on one level this multifaceted symbol encourages the development of harsh male personalities, com-

Plate 13.4   Two men stand facing one another and play a pair of phallic-like antiphonal sacred flutes.

municating the desirability of ferocious crocodile-like emotions and behaviour. On a sociological plane, this knobbly-backed creature, emulated in men's scarification, may represent the unity of those initiated together. The crocodile evokes both of these things simultaneously for initiated men. The sacred flutes that feature in initiations are another prominent symbol. We may interpret these as symbolising the rigid cultural demarcation of men from women enjoined by the entire traumatic initiation sequence, for these instruments, revealed to novices at initiation, are phallic in form and mythological origin, and phallic symbols represent the whole proud belligerent Iatmul male ethos. Furthermore, to move from the individual emotive plane to the collective one, these flutes are highly suggestive of the dual organisation of Iatmul society, men playing them in pairs (Plate 13.4). The flutes have no lateral stops to control pitch, and the intervals between their seven or so notes are too large to produce tunes. The Iatmul overcome this by playing them antiphonally in alternating pairs, one a tone higher than the other, the differences in pitch giving harmonies. When two performers blow in turn, they can play tunes. The Iatmul call the lower-pitched flute the 'elder brother', further suggestive of initiation relations and the dual organisation of society. The flutes are not mere musical instruments; they multifariously invoke and convey things about the cultural order, heightened in salience by the traumatic context in which men are first introduced to them.

While these symbolic interpretations appear neat and convincing, enormous epistemological problems attend them. These centre on the disinclination, even apparent inability, of many people to intellectualise verbally on the symbols they employ and discuss their import as metaphors. It is doubtful, for instance, that many Iatmul would discuss the paired flutes as metaphorically like socially interdigitated moieties or draw the parallel that as paired flutes are essential to play tunes so paired moieties are essential to play out social life or comment that taking away one flute or moiety would mean discord and chaos. (Indeed, it is debatable whether many Iatmul would accept or even comprehend this line of reasoning if it were explained to them.) Even where people can give an exegesis of some symbols they are unlikely to integrate them verbally into the cognitive constructs beloved of anthropologists. We assume that this is a substantive aspect of symbols – to convey things that people are disinclined or unable to put into and interpret in words. We suppose that symbols are effective on a non-verbal, unconscious plane from which anthropologists are intellectually equipped to retrieve them. But the post-modern critique seriously challenges our ability to so interpret other cultures and their symbols. If people are unable to put these matters into words, on what grounds can we legitimately do this on their behalf? We need to exercise great care and intellectual honesty if we are not to end up merely with fanciful imaginings, which is not to argue that symbolic interpretations are not worth the effort.

FURTHER READING

The ethnographic monographs on which this account draws include:

G. Bateson, 1936 *Naven*. Cambridge: Cambridge University Press.

D. B. Gewertz and F. K. Errington, 1991 *Twisted histories, altered contexts*. Cambridge: Cambridge University Press.

S. Harrison, 1990 *Stealing people's names*. Cambridge: Cambridge University Press.

M. Houseman and C. Severi, 1994 *Naven ou Le Donner à voir*. Paris: CNRS-Éditions.

J. Schmid and C. Kocher Schmid, 1992 *Söhne des Krokodils*. Basel: Basler Beiträge zur Ethnologie Band 36.

On initiation elsewhere in Melanesia see:

M. R. Allen, 1967 *Male cults and secret initiations in Melanesia*. Melbourne: Melbourne University Press.

G. H. Herdt (ed.), 1982 *Rituals of manhood*. Berkeley: University of California Press.

G. H. Herdt, 1987 *The Sambia*. Fort Worth : Holt, Rinehart and Winston.

I. Hogbin, 1970 *The island of menstruating men*. Scranton: Chandler.

N. C. Lutkehaus and P. B. Roscoe (eds.), 1995 *Gender rituals: Female initiation in Melanesia*. London: Routledge.

On rites of passage see:

J. La Fontaine, 1985 *Initiation*. Harmondsworth: Penguin.

V. W. Turner, 1969 *The ritual process*. London: Routledge.

A. van Gennep, 1909 (repr. 1977) *The rites of passage*. London: Routledge.

FILMS

Guardians of the flutes. British Broadcasting Corporation Under the Sun Series.

14 Ancestors and illness in the shadow
of the Owen Stanley Range

Throughout Melanesia people believe that the dead return as ghosts, causing their surviving kin to fall ill and sometimes to die. We have a conflation in this belief of what are for us, by and large, two virtually independent fields of experience and knowledge: the religious and the medical. We find again that our conceptual categories are inappropriate to deal with what we find in Melanesia. In the same way that our concepts of economics (chapters 5 and 6) and politics (chapters 7 and 10) demand sympathetic revision to accommodate Melanesian practices, so too do our ideas relating to religion and medicine. These categories, although difficult to apply unambiguously to many other cultures, are nonetheless firmly established in anthropological writing, and we need to review what their study encompasses before investigating their amalgamation in Melanesian practices.

Religion and medicine

The study of religion has a long history in anthropology. Indeed it was the exotic and, to early observers, bizarre beliefs found in other parts of the world that attracted many to the study of so-called primitives or savages and led in part to the founding of the discipline. The literature on the subject is vast. We have to decide what is relevant to Melanesia, notably what we shall understand the term 'religion' to refer to – which is not easy, for Melanesians have no comparable concept which we can attempt to define. Whatever our definition, it will in some senses distort indigenously voiced conceptions, but the attempt has to be made. We broadly understand religion in South-West Pacific contexts to encompass beliefs in non-empirical forces, that is, forces the existence of which we cannot detect with our senses. Many of these forces are of the kind we commonly call spirits. They can intervene, for good or bad, in the lives of human beings, and the living attempt to manipulate or control them through various rites and observances.

The early anthropologists Tylor and Frazer distinguished religion, which centres on beliefs in spirit forces which affect the living and may be appeased through ritual, from magic, which involves the belief that people can control events by certain potent techniques alone. Durkheim and Mauss maintained that religion is collective and functions to integrate a society, whereas magic is an individual matter, people engaging in it for private ends. Malinowski, whose views were strongly coloured by his Melanesian experiences, argued that religion reduces human beings' general feelings of insecurity in an unpredictable world whereas magic helps them, they think, specifically to control events and achieve some particular end. Contemporary anthropologists tend to eschew such distinctions, maintaining that in many parts of the world they interfere with our understanding of what people believe about these matters. Although this is a sound view, motivated to some extent by a wish to avoid belittling connotations of the word 'magic', there is nonetheless something in the early anthropologists' position that is relevant to Melanesia. When people here engage in actions that they believe to have a non-empirical or supernatural effect on events, they may conceive these to result from either spirit-like (religious) or ill-defined ethereal (magical) forces. Rather than impose our own cultural categories beforehand, however, we should try to draw these distinctions out of the ethnography.

The study of medicine in anthropology has a relatively short history. The field now commonly called medical anthropology has taken shape only in the past decade or so. It is characterised by two complementary approaches, which recent research attempts to synthesise:

(1) what people think about disease and how they treat it, the study of ethno-medicine; and

(2) what Western medical science diagnoses their complaints to be, the study of clinical conditions.

The former overlaps considerably with the field of religion in Melanesia, where people believe that their morbidity results from the interference of supernatural forces in their lives and attempt to control these through ritual manipulations. It is the perspective that informs this chapter's ethnographic enquiry into illness. The approach of medical science is quite different and more closely allied to physical than to social anthropology, given its emphasis on the biological condition of subjects (chapter 2). It is in this bio-technological tradition, not in the supernatural realm, that Western medical knowledge is situated, and consequently this approach is founded on our culture's idea of science.

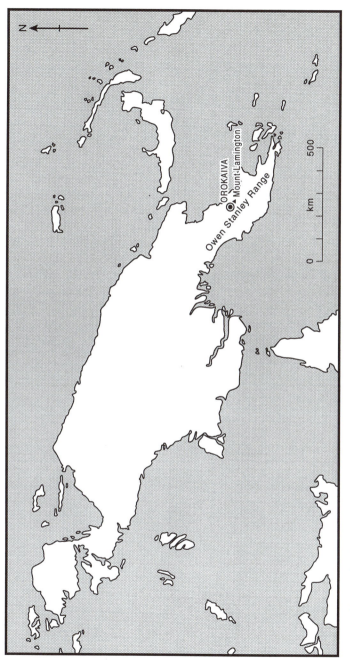

Map 14.1   The Orokaiva and the Owen Stanley Range.

Some pioneering research has been done in Melanesia in biological medicine, the best-known of which is probably the association of the degenerative brain disease *kuru* of the Eastern Highlands of Papua New Guinea with cannibalism (Lindenbaum 1979; Hornabrook 1976). It would be wrong, however, to imply that Melanesians ascribe all illness to supernatural agencies. Their practical as opposed to ritual treatment of many complaints follows sound biological reasoning, according to our science, within the limits of their technologies.

In our review of some Melanesian religico–medical beliefs we shall turn to the Orokaiva of the north-east coast of New Guinea (Map 14.1). They reside in the shadow of the Owen Stanley Range, which forms the eastern tail of the island's central cordillera. The region experiences considerable seismic activity and includes the active volcano Mount Lamington, which erupted in the 1950s with considerable loss of life. The Orokaiva occupy villages on a forested plain with many extensive grassland clearings that rises inland towards the mountains, where it is dissected by rivers and foothills, and runs down to the coast where it ends in extensive swamps. The region is hot, seasonally very wet, and mosquito-plagued. The Orokaiva's staple is taro, supplemented with other food plants, such as sago, yam, breadfruit and coconut. Fishing also supplies a significant proportion of their diet, especially on the coast. Orokaiva society features patrilineally constituted totemic clans, and people subscribe to an elaborate system of totemic observances centring on plant emblems called *heratu*. The wealth they exchange includes feather, boar's-tusk, dogs'-teeth and sea-shell ornaments and pigs. They have a war-like and cannibalistic reputation, having fiercely resisted European penetration of their region. They initiate young men, revealing ritual objects and knowledge to the novices, and believe that spirit forces are implicated in sickness.

Spirit forces

Orokaiva religious beliefs and many of their medical practices centre on two spirit concepts, *asisi* and *sovai*. The representation of these beliefs is exceedingly difficult, as Williams (1930) makes clear, revealing a sensitive awareness long ago of today's much vaunted post-modern conundrums but pushing on in a practical manner with the ethnographic job in hand as an officer of the colonial administration. According to the Orokaiva, all living things, animals and plants, have *asisi*. They call their shadows and reflections *asisi*, and another manifestation of the *asisi* is the image of a person dreamed of; the *asisi* has temporarily left the person's corporeal self in sleep to visit the dreamer.

The ethnographer glosses *asisi* as 'spiritual substitute', that is, the immaterial counterpart of living matter, which coexists with its material aspect and sometimes substitutes for its concrete representation. The *asisi* of things may impinge on human life in many ways. A man attributed a stomach ache to his having eaten some unwholesome sugarcane, saying that it was only painful when the wind blew and swayed the cane in his garden. It was the *asisi* of the plant he had consumed that connected his stomach ache with swaying sugarcane; the cane existed for him in his body simultaneously with its tangible existence in his garden.

The *sovai*, in contrast, is associated with dead creatures. When they are living, human beings possess *asisi* like other living matter: at death they become *sovai*. It is tempting to equate the *asisi* spirit force with the *sovai* one, as the living essence that survives death, but although they are closely associated this is not entirely the case. For instance, on occasion *sovai* may leave living people when they are sick and then return to them. However this only happens when they are near death, and we can legitimately think of *sovai* as spirits of the dead. The Orokaiva vary in their explanations of how and when the *sovai* departs from a corpse and even give contradictory interpretations; it may occur in a flash when the deceased takes his/her last breath, or it may be piecemeal, over a period of several weeks. The Orokaiva say that the maggots which inexplicably appear on a corpse and then disappear are manifestations of the departing *sovai*, and widows, who slept for a period under a shelter on their husband's shallow grave (Plate 14.1) would occasionally winkle out the *sovai* maggots, release them nearby in the forest where they would disappear.

It is apparent that, whereas *asisi* exist together with the physical corporeality of living things, *sovai* exist on their own. They may be invisible and ethereal, when they betray their existence by strange noises or the movement of things. Sometimes they become ghosts which, visible to the living, resemble the deceased. At other times they may take the form of an animal, such as a wallaby or a pig, a lizard or a fish; the Orokaiva particularly identify strange or abnormal creatures (for instance, a snake that wriggles oddly) as *sovai*. The exact relationship of the *sovai* to the animal is ambiguous: some people maintain that the animal *is* the *sovai*, but the belief that if the creature is killed the *sovai* survives in some other form suggests that the animal is separate. At other times *sovai* appear as fiends or hobgoblins, monstrous hairy and fanged forest creatures that attack people when alone in the bush. Finally, there are the *sovai* of legends and the Orokaiva are undecided whether they emerged long ago from deceased humans.

Plate 14.1   A group of mourners on the Embogo River sit around the shelter erected over a grave.

Although *sovai* may appear anywhere at any time, the Orokaiva believe that they frequent specific localities, which they call '*sovai* villages'. These are usually natural features such as hillocks, pools or rock outcrops. The *sovai* roam about from these bases, as living people travel away from their villages. Those of the recently dead haunt their old villages in particular, and those living there do what they can to induce them to leave, notably in the series of mortuary rites following a death. The Orokaiva are unhappy at the prospect of having them in the neighbourhood because they consider them intensely dangerous, capable of causing sickness and even death.

Occasionally the *sovai* may help the living (for example, in hunting), but usually they do them harm (e.g. hinder the hunter, ruin crops with a blight, or even cause natural disasters such as earthquakes). The malicious act most frequently attributed to *sovai* is causing human sickness, and Orokaiva ascribe illness to their malevolent interference more than to any other cause. They may enter the body in immaterial form, causing the person to become ill. They may even be held responsible for sickness by mere evil influence, for example, by touching food, and if someone is unfortunate enough to have ingested a *sovai* in the shape of an animal, then illness is almost inevitable. *Sovai* may also assault people in the forest in the guise of monsters and cause them injury.

The Orokaiva understandably have mixed feelings about the *sovai*.

They grieve for deceased relatives and remember them with affection and respect, but they fear *sovai* and regard them with aversion. The latter emotions appear to be uppermost in their minds: 'on the whole the Orokaiva regards his relatives and friends after their death as enemies' (Williams 1930: 283). The Orokaiva also believe that sickness results from sorcery, which demands curative actions of its own (chapter 11). The Orokaiva also accept many minor ailments as inevitable rather than attributable to *sovai* or sorcery attack, and they apply common-sense remedies to these without recourse to supernatural manipulations.

Dealing with spirits

It is on these spirit conceptions that Orokaiva religion and a considerable part of their lore relating to the treatment of sickness centres. When Orokaiva fall sick they withdraw from everyday life, often leaving their *sovai*-frequented village to escape the malign forces there and secluding themselves elsewhere for quiet and rest. This behaviour not only has these therapeutic effects, but also signals to relatives the need for curative action – even obliges them, in a sense, to ensure that the sick person recovers. The Orokaiva conceive of most illnesses, which they call *ambu*, as intrusive elements that enter the body and may leave it again and that may pass from one person to another. The Orokaiva remove the *sovai* presence that causes illness in one of two ways: they make it offerings to persuade it to leave or try to expel it by various ritual techniques.

Offerings of valuables, such as feather or other ornaments or food, are commonly made to appease the *sovai* and persuade them to cease making someone ill. 'It is the very essence of Orokaiva religion to placate them' (Williams 1930: 287). They suspend the wealth on verandahs or at other points in the village for the *sovai*, which, if they find it acceptable, cease their attack and allow the sick person to recover. The Orokaiva also make offerings to ward off disease-inflicting *sovai* attacks. Occasionally people leave gifts for the *sovai* around the village. Sometimes they erect little platforms on which to put offerings, with ladders leading up to them for the *sovai* to gain access (Plate 14.2). At other times men go around the village beating drums and carrying either a pig lashed to a pole or morsels of cooked food, stopping at intervals to put the animal down or deposit some food, while loudly advertising that they are for the *sovai*.

The long drawn-out series of mortuary ceremonies practised by the Orokaiva is also intended to placate the *sovai* of the recently dead, which they believe to be particularly virulent and dangerous (Plates 14.3

Plate 14.2   A woman of the Kamusi region placing a food offering for the
sovai on a *wawa* platform decorated with bark-cloth streamers.

Plate 14.3   An Orokaiva woman of the Mambare region wearing 'widow's weeds', a vest of Job's tears seeds.

Plate 14.4   Celebration of the end of the period of seclusion imposed on
widows following a husband's death in a village on the Mambare River.

and 14.4). A funeral is a dangerous time for all, especially for those who
hug the corpse in shows of grief, whom the new *sovai* is particularly
likely to enter and make sick. The funeral ceremony is marked by
exhortations to the new *sovai* from the graveside to go away and not
harm its living relatives. The Orokaiva similarly hail the *sovai* at other
times, occasionally telling them to go away and leave them alone. The
sovai, they maintain, reply from the forest with inarticulate cries.

The Orokaiva also employ a range of expulsive treatments to evict the
offending *sovai* from the body of a sick person. Most of these involve
substances called *sivo*, concoctions made of leaves, bark, fruit and so on,
which they believe have curative power. Expulsive treatments take a
variety of forms. A sick person may eat or sniff a strong-smelling
concoction (for instance, of odoriferous bark) to 'frighten away' the
ambu sickness. A variation of this treatment is fumigation with a mixture
of potent leaves and bark placed in a wooden bowl into which is
dropped a hot stone; here the patient sits under a pandanus leaf mat and
inhales the steam.

Sometimes a healer will blow on a patient's body and into orifices, such as ears and nostrils while chewing a *sivo* to drive out the illness. Sometimes the healer will massage the illness out, making throwing-away motions and perhaps calling on the *sovai* to go away as he works. An intriguing version of this technique involves the removal of some object from the patient either by sucking or by massage; in some instances the object may travel from the hand up the arm to appear in the mouth. The kinds of things 'removed' include tufts of the hair of the deceased person whose *sovai* is responsible for the illness or slivers of wallaby bone (the diagnosis in this case being that the patient had eaten wallaby when the creature was a *sovai*). In one case a woman massaged a sick baby's neck with potent *sivo* leaves until she 'removed' a mess of chewed betel nut in which there was a pig's tusk. The diagnosis was that the mother had eaten some pork that came from a pig that was a *sovai* and had passed on the spirit infection to her child in her breast milk.

In making offerings in their struggles to control the disease-inflicting *sovai*, the Orokaiva are resorting to tactics that mimic what they do when they seek to adjust disrupted relations among the living. They engage on these occasions in an exchange of some kind – of valuables, food, or whatever is appropriate. They are extending this response to relations disrupted by what they believe is supernatural interference. They offer gifts to the attacking *sovai* to induce them to relent – extending exchange to surreal transactions with the spirits of the dead. It would be incorrect to think of these offerings as sacrifices; they are not made with this intention. There is no hint of consecrating the gifts to the spirits or of identifying the donor with them, no idea of communion with the spirits or of expiation or atonement. There is no apportioning of blame, as with sorcery; the malevolent *sovai* strike down the innocent for no reason. The only parallel with sacrifice is that the offering is a symbolic gift giving to the spirit world.

What the Orokaiva receive in return is unclear. They do not think that a ghost or hobgoblin or invisible essence makes off with the feathers, sea-shells, or live pig (although some people say that the spirits eat any food put out for them, but take only enough for an ant, paralleling the fact that the food rots and eventually disappears). Everyone knows that if the steps taken to cure the sickness are successful, then the officiator at the curing rite takes the wealth given ostensibly to the *sovai*. In other words, although the Orokaiva and other Melanesians frame their actions as sociopolitical exchanges with the spirits, they do not think that they are engaging in transactions similar to those between living people. The *sovai* are unpredictable. They observe no rules of expected conduct, and people cannot exert pressure on them to reciprocate (i.e. to stop the sickness) as they can living exchange partners. People are aware that they are trying to control the uncontrollable. What is important to them is the *principle* of the action, the ethic symbolised in any exchange. It expresses the good trouble-free relations which the living desire to maintain with the dead.

The expulsive curing techniques employed by the Orokaiva are amenable to similar symbolic interpretation. Some sick people do apparently believe that objects are removed from their bodies. This is not difficult to credit. If we were sick and had limited technical resources to tackle our condition, any of us might believe such things too (it is, if you like, almost wishful thinking, of which we are all capable). But many sick people do not believe that objects are literally removed from their bodies and yet willingly have the rituals staged on their behalf. And all the practitioners know that what they do is sleight-of-hand, yet they too believe that their curing acts are efficacious, in some sense. They are not charlatans but act in culturally sanctioned good faith. What we have again is a symbolic act, not one which people necessarily believe is technically instrumental in effecting a cure. It is an expression of the desire to see the sickness expelled from the patient as is the object purportedly removed.

If, on the whole, the Orokaiva do not believe that their actions are technically instrumental in effecting a cure, what is the point of their curative acts? This is to view the issue on a physiological plane, where the Western medical system tackles sickness. The behaviour of these people has powerful emotional and psychological consequences, and as Western medicine is gradually acknowledging, these are significant for promoting recovery. Believing that in these acts one is signalling to the unseen spirit powers responsible for one's condition and that they heed such messages gives one grounds for hope and optimism. Furthermore, these people are communicating not with strange or distant powers but with deceased relatives, people who if alive would have an interest in their welfare, and we can imagine the deep emotions this arouses.

We, as social scientists, might argue that human beings are expressing a wished-for occurrence in such symbolic behaviour, and we may speculate on the possible repercussions of this for their relations with one another, but *they* believe that they can influence spirit powers. The psychological boost that this gives the sick is difficult to assess, but it must be considerable. It is the reverse of the power of suggestion that features in sorcery (chapter 11), where individuals who believe that they are the targets of sorcery can think themselves into a morbid condition. Here we have individuals whose belief in the efficacy of the steps taken to alleviate their suffering promotes their recovery. Everyone has heard of mind-over-illness recoveries resulting not apparently from the physiological manipulations of our medical technicians but the refusal of people to die. Likewise, the practices to which people like the Orokaiva resort when ill are not pointless mumbo-jumbo; they may significantly aid recovery.

But their ritual actions are amenable to a wide variety of interpretations, which brings us back to an issue that has recurred through this book, namely the problem of pinning down the fluid concepts that characterise Melanesian life, drawing firm boundaries around them. This is a very considerable problem when dealing with matters purely of the mind. We cannot postulate self-regulating or other systems based on events witnessed in the 'real world', the logical consistency of which we can test against observed facts (as we can ecological, economic, political and such issues). Religious beliefs, like symbols and related actions (chapter 13), have an independent cerebral existence; their rationale is people's interpretations.

Although the members of a society like that of the Orokaiva hold similar beliefs, there is no authority that might standardise these, ensure that they are consistent. Williams talks of the unsystematic and contradictory nature of Melanesian beliefs. It appears that their religious knowledge and practice is continually in flux, developing and changing, although certain fundamental tenets, such as beliefs in ancestor spirits, seem to remain constant. These belief systems allow extensive scope for idiosyncratic ideas, which are so considerable in Melanesian contexts that they threaten to overwhelm our conception of a body of knowledge that is transmitted between generations, independently of individual interpretations of it. It is this tradition that anthropological accounts purport to document and interpret. The continual change and adaptation which are intrinsic to these systems raise another interesting question with which the social sciences are wrestling: What sparks off change, and what is it that makes some innovations and not others take hold? Presumably certain persons occasionally come up with ideas that hit the right emotional note; if not, their privately held views and interpretations die with them.

When an individually inspired belief or practice has come into vogue, decades later people may have forgotten its origin. In this event, what are we, ignorant of its origins, to make of it? An ethnographic illustration makes the point. Some Orokaiva believe that washing a dog with an infusion from a furry-leafed orchid growing near a striated rock outcrop will help make it a good hunter. According to one old man, the hairy leaf is like a healthy dog's coat, and the plant has killer-hunting powers because it grows in a place where, as evidenced by the grooves on the rocks there, a *sovai* monster sharpened its fangs. The ethnographer's interpreter, on hearing this, dug up a few bulbs to plant in his home region. If the plant becomes a hunting-dog-enhancing specific there too, to what will people eventually attribute its powers? They may possibly remember its foreign origin, which could give it perhaps some exotic quality and power; otherwise, in all probability, they will believe that it is powerful because tradition has it that it is powerful. Its arrival could feature as oral history, perhaps being transformed over time into a mythical account about an ancestor who assisted a strange, nosy European. Any comprehension of amorphous Melanesian philosophy has limits, for insiders and outsiders alike.

FURTHER READING

The ethnographic monographs on which this account draws are:
A. Iteanu, 1983 *La ronde des échanges*. Cambridge: Cambridge University Press.
A. Iteanu, 1990 'The concept of the person and the ritual system: An Orokaiva view.' *Man* 25: 35–53.
E. Schwimmer, 1973 *Exchange in the social structure of the Orokaiva*. London: Hurst.
F. E. Williams, 1928 *Orokaiva magic*. Oxford: Oxford University Press.
F. E. Williams, 1930 *Orokaiva society*. Oxford: Oxford University Press.

On sickness and treatment elsewhere in Melanesia see:
S. J. Frankel, 1986 *The Huli response to illness*. Cambridge: Cambridge University Press.
S. J. Frankel and G. Lewis (eds.), 1989 *A continuing trial of treatment: Medical pluralism in Papua New Guinea*. Dordrecht: Kluwer Academic Publishers.
R. W. Hornabrook (ed.), 1976 *Essays on kuru*. Farringdon: E. W. Classey.
G. Lewis, 1975 *Knowledge of illness in a Sepik society*. London: Athlone.
S. Lindenbaum, 1979 *Kuru sorcery*. Palo Alto: Mayfield.

15   Myth in the Star Mountains

The traditional stories that we have inherited from our forebears, fragments of oral custom from a different time, such as 'The Emperor's New Clothes', 'Sleeping Beauty', 'Rumpelstiltskin', 'Little Red Riding Hood', and others pose intriguing cultural puzzles. Although currently relegated to the place of children's bedtime stories, they demand consideration beyond their customary explanation as moral tales. They belong to a genre that anthropologists broadly label as myth and have devoted considerable effort to examining. The origin account from the Bogaia people related in chapter 1 falls into this class of story.

Myths

Mythology has generated some unexpectedly heated debate and some subtle and difficult intellectual arguments characterise its study. There is even disagreement at the outset as to what narratives qualify as myths. The initial problems encountered in defining the field of study foreshadows the differences that follow in the analysis of texts deemed to fall within it. It is difficult to distinguish unambiguously between myths, legends, epics, fairy stories, folktales, overembellished historical accounts and so forth. Some writers consider it is fruitless to divide the tales told in other societies into such different genres. Others have tried to do so, although their distinctions have not met with universal acceptance; Malinowski (1954), for example, distinguished between fairy tales (told for entertainment, full of miraculous happenings and believed by no one), legends (told to support social claims, not miraculous or sacred in content), and history (actual episodes witnessed by people in living memory).

Myths are narratives rooted in the past which may or may not have fantastic content or relate to some actual historical event. They are part of a cultural repertoire, not open to overly imaginative embellishment by inventive individual storytellers, having an established story line and structure of events familiar to and expected by the audience. They are

229

characteristic of oral traditions, passed on by word of mouth. This manner of transmission produces gradual changes over time, each generation unintentionally introducing modifications. Myths may appear to justify contemporary institutions and practices or contain a parable-like moral message. They may help people explain themselves to themselves obliquely, addressing issues of profound and deep-rooted concern, and assist in the resolution of contradictions inherent in human life and society. They are subject to shared performance, the tellers of myths holding the attention of their audience. They entertain, and they may seem to explain. In short, myths are multifaceted tales not amenable to straightforward interpretation.

Several different approaches characterise the study of myth, each reflecting the preoccupations and intellectual concerns of particular scholars at different times. Different approaches to myth reflect to some extent a history of Western ideas; we need to remember that they are inherently ethnocentric. The various approaches may be classified as follows (after Cohen 1969): mythopoeic, viewing myth as expressive narrative and performance; intellectual, proposing that myths account for phenomena, events, etc.; sociological, relating myths to issues of social solidarity; functional, relating myths to cultural charters; psychological, relating myths to unconscious concerns; structuralist, relating myths to contradiction resolution and human cognition; and interpretive, linking myth and ritual. Our investigation of Melanesian myth applies each of these approaches with no intention of deciding that one is better than others, although where appropriate criticisms are made and shortcomings pointed out. It is not prevarication to conclude that myth may be amenable simultaneously to a range of interpretations and satisfy a range of demands. Each approach asks somewhat different questions and so comes up with different answers; all are valid in their particular contexts and in their various ways add to our appreciation and understanding of myth.

In this foray into myth analysis we shall turn to the Baktaman of the Palmer River in the centre of New Guinea. Along with other Ok speakers they inhabit a region that straddles the Irian Jaya/Papua New Guinea border across the central cordillera in the region of the Star Mountains and the Victor Emanuel Ranges (Map 15.1). These phallo-crypt-wearers traditionally had a reputation for ferocity and canni-balism. They live in small isolated hamlets in raised houses and cultivate short-term swiddens, their staple crop being taro. Population density is low and large parts of the region are under forest. Informal kin associations characterise social life. The Baktaman are renowned for their highly secretive cult activities, which centre on the transmission of

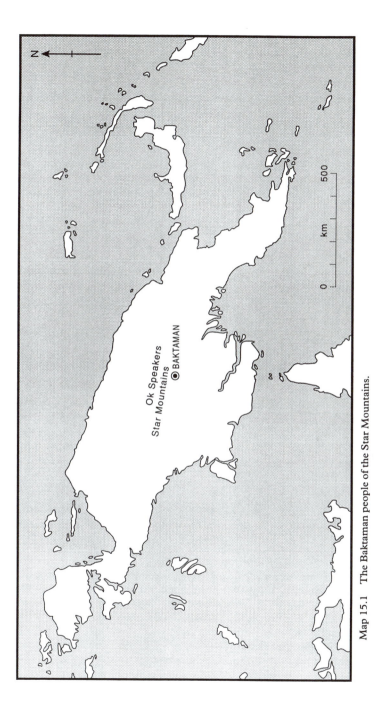

Map 15.1   The Baktaman people of the Star Mountains.

sacred knowledge by men in complex and long-drawn-out series of initiation rites.

The myth to be examined here relates to the sixth of a seven-stage series of initiation rites that are part of a hierarchy of ritually transmitted esoteric knowledge. The initiation series, with its stages establishing classlike ranks, institutionalises ritually sanctioned inequality more obviously, though less painfully and traumatically, than on the Sepik River (chapter 13), but it is equally at odds with the egalitarian principles identified as characterising Melanesian culture. The ritual secrecy that surrounds some Baktaman esoteric knowledge results in its unequal distribution. Even markedly egalitarian societies have potential inequalities; the individuals in any social group will inevitably have different skills, knowledge, abilities, experience and so on, and those with culturally salient traits at any time will consequently have a degree of respect and influence. The Baktaman initiation series formalises these differences in the ritual realm in a ranked series of age- and gender-defined revelations of knowledge. But access to this knowledge does not translate directly into sociopolitical authority in these small, isolated communities, which rely on very informal mechanisms to order themselves. Furthermore, no person is excluded culturally from any formally or informally transmitted knowledge relevant to his or her gender domain at the appropriate time in his or her life. In other words, there are no exclusive classes in the marxist sense, featuring exploitation of some by others throughout their lives, and, if we concede that women occupy a different but not to them subordinate domain (chapter 9), there is certainly no evidence that people think like this. The hierarchy is a transient and opaque Melanesian one; when individuals are old enough they are inducted into the knowledge.

A Baktaman myth

The following is a version of a myth told by the Baktaman and associated with the sacred knowledge taught during the sixth stage of their initiation sequence:

First there was a dog – he came down, went to the base of very large trees, bit off the roots, dug holes under the trees; out of such holes he pulled the first men, many places. The men were very glad to be out of the ground, and they danced and sang. But these first Baktaman had not carried any taro with them; the dance made them hungry and they wanted and needed food. Grandfather cuscus *awarek* remained below ground in his hole, clutching the taro and would not release it. Neither dog nor man dared go down into the hole to fetch the taro. Finally the swallow volunteered. He flew down into the hole, but was frightened and turned back. He tried again, but again turned back in fright.

The third time, he managed to snatch a little bit of taro, he flew out of the hole and into the air, and he deposited small bits of taro high up on the white tree trunks, and on the white cliff faces of the mountains. The men fetched down the taro and made a big feast. Then grandfather cuscus came up out of its hole bringing plenty of taro with him. He lined up the people by clans, according to which hole they had come out of, and named them, making the clans of Yeni and Minkarin and Murukmur and all. Then he went down under the ground again. (Barth 1975: 83)

The mythopoeic approach to myth considers it a vehicle of aesthetic expression broadly comparable with poetry, opera, plays and so on. The performative element is to the fore. In telling myths, people re-enact and even to some extent re-create them, linking their past to their future emotively through present-day actions and discourse. The story must be related in such a way as to engender the appropriate feelings in the audience. It may be entertaining and enjoyable, riveting attention, but it is likely also to foster an attitude of mind – perhaps awe and mystery in the case of the Baktaman myth, with its close associations with initiation into the secrets of cult lore (although according to Barth [1975] myth telling is not an important part of Baktaman ritual performance, in marked contrast to its role among some neighbouring Ok speakers). Although many anthropologists would concede that the performance of myth is significant, they would point out that this approach fails to address its form and content. Telling and hearing myths may foster certain emotional responses, but it is something beyond their mere manner of recital that makes them powerful.

The intellectual approach to myth might accept this story as an account of the genesis of the Baktaman population or the origin of their staple crop, taro. This mythical explanation is no more fantastic or unbelievable than, for example, the story of Adam and Eve in Genesis or the loaves and fishes in the Gospels. Indeed, these stories are of the same genre, and it seems reasonable to accept that on some level myths may be attempts to account for life's otherwise inexplicable mysteries. We associate this approach with armchair Victorian scholars, although the idea that myths and ritual are attempts to satisfy human curiosity about life's experiences – that they represent non-scientific cultures' attempts to answer the intractable why questions – has continued to attract advocates, who rail against the emphasis anthropologists place on the relation between myth and social action at the expense of cognitive perspectives. This neo-Tylorian perspective that myth and ritual are analogues of scientific enquiry in other cultures has some serious flaws; for example, scientists continually test and change their models, whereas myths are beyond question.

The Victorian scholars interpreted myth in the context of their effulgent new evolutionary theory. They reasoned that because people around the world tell each other myths, their study should help in the formulation of evolutionary sequences for humankind, myths being 'survivals' from dead cultures. Although later scholars have eschewed the sweeping generalisations of the nineteenth-century evolutionists, the idea that the study of myth might inform us about past events retains its appeal. The time perspective is shorter, from evolution's millennia to history's centuries. This interpretation of myths as historical narratives extends from early diffusionist speculation about them as records of past events and population movements (Rivers 1914) to more modest current expositions of them as oral history relating to more recent, local events.

Regarding historical intelligence in the Baktaman myth, it is pertinent that today these people identify the dog-dug holes of the myth with limestone sink-holes occurring at named geographical locations in their region. Indeed, the teller of the myth sometimes digresses at the opening, after referring to the holes, into an account of his region's sacred geography. It is possible that certain events occurred in the past in the vicinity of these locations of significance to the clans associated with them, perhaps related in other myths. It seems reasonable to argue that historical developments within a society may be obscurely wrapped up in some myths, especially in cultures that have different non-linear time perspectives, and that by ordering specific events these narratives anchor the present in the past. They give meaning and legitimation to social life by relating it to ancestral times. Michael Young has argued, for example, that Goodenough Islanders use myths to construct their identities, literally living their myths and recasting them through their experiences (1983).

The sociological approach to myth views it as expressing and affirming social solidarity, communicating in words what rituals convey in actions. The telling of myths contributes to social solidarity by expressing values central to social life, even reifying features of the social structure. By sharing the same corpus of myths, the members of a society experience the same cultural heritage, with all that this implies regarding acceptance of the same obligations, similar expectations, mutual responsibilities, and so on. The Baktaman myth gives this small Ok-speaking population a sense of identity. They are the people whose ancestors emerged from certain holes in their region, now metamorphosed into sink-holes. These mythical men shared a cuscus-grandfather; in their subterranean world they were brothers. Hence the myth gives prominence to the principle of sibling solidarity, a central tenet in many kin-constituted societies. Brothers stick together in facing life's difficulties, ensuring adequate food supplies, and sharing what they have in feasts. It is the recognition of common obligations and responsibilities among brothers that gives substance to Baktaman society. Those who descend from one hole, from the same ancestor, comprise the clans of their society. Although these patrilineal exogamous clans feature little in everyday life, they emerge in the context of cult activities. The myth relates further to social solidarity in being closely related to one of the stages in men's initiation to cult knowledge, a ritual sequence central to the ordering of Baktaman social life. It also refers to dancing and feasting, important social events which imply exchanges of food and valuables and all that these entail sociologically.

The social import of this myth is far from obvious. A problem with sociologically informed theories is determining how ambiguous mythical accounts operate effectively in the way proposed. They are not often obvious bulwarks of the social order; they depend upon some hit-or-miss subliminal receipt of their import, and this suggests that other devices might better serve the social purpose attributed to myths. Nonetheless, it seems reasonable to argue that sharing myths, along with other aspects of their cultural heritage, will give people a sense of common identity and solidarity. It is when writers suggest that this is the reason myths exist that they ascribe too much to the sociological perspective. Solidarity is a by-product of myths; although perhaps contributing to their existence, it hardly explains why they exist.

The functional approach to myth is a blend of the sociological and historical interpretations and centres on the legitimation of contemporary social arrangements. It is associated with Malinowski (1954), who enunciated it in his discussion of Trobriand Island mythology (see chapter 5). According to this approach myths embody a justificatory message. They recount the first performance of some act that validates a present-day claim in social relations. They are charters legitimating present arrangements and actions. Malinowski (1954: 101) asserts that myth 'is not an idle tale, but a hard-worked active force; it is not an intellectual explanation or an artistic imagery, but a pragmatic charter of primitive faith and moral wisdom'. People require a charter beyond question and outside ordinary time to legitimate their institutions. Whereas the arrangements of everyday life – actual patterns of settlement, real claims to property and title, and so on – are always open to dispute, immutable myths, set in another time and involving unreal events, indisputably affirm claims and transcend inconsistencies.

The Baktaman myth is uncannily similar to one told in the Trobriand Islands in which brother and sister pairs emerged from holes around the archipelago – now marked by physical features such as grottoes, coral outcrops and springs – and established today's clans. Both the Baktaman and the Trobriand myth, in which original people emerge from holes in the ground, can be thought to function as charters that establish and affirm today's territorial rights and clan arrangements. They legitimate the current social order and claims to land; clans are associated with territories where their members have inalienable rights of residence and land use. The myth is their title deed. Criticisms of this functional interpretation of myth target its earthy pragmatism, which leaves no room for its symbolic representations, discursive ambiguity and multi-faceted explanations. It is considered too positivistic for such equivocal subject matter, too likely to reduce the mystery of myth to life's everyday mundanity.

The psychological approach draws on psychoanalytic theory to propose that mythical themes, events and symbols are expressions of unconscious anxieties. It considers myths analogous to dreams. They embody messages from the unconscious, condensed and disguised and symbolically reconstructed, which wrestle with life's deep, unresolvable conflicts. This approach assumes myths, like dreams, use similar symbolic manipulations to express subliminal conflicts and wishes, although in myths the conscious element may be more evident, rendering them more readily comprehensible. Several unconscious themes amenable to psychoanalytic interpretation may be inferred in the Baktaman myth.

The theme of the myth comes over generally as an expression of fear of the unknown. We can suggest that the myth may originate, at least in part, in the deep-seated trauma of birth and all that this implies in psychoanalysis. The emergence of men from holes in the ground may refer to their birth. Perhaps we can see an element of mother earth identification here, today's deep dark sink-holes equating with birth canals and wombs. The fear expressed by the men in the myth about going back into the dog-dug holes and retrieving the taro invites interpretation as an expression of return-to-the-womb phobia. We may also have an expression of men's fear of the vagina and their feelings of inadequacy regarding women's reproductive powers, a culturally appo-site interpretation in the light of Melanesian male fears of menstrual blood and birth pollution (see chapters 9 and 13). In the male ancestor figure who remains in the womb it may even be possible to discern Oedipal-like father-figure conflicts, the newly born men having to wrest their staple food supply from an ancestor figure and establish their independence. And in the final episode there is possibly reference to deep-seated feelings of insecurity related to loss of one's parents, with the cuscus-ancestor disappearing underground after organising his descendants.

This summary of possible psychoanalytically informed themes could doubtless be extended, but it illustrates the approach. It depends, however, upon acceptance of the assumption that all human beings, regardless of culture, share the same deep-seated psychological anxieties (and the prior assumption that the unconscious exists and is accessible to conscious interpretation by others). Furthermore, it is not clear why human beings invent myths to cope with their unconscious conflicts – how this helps them cope with and resolve them.

The structuralist approach, associated with Lévi-Strauss, postulates that myths mediate the contradictions that characterise human life – that they reveal some of the fundamental conundrums that exercise the human intellect and that their study can help establish what makes the human animal unique. This occurs where culture displaces nature, and the structural study of myth focuses on this opposition and transition (there are strong resemblances here with the earlier nature:nurture debate [see chapter 4]). The approach borrows from linguistic theory, arguing that myth communicates something, and it is the structure as opposed to the cultural content of the message that demands attention. Different cultures draw on different experiences for content – just as French handymen (*bricoleurs*) may use different odds and ends for a job – but structure their myths similarly to resolve the same universal contradictions. It is through the analysis of several myths that structuralism reveals the repetition of contradictions and their transformations, the underlying structure clothed in different narrative content. Structuralism uses binary or paired oppositions to manipulate these relations into the desired transformations centring on nature and culture.

A structural study of the Baktaman myth requires us first to decompose it into incidents or segments:

1. Men emerge from dog-dug holes and dance in celebration until hungry.
2. The men have no food.
3. The cuscus-ancestor holds onto the taro underground.
4. Men fear going underground for taro, and a swallow goes and snatches some.
5. The swallow deposits the taro in trees and on cliffs.
6. Men collect the taro and arrange a feast.
7. The cuscus-ancestor emerges, organises the clans, and returns underground.

Next these incidents must be arranged according to universal themes identifiable in them: order (1, 6, 7), chaos (2, 3, 4), cooked (6, 7), raw

(3, 4, 5), light (1, 5, 6, 7), dark (3, 4, 7). The method arranges the themes into opposed pairs, assumed to structure contradictions, transforming them according to the universal nature:culture dichotomy – order (culture) : chaos (nature), cooked (culture) : raw (nature), and light (culture) : dark (nature). According to the structuralist approach, all myths reveal this basic polarity when analysed in this way.

The message transmitted by the Baktaman myth cannot be readily put into words; otherwise there would be no need for the circumlocution of the myth. Nonetheless, we can sense the issues at stake. A perennial concern of human beings is to manage their natural environments so as to ensure an adequate supply of food to meet their demands. They have hit upon all manner of strategies to do so, a common Melanesian one, followed by the Baktaman, is to clear and cultivate swiddens (chapter 3). The contradiction is that humans aspire to manage natural resources but can never control them. Fertility is one of nature's mysteries. The Baktaman depend on other forces besides their own industry, here symbolised by the taro-fetching swallow, to ensure their livelihoods. They cannot direct these forces of fertility, epitomised by the cuscus-ancestor. Men's fears, signalled in their refusal to return to the dark underground world to bring the taro up into the light, represent their restricted knowledge and lack of control over their destinies. They may cultivate taro and transform the raw tubers into cooked food but they have scant control over yields; the cuscus-ancestor, who returns underground after organising the newly emerged men into society, keeps the knowledge to himself. There is a danger that without adequate food supplies order might dissolve into chaos as people fight over limited resources. The fear that nature will reassert itself and chaos ensue is a perennial one; fear of the subterranean world reflects this perpetual worry. If the first men had shown more resolution, people today would have taro knowledge to ensure adequate crop yields and guarantee order.

In some regards the structuralist approach is akin to the intellectual one, although not so much explaining life's big questions as 'explaining them away' by resolving the deep conflicts to which they give rise. (An interesting expansion of this theme in a Melanesian context is Roy Wagner's work *Lethal Speech*, which argues that among the Daribi myths obviate the difficulties that surround life's contentious questions through a series of symbolic word plays and transformations centring on tropes.) The strengths of structuralism include drawing attention to the ambiguous expression of conflicts in myth – one of this genre's central characteristics – and directing enquiries to the subliminal level on which myths seem in considerable part to operate. The weaknesses of structuralism include the obscurity of its interpretations and their subjective nature. Also, by locating analysis on the level of the unconscious, it is subject to the same criticisms as psychoanalytical interpretations of myth. It compounds the ambiguity of myth with its psychologically addressed, philosophical dialectic, obscuring rather than promoting understanding. The analytical method is subjective and arbitrary, the oppositions and their mediation being chosen apparently at random rather than according to any consistent set of criteria. The result is therefore open to the full devastating critique of post-modernism. The assertion that all human beings have the same mental structures regardless of their life experiences cannot justify this loose methodology, licensing free association.

The interpretive approach to myth proposes that it symbolically corroborates ritual, even intimates the same cultural intelligence. They are both cryptic commentaries on culturally important issues, being indigenous expressions and explanations of social values and moral dilemmas. The ethnographer Barth (1975) takes this line in his analysis of the Baktaman myth. The taro-hoarding-cuscus-ancestor myth relates, as mentioned earlier, to the sixth stage in the elaborate series of initiation rites that characterise passage to manhood in Baktaman society and should not be told to anyone who has not passed through this initiatory stage.

The sixth-degree initiation centres on the rethatching of one of the Baktaman's cult houses, the *yolam* (Plates 15.1–15.4). In the opening phase of the ritual, the cult leader eviscerates a marsupial caught the night before, stretches it on a rattan frame, and suspends it over a sacred fire in the cult house to dry. Some days later, after a large marsupial hunt and the amassing of sago fronds for thatching, the main phase of the ritual begins. The novices are called into the *yolam* cult house, where the older men are standing with their arms outstretched to hide something. They can hear the cult leader growling, and suddenly the men lower their arms to reveal him brandishing a *kitëm* marsupial tied to a bow with red-feather-bedecked, shell-decorated forehead bands. He jabs the animal into the house thatch while the crowd chants a *wus-wus* war cry, and then he climbs up into the roof to slash the vine attaching the thatch to the beams. When he comes down, everyone charges out of the cult house, the cult leader carrying the *kitëm* marsupial in a quill-covered net bag of the kind used to store the sacred mandible and skull of ancestors, and they all rush around pulling up vegetation and putting it in a pile while shouting 'the ancestor's hair'. They conclude by waving their arms in the air and shouting war cries.

The next day the participants, wearing their finest shell and feather

Plate 15.1   The Tifalmin cult house at Brolemavip, featuring the characteristic houseboards of the Ok speakers, with their stylised anthropomorphic elements.

regalia, congregate outside the *yolam* cult house. The cult leader, who has painted a red and a white line on the ancestral skull inside the house, shoots an arrow into a pig tethered outside, withdraws it and yells a war cry while brandishing it. Older men blow aromatic bark and ginger over the novices assembled a little way off. Next the cult leader and some senior men climb onto the roof of the cult house. The leader carries the stretched and fire-dried marsupial, wrapped in bark cloth to hide it from the view of the uninitiated, and pushes it through the hole that he poked in the thatch the day before with the marsupial on the bow. It falls before the ancestral skull inside. At this signal the men with him strip the thatch off the roof. The spectators and novices are directed to go to the gardens and harvest and cook taro corms. Some of the senior men then

Plate 15.2   House interior: the rear wall, viewed between the supports that
surround the central fireplace, lined with the mandibles of slaughtered pigs
together with a small net bag containing ritual objects.

butcher the shot pig for cooking, while others rethatch the cult house,
burning the old thatch and the heap of 'ancestor's hair' vegetation
pulled up the day before. The cult leader and others make pork-fat
offerings on the sacred fires inside the cult house. When the food is
cooked, all the men present indulge in a feast of pork, marsupial and
taro, exchanging morsels with one another in gestures of sociability.

   When the novices return, the cult leader feeds the participants pieces
of pork, pig's liver, marsupial and taro passed through the arch of a pig's
mandible, striking them on the back with a fistful of taro and cooking
leaves as they swallow. This gesture has considerable salience; eating the
pork of a pig raised elsewhere authorises novices to accept meat from

Plate 15.3   An Ok speaker wearing decorations some of which relate to his
initiatory status; for example, only those who have passed through the
third-degree initiation may wear cassowary quills through their noses.

Plate 15.4 A man thatching a house, lashing bundles of *Imperata* grass into place along the eaves.

other, non-Baktaman communities (i.e., to take part in intercommunity politics); the taro signals their authorisation to decide as adults when to start harvesting new taro from gardens; and the back slap lifts a previously imposed taboo on eating bat meat. Next the cult leader takes the *kitëm* marsupial from his quill-decorated bag and, putting it on the floor of the cult house, beats it with a stick to break its bones, saying,

I give you this, I cook it for you. Give us many pigs. Strengthen our taro gardens, make the tubers grow large. Look after this set of men, give them plenty of food so they will be strong.

He then singes its fur over the sacred fire (men present collect tufts of the fur to burn in their taro gardens to promote taro yields) and dedicates it to the ancestral skull and long bones. Subsequently he dries the animal as before and burns pieces of it on the sacred cult-house fires over the coming weeks, together with the other dried marsupial, in offering to the ancestor. Finally, the remaining pork, marsupial flesh, and taro, together with cuts from further slaughtered pigs, are distributed among participants.

It is difficult to see how this ritual relates to the myth, except that marsupials and taro seem to feature prominently in both. It is necessary to explore the symbolism evident in both to trace connections between them. The ritual links taro, marsupials and ancestors. The vine used to lash the marsupial to the rattan drying frame is the species that spreads across the surface of taro gardens, 'binding' tubers underground. The white of the shells on the bands used to tie the *kitëm* marsupial to the bow symbolises the white flesh of taro. The white line painted on the ancestral skull is similarly equated with the colour of taro. And the cult leader carries the marsupial in a quill-decorated bag like that in which ancestral relics are kept. The association of thatch with fur, hair and vegetation and the pairing of these in opposition respectively with cult house, marsupial, ancestor's skull and earth intimate the mystery of fertility. The Baktaman feed the ancestral skull with the smoke of the burned marsupial meat and pork offered to it in the cult house, and they connect this supplication and strengthening of the ancestors with taro garden fertility by burning tufts of fur there. They also spread the power associated with the cult house and its relics over the land in billowing smoke when they burn the old thatch and torn-up 'ancestor's hair' vegetation. The imagery of regeneration is evident in the rethatching too, and the introduction of the dried marsupial, later offered to the ancestor, into the cult house presages the shedding of its old thatch-hair and replacement with new.

The myth revisits these themes, emphasising the link between ancestors, marsupials and taro. It distinguishes below-ground and above-ground worlds, which the Baktaman associate with the polluted and the clean. It is paradoxical to them that their root crop staple should come from and depend on the fertility of the polluted below-ground realm. They depend on the intercession of other agents to ensure its adequate growth, allowing them to harvest it into the pure above-ground world with no ill effects. They have been unable to enter this dangerous, dirty underworld and manage the crop themselves ever since the original Baktaman emerged into the pure overworld, when they had to depend on the swallow (which, aptly, nests in tunnels in steep hillsides) to secure their first taro. The myth records the primeval and ongoing dependence of human beings on the ancestors to ensure their taro crop, a dependency which the ritual expresses too.

Anthropological understanding

The congruence apparent between the Baktaman myth and their sixth-stage initiation ritual is compelling and suggests that this interpretive approach to myth analysis is particularly fruitful, vindicating those who advocate attention to ethnographic detail and interpretation of myths within their specific cultural contexts. But doubts arise about the extent to which we can make the myth fit with the ritual and indigenous exegesis through appropriate interpretation of symbolism. These stories are not intended to be pored over and dissected any more than rituals are amenable to logical analysis. They are for telling and performing, and participants understand them by experiencing them. They achieve their meaning in action, when lived. We distort them when we describe and organise them on paper and attempt to analyse them and unravel their mysteries in everyday words and categories. The urge is to over-organise, to impose order where it is perhaps inappropriate.

The ritual practices of the Baktaman, like those throughout Melanesia, are constantly open to change and innovation; Barth (1975: 91) reports, for example, that the senior men engaged in heated debate over the proper way to perform the sixth-stage initiation ritual and agreed to modify its performance, adopting new procedures seen among neighbouring Ok speakers. This flexible and innovative approach to ritual means that practices are unlikely to constitute a seamless liturgical whole, particularly in non-literate traditions where no records are kept of previous practices and changes. Orderliness and correspondence between different stages of rituals and associated myths are improbable. The marsupials that occur in the Baktaman myth and ritual illustrate the slippage and incongruence that can occur with no apparent embarrassment to the actors. The marsupial *kwëmnok* in the myth (probably *Gymnotis* sp.) browses in trees by day and sleeps in subterranean burrows by night (hence its suitability for the story), but the animal in the ritual is an entirely arboreal *kitëm* cuscus (probably *Phalanger* sp.). This discrepancy does not bother the cult leader, who even hints that it is the result of changes over time, because it 'is an old story' (Barth 1975: 94).

This is not just a question of interpretation. The highly suspicious and secretive behaviour of the Ok-speakers, which contrasts markedly in my experience with the aggressive openness of the Central Highlanders to the east, questions further the status of orderly and integrated anthropological accounts of such elaborate initiation rituals, in which people pass on a great deal of highly valued, secret, sacred knowledge. What credence are we to give to accounts of these sensitive practices and closely guarded information? The startling disagreements over the exegesis of the ritual practices and mythology of the Ok speakers probably reflects the difficulties encountered in learning about them (Barth 1987), different fieldworkers catching different glimpses of these guarded practices and receiving varyingly fabricated accounts of their significance. The problem is compounded when we recall that not only are these people reluctant to divulge their sacred knowledge to outsiders but also different participants will have somewhat different ideas about what goes on and its significance (chapter 13). Each will witness initiation sequences like the Baktaman ritual a little differently, and where there is no overt exegesis of the kind that anthropologists favour individuals will likely entertain somewhat different views about the significance of what they have seen and taken part in – and the cult leader is no final arbiter, only another view. These post-modernist inspired criticisms apply not only to the interpretive approach but also to every other approach to the study of myth. Indeed, they apply in some degree to all anthropology, although they take on added piquancy in the study of ritual and belief, where the rationale for action exists entirely inside others' heads and experiences.

In conclusion, this anthropological introduction to some classical issues pertaining to premodern Melanesian culture is in no sense definitive and certainly not beyond question. It is not merely a collection of potted ethnographic accounts that passes on the deficiencies evident in each, whether attributable to the accessibility of indigenous knowledge, sacred or otherwise, the fieldworker's gender, his/her particular intellectual preoccupations at the time of writing; or any other conditioning factors. It is subject to double distortion reflecting my views and experiences; it is in some regards a late-twentieth-century Englishman's New Guinea Highlands-centric interpretation. The manner in which contemporary social issues in my own materialistic and image-manipulated culture impinge on my life throws into relief my understanding of some Melanesian institutions. The morality of the gift on opposite sides of the world captures this tension. In Western culture the amoral, impersonal market rules, whereas in Melanesian society it is moral, personal exchange. The centrality of sociopolitical exchange in the social lives of Melanesians finds expression repeatedly, I think, in various aspects of their cultural existence, from subsistence behaviour to supernatural ideology. It relates to their distinctive stateless social order – the persistence of aggregations of politically sovereign, sometimes violent, equal persons that is made possible by certain material and historical circumstances and symbolised time and again in different aspects of their culture – chieflike offices in some places and radically different gender-defined cultural domains and knowledge-founded hierarchies notwithstanding. These and related assumptions account for the shape of this book – its emphasis on interpersonal relations and social process, fluid ideology and elastic boundaries, at the expense of structured corporations and social rules, authoritative cosmologies and fixed categories. In short, this is a particular vision of premodern Melanesia, and I critique others and interpret their ethnographic records from my own distinctive viewpoint. Theoretical, political, personal, regional, historical and other assumptions shape anthropology and make any introduction, like this Melanesianist one, to the discipline a compromised endeavour.

FURTHER READING

The ethnography on which this chapter draws is:
F. Barth, 1975 *Ritual and knowledge among the Baktaman of New Guinea*. New Haven: Yale University Press.
F. Barth, 1987 *Cosmologies in the making*. Cambridge: Cambridge University Press.
B. Craig and D. Hyndman (eds.), 1990 *Children of Afek*. Oceania Monograph 40.

On oral traditions see:
P. Cohen, 1969 'Theories of myth'. *Man*. 4: 333–53.
R. Finnegan, 1992 *Oral traditions and the verbal arts*. London: Routledge.
C. Lévi-Strauss, 1968 *Structural anthropology*. London: Allen Lane.

Also on Melanesian myth see:
K. Burridge, 1969 *Tangu traditions*. Oxford: Oxford University Press.

G. Gillison, 1993 *Between culture and fantasy.* Chicago: University of Chicago Press.

E. E. Facey, 1988 *Nguna voices.* Calgary: University of Calgary Press.

J. LeRoy, 1985 *Fabricated world.* Vancouver: University of British Columbia Press.

J. LeRoy, 1985 *Kewa tales.* Vancouver: University of British Columbia Press.

B. Malinowski, 1954 'Myth in primitive psychology.' In *Magic, science and religion and other essays.* New York: Doubleday Anchor: (93–148).

W. H. R. Rivers, 1914 *The history of Melanesian society.* Cambridge: Cambridge: University Press.

R. Wagner, 1978 *Lethal speech.* Ithaca: Cornell University Press.

J. F. Weiner, 1988 *The heart of the pearl shell.* Berkeley: University of California Press.

M. Young, 1983 *Magicians of Manumanua.* Berkeley: University of California Press.

On inequality in Melanesia:
R. C. Kelly, 1993 *Constructing inequality: The fabrication of a hierarchy of virtue among the Etoro.* Ann Arbor: University of Michigan Press.

Index

acephalous – see stateless
achieved status 99–100
action-sets 143
adaptation 25–27
adolescence 135
adoption 64, 66
affines and affinal relations 96, 135, 139, 140, 144, 211
African models 140–41
age 205, 232
aggression 64, 163, 185, 206
agriculture 25, 137
agriculture, origins of 15
alliance theory 209
ambush 181, 186
ancestor spirits 59
ancestors 86, 244–45
Anga 114–29
arrow-stem men 185
artifacts 117–18
ascribed status 176
asisi spirits 218
Austronesian 8–9, 14, 70, 166, 176, 177
authority 99, 108, 165, 176, 177

Baktaman 230–47
Balim River 181, 182
bark-cloth 121–22
Barth, F. 233, 239, 245, 246
Bateson, G. 206
battles 181, 186
Bayliss-Smith, T. and Feacham, R. 49
beliefs 215–28
beliefs, flexibility of 227–28, 245–46
betel nut 170, 200
betrothal gifts 94, 137
big man 99–111, 142, 143, 149, 151, 157, 158, 160, 161–62
bilateral groups 66, 142
biological anthropology 5–7, 25–26
birds 5, 92, 115, 119
birth exchange 57
Bismarck Range 36–37

Bismarck Sea 54
Black Islands xv
body heat 171, 206
Bogaia 12
Bougainville 100–11
boundaries 10–12
bows and arrows 117, 185
bride 56
bridewealth 93–96, 156, 161
Brookfield, H. and Hart, D. 2, 76
bullroarers 205
Bulolo 116
burial 219–20
burning off 39, 41
butchering 88, 90, 91, 190, 241

cane grass 119, 123–24
cannibalism 187, 190–94
capes 121
capital 126–27
case histories 151, 158–59
categories 10–12, 215, 227
ceremonial exchange – see sociopolitical exchange
Chambri Lake 199
chiefs 99, 176–77
childhood 60–63
Chowning, A. 1
clans 66, 140–41, 142, 197, 209, 218, 235
Clarke, W. 44, 46
classification 10–12, 17–18
clearing gardens 39
climate 5
co-wives 146, 151
coast 2–3
coconut 23, 218
commodity 77–79, 86, 96, 119–21
comparative method xix
compensation 157, 162, 185, 187
competitive exchange 99, 107
conflict theory 186–88
contradictions xvii, 165, 237, 238
cooking 89, 117, 137

249